CONFESSIONS OF A RENEGADE
PEACE CORPS YEARS

CONFESSIONS OF A RENEGADE PEACE CORPS YEARS

Eddie James Girdner

GYAN

ISBN: 978-81-212-1232-8

Price: ₹ 990

First Published 2015

Published by

Gyan Publishing House
23, Main Ansari Road, Daryaganj,
New Delhi - 110002
Phones : 23282060, 23261060
Fax : (011) 23285914
E-mail: books@gyanbooks.com
website: gyanbooks.com

Laser Typesetting: Rajender Vashist, Delhi
Printed at: G. Print Process, Delhi

Cataloging in Publication Data--DK
Courtesy: D.K. Agencies (P) Ltd. <docinfo@dkagencies.com>

Girdner, Eddie J.
Confessions of a renegade Peace Corps years / Eddie James Girdner.
p. cm.
Includes index.
ISBN 9788121212328

1. Girdner, Eddie J. 2. Peace Corps (U.S.)--Biography. 3. Volunteer workers in social service--India--Biography. 4. Country life--India, North. 5. Country life--India--Punjab. I. Title.

DDC 361.6092 23

Contents

Abbreviations

BDO: Block Development Officer
IUD: Intra Uterine Device
MLA: Member of Legislative Assembly
SDM: Sub-District Magistrate
SGPC: Shiromani Gurdwara Prabandhak Committee
VLW: Village Level Worker (Gram Sevak)

Glossary of Terms

Akali Dal: A Sikh-based political party in Punjab

Allu: Potato

Almari: A Cabinet set into the wall, usually with doors

Angrez: An English person

Ashram: A place to stay for members of a religious group

Ata: Flour, usually of wheat in Punjab

Aurat: Woman

Badam: Almond

Badmash: A criminal person or a person of bad character

Bahujan Samaj Party (BSP): A Dalit based political party

Baisakhi Festival: A spring festival in April to celebrate the wheat harvest

Bajra: Millet

Bakra: Goat meat

Bania: A Shopkeeper; Traditionally also money lenders

Belcha: Shovel

Bendi Tori: Green okra

Bhangra: A local dance in Punjab performed at weddings and other occasions

Bhramachari: A religious person who practices celibacy

Bolie: A dirty rhyme in Punjabi, usually sung at weddings

Bunds: Earth ridges around a field to contain and direct irrigation water

Burfi: An Indian milk sweet

Burseam: Clover

Bustee: A city slum area

Canaal: A measure of land in Punjab. One-eighth of an acre or 5445 square feet

Cha: Tea

Chamindar: Shoemaker

Chapati: Breadcake of wheat flour cooked on a flat plate

Chaprasi: A servant

Charpie: A small string bed

Chola: Fried chickpeas

Chowkidar: A night watchman

Chuney: A long piece of thin cloth worn over the shoulders and breasts of a woman

Communalism: In the Indian context, refers to favouritism of the members of one's own religious faith

Cuckerbit: A member of the family of vegetables such as cucumbers, kerala, zucchini, and so on which grow on vines

Dal: Lentils

Dalit: Members of the so-called untouchable castes

Datum: Stick from a branch of a tree which is chewed for cleaning ones teeth

Desi: Home made or unimproved

Dhaba: A small local eating place in Punjab, often found along the roads and highways

Dhobi: A washerman

Digambara: A member of the Jain sect whose members do not wear clothes

Diwala: Carpenter's festival immediately following the festival of Diwali to celebrate Visvakarma, the Hindu God of carpentry, engineering and industrial arts

Diwali: The festival of lights in November

Doaba: The triangle of land between the Sutlej and Beas Rivers in Punjab

Dolie: A screened kitchen storage cabinet for vegetables and such items

Dak Wallah: Mail Carrier

Doli: In an Indian wedding, an enclosed cot suspended by four corners from a bamboo pole and carried by male relatives in which the bride sits. Today it refers to the ceremony in which the bride leaves her parents home after the wedding.

Double Roti: Modern baked and packaged bread bought in a store

Duniya: The world

Dupatta: Same as chuney. A thin piece of cloth worn over the shoulders and breasts of a woman

Duree: A small woven carpet which is sometimes used as a matress

Dussehra: A festival

Gaddis: A hill tribe in the foot hills of Himachal Pradesh

Garbhani: Religious writings or speech

Gobi: Cabbage and cauliflower; Cabbage is bond gobi; Cauliflower is phol gobi

Godown: A building for storage of grain and so on

Gober: Bullshit, to be used as fertiliser or dung patties

Gram Sevaks: Village level workers

Gulbotting: From Punjabi; Talking or shooting the shit

Gur: Lumps of brown sugar made from sugar cane

Gurdwara: A Sikh temple

Guru Granth Sahib: The Sikh scriptures

Hava: Air

Halwai: One who makes and sells sweets

Hartal: Strike when all shops close

Hijra: A eunuch

Holi: A Spring festival where people throw coloured powder on each other

Japji: The morning prayer read from the Sikh Gurdwara

Jat: A member of the largest cultivating caste in northwest India. They are the dominant group in Punjab.

Jelebi: An Indian sweet, fried in hot oil

Kabbaddi: A game in Punjab where the object is to catch a member of the opposing side and pull them across the line, to one's own side

Kaccha: Special pair of shorts worn by Sikhs

Kali Pani: Black waters, usually thought of as being outside of India and thus sinful

Kallar: Soil which is saturated with mineral salts and has thus lost its productivity

Kamiz: A long shirt

Kanga: Comb

Kara: A steel bracelet worn by Sikhs

Karati dal: Salty and spicy lentils fried in oil and sold on bus stands and other places

Kerala: A state in south India

Kerala: Bitter gourd

Kesh: Hair

Khaddi: Home-spun cloth

Khanna: Food

Kharif: The rainy season, from July to September in Punjab

Khusra: A eunuch

Killy: A small salamander type of creature that lives on the walls and ceilings of houses in India

Kirpan: A sword

Kissan: Farmer

Kucha: Made of mud, such as a kucha house; Something of poor quality; Opposite of pucca

Kurta: A long loose shirt

Kushy: Happy

Ladu: Sweet in the shape of a yellow round ball

Lakh: 100,000

Lambardar: The collector of land revenue

Lathi: A bamboo stick used to keep order, usually by police

Loo: A hot dry wind from the west

Lucerne: Alfafa

Lussie: Buttermilk

Lunger: Feast at a festival, where food is provided free for everyone

Mali: A gardener

Mandir: A Hindu temple

Masjid: A mosque

Mela: A fair

Mirch: Pepper, Kali mirch is black pepper. Lal mirch is red pepper

Mistry: A carpenter

Miswak: Stick which is chewed for cleaning teeth

Mooli: A radish

Morcha: A campaign

Mucher dani: A mosquito net

Mucky roti: Corn bread chapati

Mudge: Water buffalo

Mukhy: Maize

Mundi: A grain market

Mung (moong): A green pulse, lentil

Mungie: A small string bed; See charpie

Namaskar: Indian greeting; see Namaste

Namaste: Indian greeting with hands folded against each other

Nan: A type of pita bread baked in an oven

Nanga: Nude

Naxalite: A member of a Maoist revolutionary organisation which had its origins in the Naxalbari District of West Bengal state

Pagal: Insane

Paisa: Indian unit of currency; 100 paisa is one rupee

Pakora: A small fried vegetable, usually of spinach or potato, coated with chickpea flour

Panch: A village elder and one of the village leaders

Panchayat: (Gram Panchayat) A council of five. A group of recognised village leaders who meet concerning judicial cases or problems, and plan undertakings and procedures. They are seen to be democratic and representative.

Panchayati Raj System: A three tier level of governance in a District for political decentralisation. At the village level is the village council or gram panchayat. At the block level is the panchayat samiti. At the district level is the zila parishad.

Panchayat Samiti: The governing panchayat council at the level of the development block.

Pani: Water

Patwari: The village keeper of records, such as births, deaths, land sales and so on

Pind: Village

Palak: Spinach

Pucca: Cemented house or something well made or excellent

Punkha: A fan

Puri: Fried bread of chickpea flour

Prasad: A gracious gift; Food which is first offered to a diety and then distributed as a sweet given at Gurdwaras. The food is considered to have the blessing of the diety.

Pyar ka Mausam: Season of love; the cool part of the year, November to February in Punjab

Rabi: The winter season for crops, from October until April

Ragy numy: Blood money, paid for death or injury

Rai: Mustard

Rajai: A heavy quilt stuffed with cotton or wool

Roti: Bread, such as chapatti or double roti

Rupee: Indian unit of money. In 1968, there were 7.5 rupees to a dollar

Ryot: A peasant

Sagh: Greens cooked, usually with ghee or butter; Sarson ka sagh is mustard greens.

Sardar: A senior person of the village, a leader

Sarpanch: The head of the panchayat or council of the village

Sarson: Mustard

Sat Shri Akal: Sikh religious acknowledgement and greeting

Scungbie: A drink made with lemon juice and water and usually containing salt and red pepper

Subzi: Vegetable

Sedougie: A Sikh man who usually wears a turban

Shalgam: A turnup

Shamiana: A tent shade erected for a party, wedding or such function

Sherab: Wine, whiskey, and so on

Sherabi: A drunkard

Sikh: Member of the Sikh religious and ethnic community

Suntra: Tangerine

Swaga: A heavy flat plank used to level a field after the planting of wheat to facilitate irrigation

Tara: A sort of long cucumber-type vegetable

Tehsil: An administrative area of a district

Tempu: A three-wheel small vehicle used for transportation

Terrai: The elevated plains area in Eastern Uttar Pradesh near the hills

Tij: A holiday

Tonga: A one horse carriage, used for local transportation

Toria: A plant, grown to improve the soil

Tumba: A piece of cloth wrapped around the waist and legs, which farmers wear in Punjab

Turie: Chopped up wheat straw

Vidhan Sabha: The State Legislative Assembly in Chandigarh in Punjab

Walla: Name attached to something one does, for example; Subzi walla—seller of vegetables. Rickshaw walla—driver of a rickshaw

Zila Parishad: The political council of the district

Synopsis

In this book, I tell the story of how I became an American Peace Corps Volunteer in India from 1968 to 1970. After training in California, our group of volunteers were sent to Delhi. I recall my early impressions of India, old Delhi, and the trip to Batala in Punjab.

After another six weeks of training in Batala, Punjab, I lived in a village in Banga Block of Jalandhar District. My supervisor was the Block Development Officer in Banga. This is all described in the chapters of this book. I also worked with the Agricultural Officers and the Village Level Workers, posted in the development block. I established contacts with local farmers and learned to communicate with them in Punjabi. I sincerely express my feelings and reactions and the reactions of the persons I worked with, to a quite strange and unique situation.

The chapters briefly but honestly, discuss the projects we worked on, such as—wheat, maize, and soybeans projects. How I found a place to live, built a latrine, made a garden and worked on various food production projects and other aspects or rural life in Punjab in the 1960s.

Also I describe my relations with friends in the village and town, farmers, students, villagers. There was a project to build a school in a poor village, under the school partnership programme.

Also described are weddings and festivals in the village and elsewhere.

The book tells how I became acculturated to the Punjab in the two years and began to feel at home with friends, and my mixed feelings of leaving to go back to the US.

The book is not just a glorification of the Peace Corps, but takes a critical view, suggesting that there was really no need for such a programme, given the Green Revolution in Punjab.

The young man who I worked with in Kariha Village, Jatinder Singh Kariha, became a leader of the Akali Dal Party in Punjab and an MLA in Chandigarh.

The book takes a critical and somewhat humurous approach, that looks at my Peace Corps experience in the nineteen sixties. Many of us joined partly to avoid the war in Vietnam. Getting an exemption from the military I joined the Peace Corps training in California. A number of memorable incidents followed, like, a trip to Delhi, early impressions of India and old Delhi, the trip to Punjab and Batala for more training and going to my local station with the Block Development officer. Problems of getting settled, getting a place to live in the local development block, and meeting agricultural officers and village level workers are recalled. I lived one month with Hardev Singh Kariha, a big farmer of the district, Sikh Jat member of Punjab Legislative Assembly (MLA) in Chandigarh. I worked with his son, Jatinder Singh Kariha, a young farmer, who later became MLA of the district in Shiromani Akali Dal Party. I worked with agricultural officers in wheat, maize and soybean projects. The bcok is about village life, friends, village festivals, weddings, students, travel, and a love story. At the same time, it shows that the cultural exchange was valuable for both me and my Indian friends.

I have included some pictures in the book. Also I have included maps of the local area.

Preface

The early Peace Corps was infused with the spirit of the sixties. Young people were idealistic. They wanted change and believed that positive change was possible. They thought that there was a better world coming and they were willing to work for it. They were encouraged by the Civil Rights Movement and the dream of Martin Luther King. By 1968, however, the catastrophe of the Vietnam War had split America right down the middle. The university campuses all across America were exploding with demonstrations against the war. Students chanted "Hell No, We Won't Go". American soldiers continued to die in Vietnam along with many more Vietnamese. Bob Dylan, Joan Baez, and the Beatles sang protest songs.

The youth of America wanted peace not war. Joining the Peace Corps seemed like a good way to work for Peace. Most of us joining the Peace Corps simply thought that the Vietnam War was wrong and that America was wrong. We refused to have anything to do with the war except to protest against it. There was only two ways out. Join the Peace Corps or go to Canada. To the other half of America that still believed that the Vietnam War was a noble enterprise for stopping Communism, those who joined the Peace Corps were just "draft dodgers."

Those who joined the Peace Corps were often looked down upon as renegades. This is the story of one of those American renegades.

Eddie James Girdner

Acknowledgements

First, I thank President John F. Kennedy and Sargent Shriver for their political vision in launching the Peace Corps. It was a vision which is sadly lacking in politics in the United States today. It is a miracle that they pulled it off, given the narrow vision, parochialism and conservatism of many members of the US Congress at the time.

I also thank the Peace Corps staff for accepting me into the India 53 programme for India. I am also thankful to those who helped me get a military deferment from the Presidential Appeals Board, when I was turned down by my local draft board in Princeton, Missouri and by the State appeals board in Missouri.

I am thankful for the Peace Corps training staff in Hemet, California and Batala, India, who whetted our appetite for India, as well as for Indian food. They also providedan opportunity for me see a little bit of America before flying off to India.

Also thanks to my supervisor, the Block Development Officer, Harbans Lal Sharma and the Agricultural officers of Banga Block in India who helped take care of me and provide for my needs.

Hardev Singh Karihaand his son Jatinder Singh Kariha and family offered me their generous hospitality. They gave me a place to live in their guest roomin Kariha village for the first month after arriving in Banga Block.

Also thanks to all my fellow volunteers in India 53, who were friends and colleagues in India. Special thinks to my travelling buddy Bob Baker in our travels around India.

There were many who helped me in India. The Sarpanch of Mahil Gaila, Swaran Singh, looked after me and often fed me on cold winter evenings when my cook was gone. He always made me drink a shot of his Binnys Sherab. Sukhdev Singh taught me a lot about India and usually had some cold beer when I arrived at his comfortable house hot and exhausted from riding my bike in the punishing heat of Punjab. My friends, Sant Ram, Prem Kumar, Karamjit Singh, Jagbadal Singh and many others kept me company and clued me in to what was happening among Punjabi youth.

Bachan and Mussie, my cooks, kept me fed.

The carpenters in the village, Gulzar Singh and brothers saved me from the mosquitos and flies with screens for my windows, made some beautiful furniture for my place, and were always for a party at my place with bukra and Binnys.

Many others friends and colleagues provided me places to rest from bicycling in the blazing Punjab sun in the hot afternoons and a warm bed on some cold winter nights in Punjab. I thank these and many others who helped me to survive and enjoy the years that I spent in India.

Eddie James Girdner

Introduction

The year was 1968. The US Embassy in Saigon had recently been attacked and taken over by Communist forces and several people killed on the grounds. This was part of the Tet Offensive. The US military officer at the Armed Forces Entering and Examining Station (AFEES) in Los Angeles on that cool foggy morning barked at me: "Move on! You are on your way to a new way of life!" He was dead right. I was. But it was not what he had in mind. He thought I was going to be sent like a sheep to the slaughter in Vietnam. Instead, I spent two years in Punjab, India. These were two of the most pleasant and interesting years of my life. Not everything was easy, but this period of my life provided an education about the larger world. It was one way for Americans, clueless about the larger world, to learn about the global birds and bees. They will never get a clue as long as they stay in their cozy cocoon listening to CNN and the rest of the American corporate press.

Most Americans have been brainwashed into believing that the United States is and always has been a great positive force in the world. They believe that America means well even when foreign policies, such as those in Vietnam and Iraq, result in colossal disasters and mass slaughter of innocent people and wreak mass destruction. The United States of America has specialised in destroying countries to save them in recent decades of history. Most Americans still believe that imperialist ventures such as the wars in Vietnam and Iraq were noble efforts for the people, but unfortunate events got in the way. Today, however, new books are bringing to light more of the war crimes in Vietnam. It would be good if those Americans steeped in these illusions about their own country would read Noam Chomsky and William Blum. I don't know about other Peace Corps Volunteers but for my part, I feel terribly lucky to have escaped that dreadful fate that fell to so many young Americans in the Vietnam War era.

It is perhaps fair to say that the American Peace Corps is also a product of this American illusion. America has long been a global empire. President John F. Kennedy had no intention of presiding over the dissolution of that empire in his presidency. The best and the brightest in his administration were out to strengthen American power and hegemony around the globe. They thought that they were rolling back Communism. They thought that the Peace Corps was a useful tool in that enterprise.

The assumption behind such thinking was the naïve notion that Americans obviously know how to do things better than others, so why not share some of their wisdom with those unfortunates who do not. "We'll teach 'em what they don't know how." English majors from the USA teaching Punjabi peasants how to grow crops? Sure, no problem. They can rise to the occasion right away once the enterprise is contracted out to a private firm. Americans are "can-do" people. There were indeed some very strange, even absurd, things going on here for sure. It stretched one's credibility, but people generally bought it. It seems that most have bought the John F. Kennedy myth of the Peace Corps. It was, after all, a part of US ideology, bringing freedom to unfortunate people and saving the world from communism, and similar pretexts. It was analogous to the white man's burden of the British Raj.

For the most part, the people we came into contact with in India did not need us. They know what they were doing. What the peasants needed, both big and small, was inputs, capital, seeds, fertiliser, tractors and so on. We could do very little in helping them got those things. Others may disagree, but this is what I believe. Is it any wonder that they were scratching their heads over why we had suddenly turned up in rural Pubjab?

Nevertheless, in the case of the Peace Corps, I believe that JFK and Sargent Shriver did mean well and that it was a good program. It was a very good thing that they did in creating the Peace Corps. Even though their thinking and vision about the world was seriously flawed, I believe it was one of the best programmes of the US Government. It was a small safety valve in an America when youth, frustrated with American policies abroad that were getting them killed, were beginning to revolt. Inducting these kinds of youth into the military, who had tasted education in the universities, was causing the military a lot of problems. People like me would have just been a nuisance to them.

On the other hand, it must be acknowledged that the Peace Corps, run by the US State Department, was part of American imperialism, to strengthen America's hand around the world. It was an effort to prove that Americans were very good and altruistic people who had nothing to gain from others. When the programme was being launched at the time the Vietnam Warwas about to begin, it can be understood why foreigners would be skeptical of American intentions.

How come Americans were helping Punjabis grow more wheat in Punjab, while destroying the rice fields and killing peasants in Vietnam? Someone might want to know that. It did not make any sense. It boggled the mind if one was aware of what was going on. It did not add up. Were those in the Peace Corps providing window dressing to cover up American imperialism in Vietnam and elsewhere? Were there two types of Americans, the good guys in the Peace Corps and the bad guys in the US military or were we all working for the same noble cause to rid the world of communism? Why should it be a concern to people in Kansas if Vietnam or India decided that it wanted to have a communist form of government? Didn't America believe in the principle of self-determination?

I don't know about other Peace Corps volunteers, but I didn't have a clue about all this when I joined. But I knew I didn't want to kill anybody. I also didn't want to get killed. The only real immediate danger facing me was the US Government. Ironically, it was also the only thing that could save me from that danger, short of leaving the country and going to Canada. That was the dilemma of thousands of America youth graduating from American universities in 1968. It was obvious that going to Vietnam probably meant getting killed or being forced to kill others. The Communists had nothing to do with putting us in such a difficult dilemma. It was a crazy situation in a crazy time. US foreign policy was driving us crazy and getting us killed. Empires always run into a brick wall at some point in their careers.

If wars like Vietnam were the hard side of American Imperialism, in which war crimes were being carried out by the US military, then the Peace Corps was the soft side of the same thrust. It was as far away as we could remove ourselves from American imperialism without becoming an outright outlaw and fleeing the country. I generally bought the hype about the Peace

Corps doing a lot of good to people in other countries. I think it was the same for other volunteers. We really did think we were doing something very good.

Consequently, I am very thankful that the programme was created which most certainly saved many young Americans from dying in Vietnam. It offered a small window of escape of youth from the military draft and the war without going to Canada. For that very reason, many Americans, mainly conservatives, opposed the Peace Corps and would have liked to have killed it.

In spite of the flawed vision of the founders about the larger world, the Peace Corps provided us a chance to learn about a fascinating country when we were very young. Surely the major benefit of this was to America rather than to India in educating some of its citizens about other countries of the world. This is true in spite of the fear of conservative members of the US Congress that we might bring back foreign ideas to America. They were right. It is much easier to see through American ideology from ten-thousand miles away and through the eyes of people on the receiving end of American foreign policy. For me it was a matter of seeing the light. I understood the role of America in the world as an imperialist country that was admired as a great and powerful country, but also feared as the Roman Empire. I cannot speak for others, but for me it was one way of knocking some sense into my ignorant head. I learned American foreign policy from the other end of the telescope. This gave me a different perspective from most when I a returned to study politics in graduate school. This was surely a beneficial feature of the Peace Corps and precisely what many in the US Congress feared would happen. It blew the cover on American ideology.

The India 53 Peace Corps group project in village level food production is described in the synopsis. This book is my story, not that of any other volunteer. It is a small part of history which should perhaps be recorded to understand more about what people were doing and thinking at the time. I hope that it will be of interest to readers too young to remember the turbulent sixties and the hope for a better world that existed among youth in those days. It should be of interest to both Americans and Indians, particularly those in Punjab. I have been told that it is the only book of its kind. I don't know if any other Peace Corps Volunteer has written a memoir about being a volunteer in Punjab. I hope that other memoirs of Peace Corps Volunteers in India will appear in future.

The names in the book have mostly been left unchanged, except in a few cases. It would be interesting to receive thoughts and comments from readers who might run across the book.

The author may be reached at eddiegirdner@gmail.com

The views expressed in this book are my own and not those of the Peace Corps or any other volunteer. As to being a renegade who believes in Peace, I plead guilty.

Eddie James Girdner

1

Dodging Bullets

"And it's one, two, three, what are we fighting for?
Don't ask me cause I don't give a damn.
Next stop is Vietnam."

—Country Joe

When John F. Kennedy was elected President of the United States in the 1960 Presidential Election, he proposed that a programme, called the Peace Corps, be established. Young university graduates as well as those who had hard skills from life would be asked to volunteer to work in developing countries around the world, which would invite volunteers. Volunteers would receive only a living allowance as compensation. The programme could be seen to follow, in part, from the famous line from President Kennedy's inaugural address: "Ask not what your country can do for you, but ask what you can do for your country."

It all sounded so idealistic. The Peter, Paul and Mary generation was ready to rise up and change the world. A new holy crusade led by bright eyed American youth was about to begin. But we shouldn't fool ourselves by all that gushing paternalistic Peace Corps balderdash. About how we were going to be missionaries, holding onto the gospel plow, and leading our little dark brothers into the glorious western light of day. We would teach'em what they don't know how. It was self-serving both for America and the

Volunteers. Kennedy and his bright young Harvard educated boys were hard-nosed anti-communists and the President had in mind preventing the further spread of communism in a revolutionary age. Nations were waking up, coming out from under colonialism, to rule themselves. The Kennedy boys were for freedom, but of a certain kind. They wanted to decide, what kind. It was clear that the Peace Corps was part of that agenda. Counter insurgency, that is. For some, what they could do for their country was to go off and shoot communists. For others, they would not be expected to shoot communists, but nevertheless, they would be labouring in the same vineyards.

From a moral standpoint, or almost any other one can think of, it was a hell of a lot better than shooting communists.

India was to be a rich ground for sending American Peace Corps volunteers, and as a fascinating country, it was an exciting opportunity for American youth who wanted to learn something about the world. Programmes began to get underway in the early 1960s in village-level food production, high school teaching, community development, poultry production and so on. Whatever Americans thought that the other people needed to get themselves civilised, and ready for the brave new world was a possibility.

By the time I joined the Peace Corps in March, 1968, it was the height of the war in Vietnam. There were more than half a million American military personnel in Vietnam at the time, and the so-called Vietcong had just managed to attack and capture the American Embassy in Saigon for a time during the Vietnamese New Year, in January 1968. This became known as the Tet Offensive. America, while not ready to admit it, had already met its Waterloo in Vietnam. But nevertheless, young men were still being drafted and sent there. A lot of them were dying in a war that was already lost. It would be another three or four years of Henry Kissinger's diplomatic table tennis with the North Vietnamese before there would be a serious winding down of the American war in Southeast Asia. President Richard Nixon would start dropping bombs in Cambodia down the Ho Chi Minh trail in early 1970.

The Peace Corps provided an opportunity to escape from the military draft and going to Vietnam in the military. When I graduated from the University of Missouri, in January 1968, the Selective Service was hot on my heels to draft me. My local draft board, in the small town of Princeton, Missouri, was determined to draft me at once into the military and chances were that I would have been sent to Vietnam. And probably killed. They had me in the sights of their guns. Not only were the Vietnamese under fire. I too was a target. They thought I ought to go and shoot some commies, like any good red-blooded American youth. But there was one thing that I was sure of. There was no way that I was going to go to Vietnam and kill Vietnamese or anybody else. I didn't have any enemies that far away. I wouldn't mind to go and make friends with them. It would be lovely to sit down and eat lunch and have a beer with them, but I would have no part in killing them. If they wanted to be communists it didn't bother me at all. Why should I care? Let freedom ring. Wasn't that the line we sang in the old song, "America the Beautiful." Yes, from "every mountain side." For me that included the mountains in Vietnam too.

If I was a coward, it was for a good, moral cause. As well as to save my skin.

Ah, the beauty of rural life. Or more perceptively, the idiocy of rural life, as Karl Marx had it. Better solipsism with a clear conscience.

So I sent in my application to the Peace Corps in Washington in the fall of 1967, while still at the university, and was accepted for a programme in India. Village level food production in Punjab. In an official way, it was meant to be just a different way of killing communists. We would show them that Americans were really good guys. It was another way of "winning hearts and minds." It was not quite that simple, however. First, I had to get an exemption from the military draft to go into the Peace Corps. I would have to do some fancy dancing to dodge the bullets of the Pentagon, and the local draft board, if I wanted to stay out of their clutches. The price of freedom is eternal vigilance, especially from those bastards in the military and the local yokels in my home-town who wanted to see me marching off.

"Johnny get your gun, get your gun, get your gun. Get those commies on the run, on the run, on the run. This will be a lot of fun, lot of fun, lot of... and so on." Bullshit.

This would take some bureaucratic wrangling, but in the end I would succeed in avoiding the draft and going to India in the Peace Corps.

Letting freedom ring was a fine platitude, but it didn't necessarily apply to my case. Not only was my freedom not ringing, it seemed that American officials were doing their darndest to strip away whatever freedom I had. My quest for freedom had to be approached in a three step process. Well, ain't it my right? Maybe, maybe not. Uncle Sam would decide that.

First, an appeal to the local draft board for an exemption. Princeton, the old home town, turned me down, flat. No surprise there. "Ours are hearts that truly love thee," the old Princeton High School ballad went. Sorry. I just couldn't find any love in my heart for those farmers on the draft board, although they were decent people, as far as that goes. But they were trying to get me killed and that was a serious proposition from my point of view. To put it bluntly, it mattered to me. I had some living to do and I wasn't ready to hang it up at a young age. They just didn't know where it was at, as Bob Dylan used to sing. Unfortunately, they knew where I was at. And I had to change that. I needed to get lost. Local small businessmen and farmers. What could one expect?

Then onward to an appeal to the great state of Missouri. They too turned me down. Flat. Of course they were hard-nosed bastards down there next to the state penitentiary in Jefferson City, Missouri. Again, no matter. They liked carrying out executions there on the banks of the Missouri River, but they were not going to get me, if I could help it. The final hope was on the man himself, the Presidential appeals board and Lyndon Baines Johnson, who was by now President. I would be saved by the great state of Texas. I hoped. But that took time for the bureaucratic wheels to move and the answer was not to come until October 1968 when I was already in India, having signed an agreement that my bacon would be shipped back and I would be drafted for war if the Presidential Appeals Board turned me down. They were keeping track of me. Just another warm body to be chewed up in the imperialist war machine.

On the 31st of March, 1968, I flew to California, for two months of Peace Corps training. After dropping down at LAX, Los Angeles Airport, there was a commuter flight to Riverside, on an old prop plane. A staff member was picking up the trainees that were flying in that day. They drove us down to Hemet, a small town in the valley. There was an old migrant labour camp for Mexicans, where we would be trained. The training programme had been contracted out to a company called Development and Resources Corporation. Just after we arrived in the evening, we heard the news that President Lyndon B. Johnson had just made his announcement that he would not seek re-election to the Presidency. This was significant, and everyone was happy that LBJ was going to be out.

We all remembered that chant at university campuses. "Hey, Hey, LBJ, How many kids did you kill today?" Great politician. His Great Society programmes were great, but he had been brought down by the war in Vietnam.

During training, they taught us some things about India, life and culture, how to grow vegetables, and some rudimentary Punjabi language. This was India 53, Food Production. Each of us was given a small plot for planting a garden. Out of the nearly forty candidates, some 23 of us were graduated and certified sane and fit enough by the Washington shrinks to go to India. We were all guys, as had to be for such a programme in Punjabi villages. Essentially, we had to prove to the company shrink that we had no objection to killing commies. Of course not. Why should we? He was scanning out brains for any fatal defects. We were not draft dodgers or anything of that sort. If that was even suspected, we would be thrown out of the programme at once. But we thought maybe it would be nice to make a little peace before going to war. That would make us more sturdy patriots and some other such another nonsense to prove that our heads were in the right place. And that we were not commies too! There was always a fear among some Congressmen back in Washington that we too might come back as commies. They had no inkling that it might be them who were driving us to perhaps be communists. There were people, patriotic Americans, putting my life in danger, and they were not communists. The communists were just minding their own business, as far as I could tell. They were not trying to get me into a war and get me killed. The disappointed other candidates in the training programme who didn't measure up were sent back home to wait for their draft notices.

The successful 23 graduates would be assigned to villages in the Doaba of Punjab, Jalandhar and Kapurthala Districts, in North India, some two hundred miles north of New Delhi, in the populous green revolution area of Punjab. The Doaba was the triangle of land between the Sutlej and Beas rivers. Eighteen of us would stay the full two years and one would stay another year. Returned Peace Corps volunteers are being completely honest when they say that their experiences changed their lives forever. The same would be true for us. What happened to each of us is a little piece of history that perhaps should be recorded somewhere and not lost. That is what I have tried to do in these pages.

2

New Way of Life

"The United States has sought to apply the imperial model to the post-imperial world."

—Richard J. Barnet

While I was in Hemet, California, in April 1968, I was ordered to go with another volunteer up to Los Angeles for a military physical examination, just in case. An ancient bus, from the early 1950s, picked us up and dumped us in a rat-infested and rancid hotel in downtown Los Angeles. Almost comical, but good enough for government work. The American soldiers might be keeping the world open and free for capital, American business, profits, bull markets and the freedom to get rich, as Ronald Reagan liked to put it. But we were a long way from being in business class. The Government was treating us like shit, which didn't provide much of incentive for trusting them when they took us into the military. At least, there were no bullets whizzing around us. In the evening we were free to enjoy the city.

Very early the next morning we headed down to the Armed Forces Entering and Examination Station (AFEES) for the military physical examination. A large crowd of rather timid looking young guys had gathered in front of the doors in the thick cold morning fog rolling in from the Pacific. Foggy times. Sheep for the slaughter, it struck me. Poor guys. Many would not make it back from

Vietnam alive. When the doors opened, an officer barked at us: "Move, you goddam motherfuckers! You are on your way to a new way of life!" Sure enough. I knew he was right. Fuck'n A. But I was hoping and praying that it was not what he had in mind for me. I would stay a free man one way or another and not be bossed around and herded like cattle on the way to slaughter. Eternal vigilance is the price of freedom. I would see that arrogant asshole in the rear view mirror. It was the second such examination I had taken. The other had been in Kansas City just before I left for the Peace Corps. Things had been a little more kindly there, but this was the top of the top, California and all that. California was always cutting edge America.

We were still young and stupid enough to enjoy Disneyland in Anaheim on a weekend diversion. Mickey Mouse and Donald Duck. One has to be versed in those central mouse and duck tenets of American culture to be a good cultural ambassador, in spite of the corporate capitalist downsides. I was not yet politically conscious enough to see through the disgusting corporate hype of Disney Corporation. We just went and had a fucking good time. The first time in Disneyland for a young guy from the Midwest is a treat and fun. It was a blessing to be that politically vacuous. Being politically challenged is part of American political culture. But it would be my fate to learn more than was good for me.

My socialisation as a young American had not been typical. Someone told me, a woman friend, after I had become a professor that I had not been properly socialised. No shit! That was true, but a gross understatement. One could not possibly imagine a more screwed up socialisation than mine. But I was bound and determined to bust out of it, even to the ends of the earth. Perhaps that was part of my project. Leave it all behind. The ultimate escape from the idiocy of rural life. The genius of Karl Marx.

The roots of that rural Bible-belt raising ran deep. Deeper than just being country bumpkins. My father, Roy Fred Girdner, came from a farming family near the small town of Princeton, in northern Missouri. Our ancestors were some of the earliest arrivals in the county in the nineteenth century, when there were still Native Americans in the area. From a family of five children, four brothers and one sister, my father bought the old family farm, when his elderly parents moved to town in the 1940s. Farming was all he knew and all he wanted to do.

The other side of it was the religious revivalism of the great depression which swept across the Midwest of America in which he was caught up. His life came to revolve around the farm, raising crops, cattle, hogs, and going to church several times a week.

He married late, meeting my mother after he was 40 years old. My mother, Kathleen Garren, had come from Arkansas with a preacher to the Assembly of God Church which he attended. My grandfather, Jim Garren, was an Irish coal miner in Arkansas. The family was dirt poor. My grandfather broke his back more than once in the mines. He was a union man, the United Mine Workers of America and swore by the union. My mother too, got into the church and made friends with others similar to her. She came with them to North Missouri and started working as a nurse at the local hospital in Princeton.

My father was drafted into the army during the Second World War, and stationed in Stockton, California. He was lucky not to be sent overseas. Once back in Missouri, they married, and he returned to farming. My older sister was born a little more than a year before me in 1943. I was the second of four, two girls and two boys. We were almost completely isolated on the farm, except for school and going to the local church. My father was a big fan of Oral Roberts, the mega-preacher from Oklahoma, who was now on TV.

My father could never be persuaded to undertake a trip off the farm when we were growing up. Except to see Oral Roberts. When he came to Des Moines, Iowa, we drove the one-hundred miles to see him in a big tent, not just once, but several days in a row. I did more travelling in a week than I had done in my whole life. Just to see a God damned preacher. Another time, the man came to Wichita Kansas and we went and spent a week in a motel, going to his tent meetings every night. He knew how to put the fear of God into us. We took out fire insurance. He persuaded us that we had to save ourselves from the hot burning flames of hell. Everybody got "saved" again.

A few years later, we didn't have a TV, but would go on Sunday to the neighbour's to watch Oral Roberts on TV. For me, it was not him I wanted to see. I didn't give a shit for that, but I did want to see some TV. We would stick as long as we could, sometimes eating popcorn, fascinated, with our eyes glued to the screen, watching innocent programmes like Lassie, and my friend Flicka. Even soaking up the commercials like wide-eyed idiots. TV was a sin, according to most of the people in our church who refused to buy a TV. But then, everything that gave one the slightest pleasure was a sin where we were coming from. Later, that made me appreciate that old definition of puritanism: the fear that somehow, somewhere, some place, someone might be happy. That streak of stupidity about TV finally broke down a few years later. Some heads were thicker than others, even within the idiocy of rural life in America in the fifties. Saved, to be sure, but not from the idiocy of rural life.

Later, I thought it was strange, how I totally missed out on American culture, music, films, kids TV shows, rock and roll dances and almost everything else. We lived in a country that we knew absolutely nothing about. We didn't have a clue as to what was going on in our own country culturally and politically.

There was a slight opening in the late 1950s when we got a TV for the first time. It came about through a sort of a revolt by my mother. One of the best things she ever did. My father was not going to go out and buy a TV, so she simply called up a big furniture store and had one delivered. The truck came and the technicians climbed up on the roof and installed the big antenna. Since the nearest station was 80 miles away, we could only get one station most of the time, KFEQ in St. Joseph Missouri. With the right weather, we could sometimes get a station in Kansas City. Other times, we only got snow. We would watch the tube up until nine o'clock every night when Lawrence Welk came on. When we saw the bubbles floating up the screen, his champagne music, we knew it was time to turn it off. Bad as it was, TV was a sort of window into sanity and regular American culture.

There were some programmes my father hated. There were the inane fake wrestling matches for St. Joseph every Saturday night. He watched them, at the same time threatening to take a post mall and bust the TV to smithereens. I was with him on the wrestling. It was truly inane TV. They had the farmers riled up, thinking that fake stuff was real. But other shows too, he watched, entertained, but not liking it much, as it interfered with his perusal of the Bible.

There were many who were rural and parochial, but our family was truly special, largely because of the religious connection. Anything that anyone wanted to do, except work was considered a sin. Cutting weeds in the garden was not a sin. Going fishing was close on Saturday and clearly a sin on Sunday. Going to a ball game was definitely a sin. It was a sin to go to a movie, a sin to dance, a sin to drink alcohol, a sin to engage in petting with a girl, a sin for a woman to cut her hair and wear lipstick, a sin to wear any kind of make-up, and so on and on. And TV was a sin, except when it was a preacher on the screen. Anything that felt good was a sin. It was perhaps a great way to demonstrate to a young person that the only good things in life were sins and that if one wanted to really live, and have some fun, then they had to go in for sin. Hell would not present much of a deterrent, in that case, since one was condemned to hell anyway, while one's friends were in heaven enjoying their sins.

My parents had few friends, and little social activity. So we lived a very sheltered life. But we did go to the library. I loved sneaking down to the library from school and the musty smell of those old books. I wanted to read them. The bookmobile came around in the summer, so I read lots of books. I naturally learned farm work and did lots of work on the farm. We were taught to work hard, but I guess I went a little too far and actually enjoyed it. That's what they called a strong back and a weak mind. The Puritan work ethic. I enjoyed long hot days of hoeing the weeds out of the garden. Driving a tractor, baling hay, picking up and piling up hay, were all just fun and not work. Doing the chores morning and evening was fine. All were enjoyable for me.

There was not much of a chance of getting close to girls. But one time in school, around the eighth grade, when one's hormones have started to pop, we had music classes. We got a chance to learn how to dance and there were girls. I even got to touch a girl and that was electric beyond description.

We were intelligent, but socially deprived or rather repressed. In high school, I excelled academically, but in sports, only participated in track. I guess that was one niche that the preachers overlooked and so I took advantage of it. I took vocational agricultural and was in the Future Farmers of America (FFA). I was good in contests, such as field crops, woodworking, and soil sciences. One needed some intelligence and some discipline. Those activities took me to the big city, Kansas City, where the national Future Farmers of America conventions were held in the huge old municipal auditorium. It was very impressive for me. It made me feel like I was part of something bigger. I could get out and have some fun with my friends. Although I was soon to realise that there was no future in farming for me. I would have liked it of course. Nothing made a farm boy more excited than to see a big shiny new and powerful tractor and want to get on it and drive it and do some serious plowing. But I did all of mine with an old 1949 model Ford Tractor, and a two-bottom plow, passing many happy hours on that old piece of junk in the field.

But I did have some spunk. They couldn't keep me down. Being somewhat of an outsider, in some ways, may have been an advantage. I had nothing to tie me to the local yokel culture. I had no girl friends in high school and no car to run around in like lots of guys. By my late high school days, I was raring to get away. I had smelled the fresh breezes of sanity outside the local slough of idiocy.

It was lucky that my older sister had enrolled at the University of Missouri in Columbia, which was 160 miles from Princeton. After High School, I followed, enrolled and was able to get away from home. I lived in the university dormitory and had friends in the university. My sister attended the local Assembly of God Church, which had the same puritanical rules we had grown up with. For a couple of years I also attended, but to be a member of the choir, one was required to sign a pledge that one would not go to movies, go to a dance, or drink alcohol. Women could not wear make-up. There were church services several nights a week. It cut in on the time one had to study and precluded having a normal social life. At some point, I could no longer tolerate such foolishness and rebelled and got away from it. I started going to the football games, and taking girl-friends out to films and pizza, but nothing very serious. Innocent things, but fun. By the time I had finished the university, I was almost normal, having sloughed off some of the damage done to me by my family. I had tasted beer, but did not really care much the taste.

One thing I knew was that I did not want to be drafted into the military and go to Vietnam. What could be more logical than avoiding that? One would be an absolute fool not to. I had not majored in social science, but had enough sense to know that what the US was doing in Vietnam was not right and made no sense for people like me. When there were big bull sessions in the dormitory about the war that went on into the night, I always argued against the war. It did not make any sense to go halfway around the world with a gun and kill people because they wanted to run their country under a different political system. They were not doing anything to bother us.

It was at Hemet, the winner's circle, that I started liking to drink a couple of cold beers in the evenings after the long day of language training. Finally away from home, away from the idiocy of rural life, there was meaning, promise and hope.

At the end of our Peace Corps training in Hemet, we were given a farewell dinner at a local restaurant. At this event, some of the Peace Corps officers, a couple of them returned volunteers, gave us pep talks about how we had to work hard not to lose the opportunity to do something wonderful while we were in India. In other words, sort of an opportunity to become a hero in helping to save the world. But if we did not give it all we had, we would miss the chance forever. It was all very American, that attitude, and I probably bought it half-way at that point, but this white man's burden stuff was a little naive really. The crusade to save Punjabi farmers, many of whom were getting rich, and become a hero, was like a football coach giving a pep talk to his players before the big game. Yes, all very American to get out there and be gung ho in the wheat and rice fields of fertile Punjab. Whopee Shit!

Well, I knew that I was going to miss the beer place across the highway from the Peace Corps Training camp when we left. It was called The Winner's Circle. When the day was over, usually after some language sessions in the evening, most of us would be over there and our weekly allowance covered enough to buy a few beers. I recall that we got some eight dollars a week. It was a place to go in the evenings. There was a pool table and one of those shuffle board games. I very much liked playing games and drinking beer. I had not had much leisure time in the university. But we did not stay terribly late. We would come back early, with a little buzz in our brains, where we slept four to a room in the building for migrant farm workers. My God! That beer was delicious.

There was another tour during the training. In May, we were taken on a trip to see California, agriculture down in the Coachella Valley, one of the big vegetable producing areas. The date palms produced juicy dates which were being made into milk shakes and ice cream. All the vegetable area was irrigated, of course. There were alfalfa fields, which I knew something about from Missouri. They showed us how crops like radishes and carrots were planted, grown and harvested. This was mostly done by big machines but they still needed Mexican labour for some of the harvesting. I am not sure that it had much to do with agriculture in Punjab. But we got to see some of our own country. This was the first time I had travelled in California.

There was a Sunday trip to Baldwin Hills in Los Angeles for the Baisakhi Festival. This is a harvest festival held in Punjab to celebrate the end of the wheat harvest. We were invited to the house of a well-off Sikh in the hills above the city. That day, his house was made into a sort of *Gurdwara*, as there was a religious ceremony. It was very liberal. Mahatma Gandhi was honoured, along with Martin Luther King, who had just been assassinated a few days before. They gave us *prasad*, the sweet, at the end of the ceremony. One had to sit on the floor, cross legged, which was difficult for me, as I was not used to buckling my legs under me.

The Beautiful House in the Hills had a Beautiful Expansive View of Los Angeles

After the ceremony, there was a large spread of Indian, mostly Punjabi food. It looked delicious, but when I began to taste the various dishes, the flavours were strange to my taste and it didn't quite satisfy me, like I thought, it would. It was my initiation to Indian food. The first time for these tastes and it would take a while before I would start loving Indian food. In the evening, it was back to Hemet by the bus and I remember sort of wishing that I could have a McDonalds Hamburger. Every American needs to be cured of that frigging disease. I had a long way to go at that time.

One evening, the camp decided to give us a full Indian meal, a Punjabi meal, of curried goat and rice. I thought it was delicious, but it seems there were some complaints among those running the training camp about the cost which was going over their budget. They preferred giving us watery green pea soup. Have to keep the profits up for D and R in New York.

We also made garden plots and grew some vegetables at the camp with irrigation. The soil was sandy and easy to work. We also plowed up a field across the road and I taught several of the guys how to drive the tractor and plow with the little two-bottom moldboard plow. Having come from the farm in Missouri, I knew how to plow with a tractor. I guess most of the guys learned something from it but it was a useless skill for India. Moldboard plows were not used.

It seems that around the town of Hemet, we were considered to be weirdoes, those nut cases down at the Peace Corps camp. Believing in peace, as opposed to saying you believe in peace, would not get you very far in America. We would walk down town to do our laundry on weekends. The Peace Corps also fixed my teeth. I needed a lot of dental work, and I thought it would never be finished in time, but by the end of the training, it was done. There were also a series of injections, in those days, to get us ready for India. Particularly, I remember the painful shots in the ass, gamma globulin, they were called. This was back in the days when one had to carry an injection record with them, that little yellow booklet, when travelling to and from areas like India. We were taken to military bases in the area for some shots.

The terrible fear of all of us, of course, is that we would be "deselected" and sent back home. We dreaded to see the final result. So I was elated that I "made it" and was much surprised at some of those who got sent back, who I was pretty sure, had a better chance than me. I felt bad for them and knew that I was lucky. I think I had a pretty steady and strong character and had worked pretty hard and so looked like I could stick to it out in the field. Also I knew something about farming and growing crops. Maybe that helped. I think it was mostly for psychological reasons that some were sent back. They wanted us to be mentally sound, as some guys would crack up, being so far away from home for a long period.

Perhaps they thought my weakest point was my motivation. They seemed to think that I was mainly doing it to avoid the Vietnam War. Well, weren't we all? Anyway, if it was true, then wouldn't that show that we could make rational decisions?

Later, I would have some bouts of homesickness in India, but not so strong that I would have given up the experience. For me it just lasted for a short period and once that was over, the feeling went away. Then one really gets out of America. Later, at some point, one begins to dread the prospect of actually going back home to America. Back into the belly of the beast.

The truth is that I could never really go back home, and would realise that very quickly once I was back in America. India was much more exciting and interesting than anything I had ever experienced in America. And I had more friends there. The best thing that could happen to an American is to really get out of America. Now we were getting out, at least most of us, and we would acculturate ourselves to a new way of life over the next two years.

The Peace Corps got us out of America and away from other Americans for a long enough period of time that we were forced to understand how things work in another country. That makes one realise ultimately the myth that everything is best in America and that it is up to America to tell others how to run their business. It shatters the myth of American exceptionalism that most Americans hold. It is a truism and taken for granted. One would never be challenged spouting such nonsense in America. Since they have no foreign experience, most Americans are arrogant and ethnocentric, without even knowing it. I think that the Indians didn't learn very much from us, but we learned a hell of a lot from India and Indians. Also we made a lot of Indian friends. The cultural exchange was very good on both sides.

Even though I think that the programme was based upon arrogant and ethnocentric assumptions by many involved, it taught a lot of Americans of that generation much about the rest of the world. That was a great thing for the people who were in the Peace Corps and helped to open our minds.

We cannot deny that John F. Kennedy's Peace Corps was an arm of US imperialism, or at least intended as such by many of the congressmen who voted to fund it. If it had not been, Congress would probably never have given the programme a dime. But while some Americans in the Peace Corps were patriotic and proud that they were Americans, they came to also love the countries in which they served. I wish it could happen to a lot more Americans and have always thought that if it could, America would have to stop following such an imperialistic foreign policy. American would have to use more, of its wealth for its own people and not peddle them self-serving hogwash about keeping them free. Sometimes I wish passionately that America could be just a normal country, like any other country, going about its own business and doing something for its own people, instead of acting as if God had given Americans the burden of ruling the whole world. That is what many Americans believe, after all, and surely this is the root of many of America's problems around the world. Just be a decent country and other countries will leave you alone. But an imperialist country that takes on the white man's burden just cannot do that. The needs of corporate capitalism drive American imperialism and create reactions abroad.

3

Cornucopia of Chaos

"I start on my journey with empty hands and expectant heart."

—Rabindranath Tagore

Our Peace Corps training was over on May 25, 1968. We were given a week off to enjoy the beach in Santa Monica, chug a little beer, meditate on the suspension of life as we knew it, and watch the glorious California girls, for one last time. A few volunteers who were more well-healed than me flew back home to say goodbye to their parents and friends. Then one early morning, at the beginning of June, we piled into a taxi and were off to Los Angeles International Airport for the trip to India. The flight was on the old Pan Am One, round the world flight, a big Boeing 707 going west. Those were the days when people put on ties to fly, before the airlines began to look more like Greyhound Bus Lines or Punjab Roadways, with passangers packed like sardines. Los Angeles to Delhi, with stops in Honolulu, Tokyo, Hong Kong, and Bangkok. That took some thirty hours in those days. Each stop, where we were herded into the airport and then back to the plane, was just a little more exotic and exciting. Sometimes forboding, and boring too as we grew more tired. We bought a lot of transister radios, recorders, and cameras in Tokyo. I remember the hills and lights in Hong Kong, and the heat and smells. We had reached the real

Asia. I, at least, wondered what the hell I was doing, off on a wild goose chase, but it was too late. We were flying on off the edge of the earth. And it would be a long time before we would be back. What the hell. What an adventure. I loved it. Some guys on the plane thought they could see bombs going off when we flew over Vietnam. I was not sure about that.

We then flew across India, in the clear June night, all those small villages dotting the countryside in dim lights in the early morning darkness. An awesome sight, and then we came down and landed at Palam Airport at four o'clock in the morning. The airport was later renamed Indira Gandhi International Airport. The airport was under construction, as it has been, I guess, for the last fifty years, never getting done. A very strange place for most of us who had never been outside the United States. Some Peace Corps officials and a couple of volunteers came out to meet us. It was hot, hot, hot, in the coolest part of the day, just before the sun came up. The volunteers looked thin and run down to us. Scrawny and tired. Thats the way we will look, after two years, we thought. We looked flush, beefy, and healthy to them, having just embarked from hamburger, french fry, fast-food America.

The bus looked shabby and the road from Palam appeared dim and deserted in the early morning as if passing through a stretch of near desert. But it was more luxury than we would see in months. The dry shrubs along the road, the dust and rough road were not very inviting. We bounced along to the western part of the city in the dusty air, arriving near the foreign embassies.

We were taken to the elegant International Centre on Lodhi Road, where we were given a little orientation and some pocket change in rupees to spend in the city. One purpose was to frighten us about eating the food in India. I suppose the Peace Corps doctor had a vested interest in this. He did not want too many of us falling ill. I remember him telling us to treat all fruits and vegetables as if they were covered by a fine film of feces. I don't know about the vegetables being full of shit, but I think he was to a considerable extent. But I suppose it was not bad to warn us to wash the fruit before eating. It was an exaggeration, and I often thought about all that shit on the outside of my apples and radishes and wondered who was that son of a bitch smearing them with shit before they reached the market. One had to learn how to function in society without worrying about things like that.

After a good day's sleep, dead out, among the strange aromas, some us headed down to Connaught place in the evening. I remember it quite well. It was indeed all very exotic for us. We met some Americans around Gaylords Restaurant who were living in the city, but more interesting, were some young Indians, who took us to old Delhi and to their home. Here was chaos. Here was heaven. Here was hell. It was most fascinting to us.

It was our first acquaintance with the old-fashioned Hindustan Ambassador taxis, Morris Minor automobiles. Great old cars straight out of the l940s. The exact original model, although the cars were being manufactured new in India. The streets looked dim and dusty and hot. We moved through them as if in the Twilight Zone. Orientation would take some time, until Delhi would appear bright and sparkling and inviting after months up in a remote village in the Punjab.

On a Sunday, some of us caught a bus and headed down to old Delhi and walked around the bazaars. The streets were terribly crowded and full of all kinds of things to buy. Full of everything that we had not seen before. We were not used to such a cornucopia of chaos. Poignant strange smells. Mass confusion, part of the timeless beauty of India. John Kenneth Galbriath, when he was American Ambassador to India, called the country a functioning anarchy. A good description, when it does indeed function. And it does, after a fashion. It seemed crazy at the time, but the hell of it is that Americans, and many Europeans, who stay around long enough come to love India and keep coming back again and again. One can spot those old hippy couples boarding planes in Istanbul and other cities. And then sure enough, there they are, getting off the plane at Delhi Airport, renewing their acquaintance with the heaven and hell that is Delhi. Many of them made their first trip there back in the hippy days of the sixties. India gets into their blood. Perhaps it is the natural human love of anarchy. Or perhaps they have an old soul, reincarnated from a former Indian life.

But not all was bright, of course. Vast numbers of people, markets, street sellers, foods, chappels, drinks, and beggars, and everyone going on and doing their thing, as normal as could be, but very confusing to us at the time. Some things seemed truly wierd, and it would take some time to get used to the country. Our language training was not of much use at that stage, but better than nothing. Fortunately India was an English speaking country, along with all the other languages which were spoken. It was all a little overwhelming those first days. In America, we had been deprived of such a rich cultural mixture, especially those of us from small towns. All of us coming from rural America had lived in a virtual cultural vacuum, only slightly broadened by being a student at the state university. But we were young and adaptable.

I remember looking out from the lobby of the International Centre one morning at the constant stream of bicycles in each direction and white-clad riders. Galbraith suggested that the greater number of bicycles was a measure of rising affluence in the 1960s. Now the country was starting to move beyond the era of bicycles, but they were certainly the common man's mode of transportation in India at that time.

In the next week, we were taken by bus to Punjab, our first time in rural India. Along the Grand Trunk Road, we stopped for lunch in Green's Restaurant in a district town along the way in Harayana. I remember the streets full of people, rickshaws, bullock carts pulled by lumbering oxen, tongas, vegetable and fruit sellers, peasants with beards and turbans, young students, all in motion. Heat, terrible burning heat of June, as most of us had never felt before. It was incredibly fascinating. It was wonderful but what the hell were we doing here? I still don't know, but I think every young American should be sent straight to some village in India to learn something about the world outside America. They should go as students and not teachers and learn. It would be good for their minds and souls. It would help them get their head screwed on straight. And it might even keep them out of the US military which was surely a good thing in those days.

4

School of Hard Knocks

"...though they won't change the face of India, they might have an effect upon their own small corner."

—John Kenneth Galbraith on the Peace Corps, 1961

On June 6, 1968, while we were still in Delhi, we learned that Robert Kennedy had been shot in Los Angeles. This was just after midnight in the US. He was running for President as an antiwar candidate on the Democratic ticket, and the California Primary Election was coming up. The next evening, June 7, we stayed in a rest house in Chandigarh. When we arrived, Pete Backry, a volunteer in our group, tuned in to a radio station and we learned that Bobby Kennedy had just died. It was sad news for us and very disturbing. He was the main antiwar candidate and his killing came just a few weeks after Martin Luther King had been assassinated in Memphis. It seemed sure that there were sinister forces on the prowl in America and that all the good people in favour of peace and progress were being eliminated from the scene. It was thought that Martin Luther King was not much of a problem as long as he was just a black southern preacher and civil rights leader. But when he began to speak out strongly against the Vietnam War and US imperialism in 1968, the FBI set its sights on him. He was eliminated. What happened in those days with the assassinations of the Kennedys and King is still not clear. Someday the truth may be unearthed. But that was a sad day for us in the group on the very day that we crossed the border into Punjab. Truly, we were on the way to a new way of life.

After spending the night in the rest house in Chandigarh, we proceeded on to the agricultural training centre at Batala in Punjab. The Peace Corps officials had arranged a dinner on the lawn for the invited Block Development Officers (BDOs) from the development blocks where we would be posted for two years. I think the dinner was meant for us too, but we didn't get much of it. Most of it was gone by the time that we got there.

We found at once that the food was great and delicious but that Punjabis had enormous appetites. Most of the food disappeared before we had a chance to get up to the tables. We were given mungies to sleep on in a big dormitory room in the Gram Sevak Training Centre. It would be our home for another six weeks of training at Batala. It was mostly, lectures and language training, with some instruction in how fields were plowed and rice was planted and so on. Planting rice was a back-breaking task and they let us get a little taste of it in the hot Punjab sun.

Our training in Punjab began on June 9, 1968. Early in the morning, we were given bicycles and told to ride out following the leader, for a tour of the area. It was a harsh initiation for me. I think there was only one other guy in my shoes. We were in a world of shit; at least I was, because we had not learned how to ride a bicycle. I don't know how many times I fell into the ditch that day, but I certainly suffered some hard knocks and bruises. I brought up the rear, along with my friend, but we eventually got there. I learned it, but the hard way. I had no choice.

I regret to have to say that I put much of the blame for the bicycle debacle on my dear mother. She would never let me have a bicycle and learn to ride it, as most children do, and so when I needed that skill later in life, I was up shit creek without a paddle. So I had to learn it the hard way. I guess she never thought of that. Of course I have to blame myself too. I should have revolted like a normal kid and held out for a bicycle. There is no progress in this world without revolt.

I have to say that she made the same mistake when it came to swimming. I didn't learn to swim as a child and so had to learn to float on my back in a week when I joined the US Navy. I didn't really learn to swim well until later, but it would have been much easier if I had learned it as a child and not under the whip of the US Navy drill commander. But better late than never.

As a laggard along the bicycle route to industrial training centres, factories, offices, and other points in the crowded and chaotic district town, through the bullock carts, cars, trucks and so on, I sometimes fell into walking and so met up with groups of young students from the local colleges along the road. They started asking me sharp questions about US foreign policy towards India and Pakistan, asking why the US supported Pakistan with so much military assistance and not India. At the time, I was very much unaware of all these things they were asking and could not explain why. I simply didn't even know about these policies, but my inclination in those days was to doubt what they said until I knew more about the situation. Later, I discovered that what they said was largely true. They were starting to educate me about my own country. The Peace Corps works both ways even though it might not have been designed that way. How many missionaries have been converted to other faiths?

The training at Batala lasted a month and a half and then the Block Development Officers came from the towns where we were to be posted. There was a final programme on the last day, July 15. I was to be posted in Banga Block of Jalandhar District. The major town in the block was Banga.

There was a love story in progress too. While we were at Batala, one of our volunteers, an older guy around thirty, fell in love with one of the young language instructors from Delhi. Russ was a rather strange guy who had already spent several years in the US military, including a tour in Vietnam. He had travelled more than most of us, but was not immune from affairs of the heart. His love affair with Rani was doomed from the start and could never work out, although he did his best to court her. Poor guy, I don't know if she had any interest in him, but when she left for Delhi at the end of the training, Russ was broken hearted and he decided to go back to the US after that. He was one of the earliest to return to America just after a couple of months. I don't know if this was related to his broken heart.

At Batala we were also warned by some American members of the staff to watch out for the women. Good advice everywhere, of course, not just India. Some of them might try to latch onto us and marry us just for the chance of getting to America, we were told. Well, I suppose there are all kinds of gold diggers, but this was hardly giving the women credit. People can be attracted to each other for lots of reasons other than money and visas. And we were going to be there quite a long time if we were successful volunteers.

There was a building at the training centre where the women were housed. One of the American Peace Corps staff designated it as "the harem" and put it off limits for visits by all of us male volunteers.

About half of the time was spent in language training. One day our language teacher took us to the bazaar, which was a more interesting place to learn some of the language. There was an extensive traditional market in Batala, as in all sizable Punjab towns. We had some tea and burfy, the milk sweet. The outside was covered with a very fine layer of silver paper. I thought this was very strange to eat silver with one's food and wondered about it.

At Batala, at the agricultural training centre, in order to prepare us for the village, and our work visiting farmers, we were required to go and visit a farmer for an overnight stay during training. The farmers had already been selected. I was sent to Asa Singh's place near Batala on 27 June. We had to travel by bike, perhaps five miles or so and were supposed to be at the farmer's house by noon. We were given the name of the farmer and the name of the village and general directions on how to get to his place. We were to stay overnight with him, see his farming operation and collect some information about his farming practices. This would give us a chance to use our Punjabi in a conversation with a local farmer. We were given a list of questions which we were to ask him about his farming operations. For example, the size of his farm, his principal crop, irrigation facilities, fertiliser practices, number of bullocks, number of buffaloes, how much of each crop he produced and so on. Of course, we were to ask it all in Punjabi. My farmer, at least, did not know English, but many farmers did. It was not really so bad, because it is really a quite easy language, once you get the vocabulary and verb forms. The syntax and grammar is pretty much the same as English.

I remember that day in June quite well. It was hellishly hot. Yes, the very hottest time of the year before the monsoon begins. I think finding the location of the place was the hardest part. I rode out on my bike and had to stop quite a number of times and turn back to find Asa Singh's place. But I did find it by noon or a little after, riding in the blazing heat. I met Asa Singh, who was an elderly farmer, and his son who would show me around and bring me some food for lunch.

The house was not inside a village but a newer house out near the fields. This tended to make it more open and airy, so a somewhat pleasant place. On one side was a big mango orchard full of large trees with ripening mangoes. A watchman was there to keep making noises to scare the crows away from the trees. It was very pleasant and cool under the trees on a charpoy, and as in every farm house, they invited me to lie down and rest under the trees after lunch in the afternoon. I sat down and after a while one sort of keels over and goes to sleep in the heat of the afternoon. Then they brought me lemonade to drink, a scungbie, which is not sweet but salty and spicy with pepper. I was not sure if I should drink it, as we had been warned about drinking the water without boiling it. This is very impractical, however, because what is one to do when one is offered a refreshing drink? It is not polite to turn it down on the basis that it might not be sanitary. One's hosts would not understand. And one cannot boil lemonade for sanitation. The Peace Corps had given us small pills to purify the water and a small plastic canteen for carrying boiled water. That was before the age of bottled water in the market. The first time I saw bottled water in India was in 1989, many years later in Hyderabad. But for the Peace Corps method, one had to wait for several minutes for the water to be purified, so I decided that it was not very practical and that I would just go ahead and take my chances and drink the water. One would either sink or swim. I threw the canteen and pills away and drank the scungbie, even though the taste was a little strange. It is good because it replaces some of the salt that sweating takes out of the body. Probably lussie, buttermilk, or yogurt, is actually the best, but at that time, I had not yet developed a liking for yogurt.

On the other side of the house, there was a very old man, Asa Singh's father, who was sleeping on a mungie in the shade. People actually tended to live to a ripe old age in these villages as it was in many ways a healthy atmosphere, except for the terrible summer heat which tended to make one weak. The man was almost naked and that impressed me. I clandestinely took a picture.

When it became a little cooler in the evening, Asa Singh's son took me for a tour of the fields. The wheat crop had long been harvested, but there were fruit trees and grapes and a field where garden crops were being grown. There was a nearby canal for irrigation. When we returned to the house, tea was brought, always Punjabi tea. I was just getting used to this. A variety of British style tea, with the milk and sugar already boiled into it. I thought it was a very useful drink for the winter time, but at the time, I would have preferred to have it black with a real tea taste.

As soon as the sun goes down, it becomes somewhat cooler, but still hot. Punjab stays hot all night in this season before the summer monsoon has come and brought the miserable humidity. The compound was a clean place because there were no buffaloes and cows. One usually ends up sleeping near the buffaloes and cows when one stays with a farmer in the summer time. Of course, the men were outside, while the women generally stayed inside the house, in their relatively secluded quarters, or up on top of the flat roof. Asa Singh also had a pretty young daughter, who I remember just catching a glimpse of from time to time in a bright yellow Punjabi outfit, but she did bring my food in the evening. This was generally the way with young women. One could only catch a glimpse of them and their bodies were almost entirely hidden by the loose clothes they wore. This was especially true of peasant girls.

In this season, it is common to sleep outside under the stars, either on the ground in the courtyard, or on the roof. This way, one can catch any relatively cool breezes that blow through, a relief from the hot loo wind from the west during the day.

Sometimes terrible dust storms would practically black out the sun, but these were rare and usually occurred just before the monsoon season.

Generally in a farmer's compound, the flies which accompany livestock, fall silent at dark and the mosquitoes take over. In the morning, it is the opposite. The mosquitoes retire to the shade and the flies take over. The Lord will provide, even when it comes to pestilence. But such activity is most bothersome when one sleeps out near the livestock. It is like sleeping on piles of cow shit. The scent is bothersome for some time for the uninitiated but it was not the first time I had known cow shit, coming from a farm. I had been exposed bullshit all my life, in more ways than one. It is, after all, a cradle to grave problem in every society that I am aware of.

In the early morning, it is a cold shower at the well, after pumping the water with a hand pump into a metal or plastic bucket. One undresses down to underwear, and dumps the cold water over one's head, soaps one's skin and pours over more water. It is cold but refreshing and a completely necessary way to start the day in the hot summer time. No more comfort for the rest of the day.

In the evening, I collected the information on Asa Singh's farming operation. This was relatively simple, but in the real world, things were not so cut and dried. Fortunately it was not rare that when one tried to conduct a conversation in Punjabi, the farmer, if he was a young farmer, would cut one off in perfect English and make one feel like a damned fool.

After lunch, I thanked Asa Singh and his son, said goodbye and returned to the training centre by bike. There was no farewell to the women, as they would remain secluded. I would have enjoyed seeing his cute daughter again in her bright yellow kamiz and pajama, but that was just wishful thinking. I am sure that I learned much from the exercise, although just what one has learned, does not strike one at the time.

While we were still at Batala, before the end of the Peace Corps training, there was a trip by bus to the hills. It was a rather small and crowded bus, up the steep hilly roads. Some of the Peace Corps staff came along with us to Palampur. This was a welcome respite from the heat of the plains. We stayed in a lovely old hotel on a hill under big shady trees. The road wound down to the main part of town through large trees. It was cool enough in the hills that the local stores were selling Cadbury's chocolate bars, which were not available down on the plains in the summer. It would have melted straight away on the plains without air conditioning. The cool, hilly, air was refreshing. One could trek up the mountain from the hotel into the rural areas in the hills. Near small terraced rice fields, there were small streams of icy cold water running over big rocks. This was terribly refreshing. This was the first time that we had been in the hills, and it suggested a lovely place to spend some time if one could get away. But one must be ready to bathe in ice cold water in the hills. It was such a beautiful place, but soon we would be back on the hot plains of Punjab to hit the dusty village roads on our bicycles.

5

Under the Stars

"The white ants are on the march."

—Nirad C. Chaudhuri

The day after the closing ceremony at the end of training on July 15, 1968 our group split up. I made my way to Banga, the major town in Banga Development Block, with the Block Development Officer (BDO), Mr Harbans Lal Sharma. We had to shift buses at Jalandhar along the GT Road. While we were waiting for the Banga bus, some men came running down the side of the road carrying a mungie with a body on it. His clothes were wet with sweat and the poor man had just passed away in the tremendous heat. They were saying "kuttem hoigee." (He is finished.) They set the body down not far from us. I was sitting in the shade near some coke wallas who were selling cold drinks. That sad scene made an impression on me, how easily one could come to the edge of life in the tremendous milieu of heat, dust, flies and mosquitoes.

We caught the bus to Banga, arriving a little after noon. It was a small town of ten thousand in the 1960s and the only town in Banga Development Block. After taking my baggage to the Panchayat Rest House, we arrive at Mr Sharma's house by rickshaw. It was on the edge of the town near some green fields. The courtyard of the house was pleasant although there is no escape from the heat in Punjab in June. Mr Sharma invited me to take a bath and freshen up before lunch. There was a small bath house in the courtyard for bathing. One strips down and pours cold water over one's body. The meal was rice and dal and vegetables which was quite delicious. His small daughter of about three years old was playing around and I made some pictures of her to give to the BDO later. In those days, not many people in Punjab had cameras and everybody always wanted their pictures made and asked for copies. After lunch, the BDO asked me to take rest inside during the hottest part of the day.

The next day, Mr Sharma would take me to the Block Development Office to meet some members of the agricultural staff. They were friendly young guys and we would become friends and travel around to the local villages in our work. They taught me what was going on with the peasants in the villages. The main constraint, of course, was a lack of resources, but Punjab was dynamic and moving forward in agriculture. The peasants mostly knew what they had to do, if they could just get the inputs they needed. They needed capital and resources but the Government could not provide enough of these.

The block jeep was broken down that day, so it was decided that I would spend the night with the BDO. That night, we slept on the roof, which is normal in Punjab in that season. The women slept elsewhere, since I was there. This was my first experience sleeping on a roof in Punjab, but I found it to be very pleasant sleeping under the stars and feeling the cool night air. The sky was so clear and the stars so bright that one seemed to be peering into the infinite Milky Way, the Big Dipper just to my right. It is an experience that one generally does not have in the West. Sleeping is pleasant under the stars, in Punjab particularly in the summer.

During the night, a rain came up, as the monsoon had just started a few days before. We had to get up and carry our mungies downstairs into the veranda.

Mr Sharma rose at five o'clock in the morning, just after daylight, and took me to the fields. It is 17 July. There was already a constant stream of people coming from the surrounding houses for their "nature call." This was very strange to see. Not being accustomed to an Indian life style, it was impossible to quickly train my bowels to move at the break of dawn. I remember going to the fields but with a quite disappointing result. Later in the day, it would be more difficult as there was practically no cover in the fields, except for hiding in the patches of sugar cane that had now grown up. This did not present a very bright prospect for me, at the time, but I would do what I had to do. For all practical purposes, one could not expect to have access to a toilet in rural Punjab, in those days with rare exceptions. There was one behind the BDO office in Banga. But for all practical purposes, unless one was in a city where there were restaurants, it was the field or nothing at all. If one was suffering diarrhoea, there was a medicine called paregoric, which worked like a cork. And some people actually suggested a cork, which might have worked better. Anyway, it was a new way of life. And I would not be killing any commies.

I had arrived and it was truly another dimension. We were cut off with only the mail for any communication with the outside world. Telephones were primitive and out of the question, except from a hotel in the city. When the skies clouded, lovely cool drops of rain came down, as a refreshing gift from the Gods. And all the scents, the wonderful scents of India, came alive to fill the air.

As E.M. Forster wrote: "The sky settles everything."

As a Guest of the Sardar I remember Tagore, "Thou has brought the distant near and made a brother of the stranger."

In many ways, Punjab was a lovely place in the 1960s, once one got settled, but getting a place to live was not so easy. After all, we were in a position that was not only strange for us but probably even stranger for the locals who had to put up with us. Our place in an Indian village would be a little one-man outpost, an extension, whether we liked it or not, of the American presence in other countries. This made some people wonder what we were doing there. It was easy to believe that we might be encroaching on the local village for some sinister purpose. But what could that be? I have thought about it and it beats the hell out of me. We were just nice guys in a very strange place. We took a wrong left turn some place, I guess. We were part of the sixties generation of live and let live and do your own thing. And keep away from the military. It is indeed ironic that we were forced to rely upon Uncle Sam, the US Government, to save us from the American military machine. Only Uncle Sam could save us from Uncle Sam.

I thanked the BDO and his wife for their generous hospitality. Later in the day, I was taken in the office jeep to the village where I was scheduled to be living. It was a small village some five miles to the east of Banga, called Kariha. It is not far from

Khatkar Kalan, where the Indian nationalist Bhagat Singh was born. There is a statue of him along the Banga-Newanshahr road.

I was taken to the large courtyard and the new pucca (brick and cement) house of one of the big farmers of the village and Banga Block. This was Hardev Singh, who was the Sarpanch of the village and also the Chairman of the Panchayat Samati of Banga Block. He was into politics and with the Green Revolution; the farmer class was gaining more political power in the state, particularly the Sikh Jats. He was a link for their interests in the state government in Chandigarh.

I am not sure how it was arranged that I would be taken to Hardev Singh's place. It is logical, however. I was coming from America and so would be honoured by being the guest of one of the prominent local political men in the block. That was all fine and understandable, except that it was completely wrong and unworkable from the perspective of getting me settled in and allowing me to work as a Peace Corps Volunteer. We were supposed to live a simple life-style on the same level as the people, relatively speaking, not to be housed in a rich farmer's house. It was the responsibility of the Indian Government, through the Block Development Office, to provide me with a place to live. It should be an independent dwelling, where the volunteer would have some privacy, rather than being the guest of someone. So this was a wrong move on the part of the officials, but they were just trying to do what they thought they had to do. Or more likely, they had not moved quickly to solve the problem of finding me a house and so just parked me there in the meantime.

Under the circumstances, I ended up staying in Hardev Singh's guest house for about a month. But this would not work, except as a temporary place to stay until an appropriate place could be found. I was hesitant to push the block officials to find me an appropriate place, which I really should have done. In the meantime, I enjoyed the relative comfort.

Kariha was a rather poor village, compared to many others and Hardev's Singh's big new pucca house stood out as a sort of mansion at the edge of the village. He had a new car, a pale green Hindustan Ambassador, with a driver, which marked him as a very big man indeed. Almost every day, he was on the road for some meeting or errand. Hardev Singh owned quite a lot of land in the village and had two tractors. One was a Hindustan Tractor and another was a Massy Ferguson. Most farmers had no tractor or owned only part interest in one. His son, Jatinder, a young man my age who knew good English, was mostly in charge of the farming operations. He would later be elected to the Punjab State Legislative Assembly in Chandigarh, the *Vidhan Sabha*, on the Akali Dal Party ticket in 1977 and become a prominent member of the Akali Dal Party in the state.

In the kharif or summer season, which begins with the Monsoon in July, they were growing mainly fields of bendi tori (okra), and maize to produce hybrid seed. I spent some time driving one of his tractors in the fields, just for a diversion, as if I was going to be one of his hired hands, working for board and keep. Maybe they thought it would be a good deal to have an American in that capacity. But Jatinder had several men working for him. That way, I learned something about the farming operations of a big farmer. Of course most of the peasants did not own a tractor at that time and were farming the old fashioned way with bullocks.

It was a short walk out to the main road or to the small railway station. There was a small train that one could take from Kariha to Banga. I took this train several times to Banga while I was waiting to get my bicycle, which the Block Office was also supposed to supply. But it took a good deal of bureaucracy to somehow appropriate the money and go to Ludhiana and purchase the bicycle. If I missed the train, I could walk out to the main road and catch the bus coming from Newanshahr.

It was a pleasant stay, in any event. The room had an inside shower and latrine, which was true luxury in a Punjab village. I was able to do some reading when I got my books from the Peace Corps. Some days were rainy and cool, and it was pleasant to relax with a good book. The food was simple, but delicious village food. Lovely vegetable dishes and chapatis. By this time, I had developed a taste for Punjabi food.

One day Jatinder asked me to go with him to Rupar, a town to the east on the Chandigarh road. He drove and we went in his father's new Hindustan Ambassador car. He was going to collect payment for some wheat which he had sold. I remember that the payment was in the form of a huge bundle of rupee notes, I don't know how much. Perhaps a couple of lakhs of rupees, which was a lot of money in those days. The money was wrapped up in newspapers and he put it on the front seat of the car between us as we drove back to the village. It struck me as a strange way to handle money, but it seems that it was relatively safe in Punjab in those days.

The family had a servant boy who came from the hills. These young guys, paharis from the mountains, work for room and board and low wages. Sometimes he would bring my food, as the women usually stayed hidden in the back rooms of the house. I very rarely saw any of the women. They must have been peeved at having another man to cook for when I arrived. One day this young guy came to me and took me to the small wooden building, a sort of shed, where he was staying, next to where they kept the car. It was at the side of the compound next to the wall. He pointed inside and said: "Sahib, your house." I was quite surprised, but then realised the meaning. I was being a nuisance and the Sardar was looking for a way to get me out of his guest room. In other words, I was being kicked out. There were six or more beds in the guest room where I was staying and where his overnight guests often stayed, and it was a problem having me in the way. I was being removed from the guest house and so had to discuss it with the BDO and urge him to find me an appropriate place to stay. I needed an independent house, where I could do my own thing and this was up to the block office.

I would go and discuss this with Mr Sharma, the BDO every few days and he would keep saying "Yes, yes, yes, of course, of course, it will be done and wagging his head from side to side." And he would go on shuffling the thin papers under the punkha, placing glass paper weights on them to keep them from blowing away, and removing straight pins from them and sticking them back in, and calling his *chaprassi* to bring in tea. A nice and kind man, a middle class Hindu bureaucrat, Mr Sharma was just trying to get on in the world and make a good life for himself. And all the time, old and timid peasants would be creeping timidly into the office where the big government official sat and greet him with a humble Sat Shri Akal or Namaste and make a humble request in a barely audible voice. They were invariably promised results, although I doubt if many got anything.

The promises would go on, from day to day. And then I would try again, and then again nothing would happen, and I would remain in limbo, my house just now coming, just now coming, but never arriving.

"Just now coming" became a joke among us.

6

Punjabi Tea

"The Punjabis... were puzzled at the first sight of the Englishmen because they had never seen any people look so implausible."

—Prakash Tandon

Kariha was a quite small village with some 1000 people. The bigger villages had a population of 3000 or more. There were basically two types of houses in the village. The old traditional mud and cow dung houses were called kuccha houses. The new cement houses were called pucca houses. In Kariha, as in most villages in the 1960s, the richer families were building new pucca houses, especially those that could get funds from abroad from a family member who had emigrated to England, Australia, or America. There were still many mud houses in Kariha in 1968. These houses were usually connected to each other with a continuous outside wall that ran along several houses. Besides these, on the south side of the village near the village lagoon, there were the thatched huts of low-caste agricultural labourers who had migrated to Punjab from further south. Many from Bihar. They worked in the fields of the big farmers. They were mostly Dalits and had come in the last couple of years and constructed their crude and rather miserable dwellings.

The village had a post office and some small stores. There was a small one-room store across from the post office, which was also in a traditional mud building. An old man was running the small store with a boy of around eighteen helping him. The store sold the basic needs of the villagers such as cigarettes, soap, rice, dal, cooking oil, ghee, butter, rice, flour, spices, notebooks, letters and stamps. Some supplies were kept in rusty cans in the store. The shop appeared to be very dirty but was a typical small village shop.

Just inside the door was a small entrance room with a mungie where the shopkeeper sometimes rests or sleeps. When I go to the shop to buy a copy book for a journal, they invite me to sit on the mungie and offer me tea. I try out my Punjabi, but am not very successful. Village Punjabi is harder to understand and so I am at a loss. The tea is Punjabi tea with the milk and sugar already boiled into it. It is very sweet and good and it is offered everywhere one goes.

There are many big black water buffaloes in the village. One can say that they are the backbone of the village. The *mudge* or water buffalo is essential for milk which is high in butterfat. They provide dung for dung patties. When they die, they provide leather for shoes. A Punjab village could not function without these cattle. The women go to the fields at five in the morning to cut fodder for them and the other cattle. They cut *burseam* (clover), *lucerne* (alfalfa), and young maize. Then the fodder is chopped with a fodder chopper, a big wheel with knives which spin around and chop the stems. The most common type is the old had cranked type, which came to the villages some thirty years ago. But the richer farmers now have the new type which is powered by an electric motor. After the fodder is chopped, it is mixed with *turee* (straw) and fed to the animals. The *turee* is left over after the wheat is threshed and stored in covered stacks around the village. The straw tends to provide bulk in the food so that the manure comes light and fluffy and good for making dung patties, the essential fuel in the village for cooking. The mixture makes the perfect gober patty for burning nicely, slow and even to cook the food just right. So the cattle are actually fuel producing machines without which life in the village could not go on. The women collect the gober every day in baskets and shape the dung patties with their hands and place them to dry on the ground or sometimes stick them on a wall. Then the patties are collected and stacked. There is a severe lack of wood in Punjab and this is the only way the food can be cooked. Kerosene is too expensive and not as convenient as manure.

There are also many bullocks, the big white Sahiwal type that are still used for plowing the fields and planting crops. Most farmers did not have a tractor or access to a tractor and still relied upon human and animal power to till their land. They were also used to pull bullock carts to take the harvested grain to the market to sell.

Just outside Hardev's compound was a low mud shed, with a thatched roof, where cows were kept. It provided shelter for buffaloes and cows. Today, I see a dead cow lying in this shed which has been there for at least a week, the carcass of a water buffalo. It is apparently starting to decompose as it is getting spots on it.

Everything in the village strikes me as being done in a very inefficient manner at this stage. This must say something about my American psyche that I would actually think about efficiency in a relatively poor rural village in Punjab.

In the BDO office in Banga, I meet the Village Level Workers (VLWs) and arrange for tour with Balwinder Singh, the Sub district Agriculture Inspector, to some local farms the next day. Each VLW has a circle of ten villages that he is assigned to. He is to give the villagers information about improved seeds and farming techniques. He also informs them of new programmes provided by the government, including population control. Sometimes it is only the bigger farmers who can take advantage of this assistance. It is late July and still hot. The humidity has zoomed, making the air super saturated with moisture. The only relief comes when the cool monsoon rains burst from the sky.

On July 26, Hardev Singh asks me to go with him to the Golden Temple in Amritsar, the Sikh holy shrine. He says that he has talked to the BDO the day before and that the tour to the villages has been canceled. I am not sure about that, but stay and wait for them to come anyway. However, he is right, the guys never come and the day is a loss for me.

The next morning, I take the early train at seven and go to the BDO office. Things start early in the summer season. I find that the BDO is just preparing to go on a tour and I am invited to come along in the block jeep to a Karnana village just to the south of Banga. We drive out to the village, dodging bullock carts and trucks and running everything else off the road. The only rule is mass and speed. Mass and speed rules and everything else flees out of the way, or they better.

We meet the Sarpanch, the head man of the village. Almost invariably, a Sikh jat, the dominant caste and dominant economic group in Punjab. They have recently gained more wealth and power due to the green revolution. The wheat and rice revolution puts a lot more rupees into their pockets. Sukhdev Singh raises good hybrid corn. Being from the Midwest of the USA, I know good corn when I see it and he has a good crop of corn. Obviously he has the ability to finance the fertiliser, which is mainly what makes for good corn, in addition to the hybrid seeds.

He invites us to his house for tea. Some farmers will even invite one to have some *desi sherab* early in the morning, local liquor, made of sugar cane, but that is the exception. It is generally the sweet gooey concoction of Punjabi tea, which quickly forms a scum on top if one does not drink it off at once. While the women are boiling up the cha, we get a chance to gawk around the room. There is usually a mantle for pictures and small curios, but no fireplace below. The walls will sport bright coloured ageing calendars of Guru Nanak, the founder of the Sikh faith with halo and garlands and offering peace, the raised hand with palm turned outward. A lot of red, yellow, and blue and sparkling gold colours. As things move on, one is offered the sword as the faith turns militant. Guru Gobind Singh occupies a prominent position in the Sikh Pantheon. One must be brave to be a Sikh. A Sikh is very brave, one is forever reminded. Well, good for them, they fought off the imperialists, including the British, but not always winning. Some of the Hindu deities may also appear, but it is generally Sikhs. The Golden Temple in Amritsar appears on a picture. The calendars may be years old, but it is not important, as they are treasures, regardless how tacky. They grace the walls of village houses.

There are some family pictures, of couples, staring straight forward, sober faced, a little terrified by the camera, Sikhs in turbans, and perhaps their wife in an earlier phase of life. Or sometimes there is a picture of the elders of the family standing around the body of a dead elder. If it is a modern farmer with some recent good income, the furniture, made locally, may be fairly new in his front guest room or sitting room, which is generally reserved for the men.

The *cha* will be brought in, sometimes, by a young woman of the family, daughter or daughter in law, heavily covered by *dupatta*. Along with the sweet Punjabi tea, perhaps some biscuits (cookies), if they are on hand, or some snack such as *karati dal*, a spicy treat that goes along well with the *cha*. One should nurse the first cup conservatively, as one cannot generally get by with drinking just one cup. When one is offered more tea, the first refusal is taken as mere politeness and probably the second declination as well, as it is considered that one really wants more, but is too polite to acknowledge this. It would seem to be bad manners. The ceremony goes on. I begin to think that Americans would indeed be better off if they would forget about some of their efficiency and have more tea ceremonies. Not much chance of that, however.

The topic of discussion turns to maize. I mention that in the US, we use 2-4 D to control weeds in corn. The BDO suggests that I do a demonstration plot at once and also start a programme to teach farmers about how to use pesticide to control maize borer.

It is a great idea. I realise later at some point in my life, however, that it is actually a terrible idea. All this chemical pollution, but one lives and learns.

I return with the BDO, with a little more resolve to be gung-ho. I feel like I must work harder at this point. The BDO again assures me that he will find me a cook, but the cook is just now coming, just now coming, just now coming. Always just coming but never arriving.

Feeling Like a Martian

It is now late July. The days are hot and sultry between the frequent monsoon downpours. The next day, early morning, I listen to the Voice of America (VOA) in bed in Hardev Singh's comfortable guest room. I am still here in the lap of luxury, but soon to be booted out. The servant boy knocks on my door and brings my mail. I get my check from the Peace Corps in Delhi, my bread money, and four letters from the US which have finally caught up with me. It is comforting to get some news from home, the first in a month. My older sister is preparing for her wedding to a Chinese engineer, which is something of a bomb shell in the small north Missouri town and church where the wedding will be held.

It is comforting to think how things never change. Not much. But we were out to change the world in the face of all the evidence against the possibility of making any difference whatsoever. The twelve labours of Hercules would not even be a start. But better than killing communists.

The morning weather feels quite cool and cloudy on this morning in monsoon season. But the sun comes out and puts an end to that in a hurry.

After breakfast, I go to the fields where the corn planting is starting with the big four-row planter. It would just be a wonder to the average peasant, who is dropping the seed by hand behind the furrow that his bullocks are making with a wooden desi plow. But Hardev Singh is no ordinary farmer. He is growing maize to produce hybrid seed. I try my hand at driving the tractor and run the planter. The hired hand does not mind. He sees that I am careful and know how to do it. I get the job and plant corn for the rest of the day, finishing the four plots which have been prepared so far. It's not my job. I am just killing time. It is one way to feel at home for a poor old farm boy like me ten thousand miles away from home. Hell, it could have been right down in our old river bottom for the joy of planting that corn that day. I enjoyed the hell out of it and felt right at home.

After having tea with the village school master, we again hitch up the cultivator and I take the tractor to the village Panchayat plot, some distance on the other side of the village, a thirty acre field which had previously been planted. The field got water logged, and the maize has drowned out. We start tilling up the field to replant it.

It rains heavily in the night and continues into the morning, so I study Punjabi in the morning, but am not making much progress. One cannot learn a language that way, especially when one is trying to communicate with villagers who hardly seem to speak the same language.

When the rains let up, I head out for the railway station, a cute little station that I loved, which is very convenient for catching the train to Banga, just five miles away. I have the urge to do some shopping. But today I cannot help being bothered by the constant staring. I am still very sensitive to it, something that it takes some time to get used to. Maybe some even start to like it at some point, but I don't think that I ever will. They know that I do not belong here. There's a son of a bitch that took a wrong left turn somewhere is what they are thinking. And they are right. But what the hell. I am here now, and this is where I am going to stay. Sure as hell, so just get used to it, country bumpkin. Don't look at me like a cow looking at a train, asshole. There's a bigger world than motherfucking Kariha *pind*, India, you dumb shit. So just leave me the hell alone. Well, who can blame them? A Martian does not drop out of the sky every day. Forgive me for my hostile thoughts, you parochial sons of bitches.

In Banga, I take a walk up Railway Road, the street that runs straight north up to the main road. I stop at the stationary shop. I always loved those little crowded shops with all the different kinds of copy books for students. I buy some paper, envelopes, ball-point pens, and a journal. The pens do not work very well, but they are different. I spot some delicious looking candies, wrapped toffees in a shop and fill up a bag. But when I try them, I am disappointed, as the taste is quite different from what I had expected.

The next day, July 30, I catch the bus to the BDO office. The VLW for my circle has come. His name is Swaran Singh, and I take the opportunity to visit two farmers with him. It is a good start, I think. But it strikes my attention that we, the block people, are only visiting the progressive farmers, the rather rich ones. And so they will naturally benefit disproportionately from the block development programmes and bureaucracy if that is the case. This is the normal pattern of agricultural extension work, I suppose. But perhaps it is not the optimal pattern of development. So I start to think that perhaps I should try to work with more of the poorer farmers. But this will be a challenge, as they will not know English, or very little.

We go to Khatkar Kalan, along the main road to Newanshahr, the famous ancestral home of the Punjabi nationalist Bhagat Singh who was hung by the British in 1931 for throwing a bomb into the Central Assembly Hall. Here we go to the house of Surgit Singh. Then we see Kishin Singh. Surgit Singh is a modern farmer and raises wheat and potatoes.

Kishin Singh is older in his sixties, and knows good English. A sort of gentleman farmer. At his place we meet an old man, sort of an intellectual, who looks like Gandhi. That day, I thought he was nutty as a fruit cake, but it was more likely me that was the nuttiest, I think, now that I am older and wiser. Now I do not think he was nutty, but that insight was to come later. He makes a strong argument to me, because clearly he is opposed to my programme, my agenda. In fact, he thinks that I am a menace to the country and would like to set me straight. He is certainly right to some extent. He argues that chemical fertilisers cause heart disease. At the time, I thought that chemical fertilisers were probably just what India needed to produce big crops of food for the masses. I don't think now that my argument was very sound, but I did in those days. I argued that if these fertilisers are so dangerous, then why were Americans the healthiest people on earth? That was bullshit, of course, but I did believe it in those days. The truth is that I was still a little wet behind the ears, but had certainly been brought up using fertilisers and chemical insecticides on the Missouri farm. I now know that the insecticides we were advocating, and that the Indian Government was advocating, were positively dangerous. After Rachal Carson's book, *Silent Spring*, many of them were banned in the US. But they continued to be produced and used in many countries around the world, including India.

This old gentleman wanted to grow some soybeans but could not get the seeds. So I wanted to help on that and would work on that project later with Kishin Singh.

After the visits and having lunch with Kishin Singh, we went back to Banga and I said goodbye to Swaran Singh. I then met some guys from Sikh National College, young students, who wanted to talk to me. So they took me to Kartar Sweet Shop. This was my first time there, although I would go there many times more in the next couple of years. It was a completely traditional north Indian sweet shop. There were no screens. The flies were just thick and swarming. The multicoloured sweets, looking delicious, were displayed out front, to the edification of the flies, where they were being prepared. A *halvai* was sitting out front frying jelabies in hot oil. It was damp and dark inside with the old crude wooden tables just filthy, soaked with milk and sticky sugar and oil, and attracting the grateful winged hoards. One could clap their hands above the table and drop half a dozen dead flies, sometimes closer to a dozen, a vulgar move, but nevertheless gratifying when one had a chance. It was a way to make a point in a crude way. Maybe these creatures do not come up to the level of mosquitoes in perfidy, but they are pretty damn close. I would go for extinction. Well, that might be a tad over the top, but they certainly got on my nerves in Punjab. Flies, black flies. Fresh out of those piles of human and animal shit that were spread over the fields from here to kingdom come. A thought that was difficult to keep out of my mind. I would go for a coke, which I thought was safe. Most would drink *lussie*. The vegetable samosas and pakoras here were delicious and the sweets were too, of course, if one ignored the likelihood of the bacteria that they camouflaged in their tasty flavours. I came to ignore it like everybody else and just enjoyed the hell out of the delicacies. Let nature take its course. Shit flows downhill.

The new friends I had made examined and cross examined me about the wondrous ways of America and also had to find out the price of everything I had on me, including shoes, watch, clothes and whatever and converted it into rupees which made it sound awfully expensive. But it was all cheap shit. Everyone always had to know the price in those days. I was politically naive in those days, so I gradually expanded my knowledge and cynicism of American and Western politics as time went along. You can't have one without the other.

Then, they wanted to take me and show me the college which was on the east edge of Banga in those days. We went to a sort of recreational centre where there was a Ping-Pong table set up. We played some games. They were far better than me in table tennis. After they had tuckered me out, and I had lost every game, I got the bus back to my place in the evening.

I had another programme with the BDO the next day on which my new friend, Swaran Singh, was supposed to go. The programme got canceled so I spent the time gulbotting (shooting the shit) with the guys in the office. In the afternoon, they decided to go to the cinema in Banga and asked me to come along. It would not be polite to turn them down, so I felt I should share the fun, and the boredom, and went with them. The film was *"Aurat"* or "Woman." The local theater was very bad. It was filthy and full of smelly peasants. I was quickly bored and dropped off to sleep for a good part of the time. I don't know if I snored. These films invariably droned on for a good three hours with an intermission. Give them their money's worth. The torture ended, mercifully, around half past five, and I was again liberated to my own devices. Hell, why bother. I would rather bore myself than pay Bollywood for the service. But, being the roving ambassador for America that I was, I would be a good sport and let the Bollywood stars titillate me from every mountain side. Ambassador, my ass. Oh well. From every mountain side, let Bollywood ring.

Back home, I could open a book. Something I understood, or at least could read. The beauty of privacy, relaxation and reading. All of which are going to be somewhat rare if I am to do my job faithfully.

7

The Idiocy of Rural Life

"....a man who cannot endure dirt, dust, stench, noise, ugliness, disorder, heat, and cold has no right to live in India."

—Nirad C. Chaudhuri

"Clouds heap upon clouds and it darkens."

—Rabindranath Tagore

August has arrived exactly one week ago. Summer may be on the wane, but not the heat, flies, rain, dust, mosquitoes and hoards of all kinds of flying insects. It seems that I have made some progress in the first two weeks since arriving. I don't realise it at the time, but it will be mid-October before I really begin to get settled in seriously. I decide to go to Newanshahr and look up a couple of the guys, Chris Klose and Russ Kenyon. They are still staying in the Panchayat Rest House as they too are waiting for their living quarters to be located. Up to this point, I have actually fared somewhat better than them. I find their location from the BDO Office in Newanshahr. I find Frank Rojas there, as well. We spend the day with a lot of card playing and some reading.

The highlights are the cheese and crackers we buy at the local government co-operative store and eat in the evening. We were not yet completely attuned to a constant regimen of Punjabi food. I spend the night at the rest house and the next day take a walk around the town with Russ and Frank. We tour the old Moslem quarters of the town, before partition in 1947. Here there are narrow streets and small shops. It is interesting architecture, a throwback to the past.

I get mail from the US, coming from Princeton, Missouri, in just four days. It is sobering to consider how the mail services have deteriorated in the age of internet, face book and privatisation.

Back in Banga, I put in my time with the BDO, still waiting for the block accountant, Ajit Singh, to buy my bicycle. But with no development on that front, I return to the market and buy some tasty fruit, pears, apples, plums. But just then, with my precious fruit in paper bags made of some local recycled paper, a huge black cloud appears in the sky. The rain begins as I wait for the bus. Big drops, as in monsoon season, mount, and then wind too, and driving sheets of rain. I have no shelter. In the quarter of an hour until the bus appears, my bags are soaked. Will they hold? Inside, the bus starts and jogs over the rough road, through potholes, as my bags quickly begin to disintegrate and break open. I see my fruit about to drop away. There is only one radical solution to salvage my fruit. And that is one which is not exactly socially acceptable in Punjab, but what the hell. I remove my shirt and tie up the fruit in a pouch. The hell of it is that men are not supposed to go without their shirts in Punjab. Not unless one is a naked Sadhu or some religious saint. When some volunteers would ride their bikes without a shirt, American style, the villagers would yell out "*Kamiz Karo*." (Put on your Shirt). But now I have little choice. There is an old woman on the same seat next to me, but there is no reaction. When we get to Kariha Junction, I get out of the bus and walk the mile to the village through the pouring monsoon rain, a lovely cool shower, and arrive at my quarters like a drowned rat. I realised what a mistake it was to come out in an approaching monsoon rain storm. Nothing hurt. I just took my refreshing shower on the road. And now I can dry myself off and eat my delicious fruit while I read a novel.

Good News

It is the seventh of August, 1968. This morning the sky let go and the rain came down in torrents. When it began to clear around eleven, I decided to go to Banga as Ajit Singh, the Block Accountant, was supposed to return from Ludhiana with my bicycle. I started walking the mile out to the road to catch the bus avoiding the large puddles in the road. A young Sikh came past and gave me a ride on the back of his bike. We have to swerve around slow moving bullock carts. I wait at the bus stop with some others on a small cement bench under the large trees. All the valuable trees are numbered and registered with the village *patwari* who keeps all the records. One of the men who worked in the BDO office told me that they had purchased my bike and I hoped it would come that day. After about ten minutes an old rumbling and chattering bus approaches. We prepare to run and catch it, but before we can, it picks up speed, too crammed to accommodate more bodies. It seemed to me that people in India were always going somewhere, always on the move.

Across the road was a village well and a traditional village mud house and some piles of straw. Across from this was a small bicycle repair shop. Another bus passed going to the east, driving bicycles off the road on both sides, but did not stop. The bus threw up a cloud of damp dust into our eyes. Two well-dressed young Sikhs passed us by on a new shiny motorcycle.

Across the road, a young girl of around fifteen was leading a water buffalo to the well. Her smaller sister, looking to be around six, held the chain attached to the buffalo's neck while the older girl dipped up water and poured it over the animal's back. The girl stood on the well curb and rubbed the back of the buffalo. They are terribly valuable animals, essential, for milk and dung patties. Several more buffaloes were tied to stakes along the road.

Another young woman came to the well. More bicycles. Then two bullock carts loaded with bricks. Across the road, a man pumped up a tire on an old bicycle with a hand air pump. It seemed that all of his body remained rigid, except his knees, which bent as he forced the handle down. A large man with a huge belly walked along the road. Huge veins stood out on his legs, as big as lead pencils. More bicycles and buses passed. A small child, totally naked, tottered around the well and splashed in the cold water. The air was terribly damp. Steam rose from the ground. Sweat rolled down my face. Black flies attacked my eyes. The small boy tottered across the muddy road and into the bicycle shop.

An old woman came to the well. Her clothes were in rags. She wore two pieces of cloth. One was a sort of skirt, worn like a tumba, and another piece of cloth on top worn like a shawl and tied by the corners at the waist. The cloth was a filthy brown, the colour of muddy water. Her hair was wet and stringing down. When she bent over at the well, her rag slipped down and her breasts were seen hanging limp and flat against her chest. When she bent over, they flopped like a sow's ears. Empty pouches, flat and lifeless. She squatted so that her knees were on her chest and washed her hair and upper garment. She seemed to draw no attention and evidently did not feel that any attention was being given to her. She performed the whole operation in the same manner as if it had been in the privacy of her own house.

Two more men came on bicycles. They talked to those who were waiting, and asked who the angrez, or English man, was. They were gazing at me with wrinkled brows and open mouths. Then they went on. The big man wandered back down the road, resembling a huge toddler just learning to walk, his legs stiff and his feet bare. The pestering from the flies became more intense as I attempted to fight them off. An old man came running down the road beating a buffalo and shouting obscenities to it. "*O tierre pan...*" (A Punjabi curse which means "fuck your sister.)" The animal was pulling a cart with a young man lying on it with wild eyes and evidently in pain. It seemed the boy was sick and the man was trying to get him to a doctor or hospital. He could not get the buffalo to go straight or fast enough. This is a crazy country. A crazy fucking country and sometimes pitiful in so many ways too. Often sad, but terribly vibrant and dynamic too. Everything is there. Everything under the sun.

Another bus roared down the road towards Newanshahr, clearing the road of bicycles. A woman's head emerged from a window as she vomited. Then a bus from the east approaches. We prepared to catch this one but a large truck was approaching from the opposite direction. The bus only veered off the road through a puddle, sending mud into the air for twenty feet and roared ahead, then slowed to let some passengers down. Again we ran to catch it, but it started up again. Not a chance. The driver had faked us out. A typical move, when the bus is crammed. We gave it up, but then the bus stopped and waited. Again we ran to catch it and clamored in. There were no seats. Literally packed. Is the driver playing games with us?

Then I recogniseda guy on the bus who I had met in Banga. He was a young guy studying auto-mechanics at Newanshehr. He invited me to sit with him, although the seat was full. I had to cling to the edge of the seat. He tried his English out on me and I tried my poor Punjabi out on him, neither of us being very successful.

Out of the bus at Banga, I repaired to the BDO office and was greeted by some of the staff, Surrinder Singh and Avtar Singh, who are agricultural inspectors. They were just ready to go out so they invited me to go with them to a *dhaba* for lunch. We walked the short distance to the shops. The *dhaba* was through a small courtyard, a small room, where two Indians sat eating. There were no screens on the door, so flies buzzed over the food in a huge swarm. They had found a plate of *chapatis* and blackened it. One of the diners brushed them away and took a chapati. A *killy*, or one of those small Asian wall lizards, crawled up the wall to the ceiling and peered at us. The food was being prepared over an open fire near the street. The waiter brought bowls of curry and potato, and vegetable stew. I broke up a chapati and dropped it into the stew. That is not the way one is supposed to do it, of course. I dipped one piece out and ate it. It was terribly spicy and burned my mouth. I drank some water. A good time to catch dysentery, I thought. We were supposed to drink only Coke or boiled water, but this was not practical in daily life.

We finished the food and washed out hands and mouths at the well outside in the courtyard, which had a hand pump. Then we walked back to the Development Office. Ajit Singh had not returned from Ludhiana. My bike was still "just now coming." Just like my house and cook. They too were just now coming.

I socialised in the office for a while. A man who lived in Kariha came into the office and said he was going to Kariha and that I could go with him. He had left his bike on the bus stop and I rode behind on his bike from the stop. When we got to Kariha he revealed that he had a letter for me. I looked at the envelope and saw that it was from the US Selective Service in Washington. My fate was sealed. This was it. The decision had come from the Presidential Appeals Board. I quickly ripped the letter open and looked at the classification card. It said, "2-a", which meant "occupational deferment." I had won my case. Free at last. I walked on to Hardev Singh's house with a little more spring in my steps. Thanks LBJ. You made my day.

8

Kismet

> "The Peace Corps had to succeed so as to prove that idealism was still worthwhile..."
>
> **—John Kenneth Galbraith, 1961**

The next week, mid-August now, Dee Wolf, a member of the Peace Corps staff, brings our trunks from Delhi by jeep. He is accompanied by a driver. We had packed our one-hundred pounds allowance of personal belongings in them before leaving the US. I have some necessary winter gear in mine, such as a heavy denim jacket, which I will need by November.

It was a rainy Saturday morning in the fall and I was not making much progress studying Punjabi. The second Saturday in every month was a holiday so I decided to take a trip down to Ludhiana to Lyall Book Stall, a big old interesting book store. I walked out and caught the bus. At the bookstore, I found the old novel *Gone with the Wind.* I was not from the South, but it was a nice story about America to read. I sometimes spent the night in a hotel there, just to get away from the village for some time. I remember reading Henry Miller's crazy books, *Sexus, Plexus* and *Nexus.* Somehow, these seemed to be popular in India.

Green's Restaurant was beautifully air conditioned. I had chicken pilaf and a big bottle of cold Golden Eagle beer followed with a double Sunday and tea. It was a beautiful little respite from the idiocy of rural life.

The rain had kept up pretty steady all day and the mud was ankle deep around the old bus depot that was in the centre of the city in those days. I got a seat in a packed bus, still fighting flies, to come back to the village and the driver drove like a maniac. At the Sutlej River, we had to wait for half an hour so that the road could be cleared after a truck got stuck crossways on the bridge. Then at Aur Village, a young man sat down behind me who apparently had had too much to drink. When he saw me, he started saying "Oh My Dear" and feeling of me. "Are you American or Russian. What are you doing here?" Then he asked me to give him a namaste. This was starting to become quite annoying to me. Finally another somewhat older guy, Mohan, came near and told him to leave me alone. Instead, the guy started getting louder and feeling of me more. The people on the bus were staring at us and it seemed that they were rather enjoying seeing me being pestered by the guy. I just wanted to get off the bus and be done with it, but had to first get to Newanshahr.

This encounter was a strange experience and the only time it ever happened to me in India. I think the guy was just a little sick mentally. A little *pagal*, as is said in Punjab. Possibly he was just drunk and affection gets expressed towards members of the same sex in a puritanical society. It has nothing to do with homosexuality, as is sometimes believed in the West, but is a result of sexual repression in the society, as far as I could tell. It always made me uncomfortable when my friend Sant Ram wanted to kiss me on the lips, as he would like to do his girl-friend, if it was acceptable. He was just expressing affection, rather than being gay.

When guys walked in the street, holding hands, it was sometimes mistaken for gay tendencies, when it was just affection. A way of expressing friendship as far as I could tell.

When we got to Newanshahr, Mohan asked me to come and spend the night with him. He had also been drinking. We went to his house and he kept telling me not to worry about what had happened. He lived in a rather nice house in the old part of Newanshahr. I was happy not to have to go back to my village in the dark. He had a comfortable house and gave me a big bed to sleep in. He said he was a government contractor and had been building roads in Jadla village and knew Chris Klose, my fellow volunteer just to the east. We had dinner. He sent his little brother out for a beer and he had a bottle of Black Night Whiskey.

Then we had a drink of whiskey, mixed with the beer. He was getting more drunk and said he would go to the cinema with his friend. I didn't want to go, but agreed to go with him. By this time, he was quite drunk and when we walked down the street, I put my arm around him to help him walk. It was the accepted custom, anyway.

We got to the cinema and got a box seat at the back in the balcony. In a little bit, Mohan got uncomfortable and turned his head to the wall and vomited. The film dragged on and on. I wanted it to end, so we could get out of there. Around half past ten, there was an intermission and I went out and relieved myself behind the theater wall.

The film took up where it had left off. The star looked to me like a wrestler with his silly girl-friend in a sari. The scene had been filmed in Kashmir and the guy and his girl-friend were dancing and singing on the hills in the cloudy and rainy weather. It seemed a little absurd to my sensibility. They were wearing so many clothes that you couldn't see any skin and then when the girl started dancing and singing and touched the boy's hand, the guys in the theater started yelling and whistling. There were no women in the audience, just guys. I felt like yelling out "Skin! Skin". The whole thing struck me as a big stag show. The emotions aroused by the film had to be expiated on their companions, at least until they got back home to their wives. They seemed to me a prudish lot who loved their male friends and just used their wives as instruments for sexual release. It seemed to me that their affections were not wasted on the women as they occupy too low a position on the social scale. They did not generally go out in public with their wives in this culture.

Such was Saturday night fever in Punjab. We repaired to my friend's house and I got a good sleep. The next day I would get a bus back to my Banga and go to the village. These experiences began to give me an insight into the culture of Punjabi society.

I remember Rabindranath Tagore, "Alas, why are my nights all thus lost?" Meanwhile, back at the ranch, I work with Jatinder Singh to help him adjust the potato cultivator to cultivate corn. I had suggested to him earlier that it could be used for that. He is interested as he would save the cost of hand weeding, which is running at forty rupees an acre. We just have to adjust the shovels and change the width between the tractor wheels. In the end, it works pretty well and would work better with some wing-tip shovels, which he says are available in Banga. He wants to use it on all his corn along with 2-4 D. A few days later, I do a small demonstration on a plot with 2-4 D weed killer.

I have been informed officially that Hardev Singh wants me to go to the Panchayat Rest House in Banga. The BDO tells me that my things will be moved by the block jeep. But the next day when I visit the office, he is off to inspect flooding in the local villages. He invites me to come along. A culvert is stopped up flooding a peasant's field. The peasant thinks someone has stopped it up. But when the passage is probed with a long pole, a big turtle comes out. We then go to a village that is seriously flooded with more than a foot of water. A peasant has failed to close the bunds properly and the water has rushed into the village from the surrounding fields.

Around half past five, on August 21, the overseer sahib comes with the jeep and my things are moved to the Panchayat Rest House in Banga. I have been ousted. This place is like a prison or dungeon, it seems to me, and rather depressing. The big room where I will be housed for some time has seven sides and five doors. It is the weirdest place I have ever seen. There is a high ceiling with I-beams to hold up the bricks for the ceiling.

Pukhar Singh is the old *chowkidar*. He helps me out and brings me breakfast. There is no flush toilet, but a place to piss and shit in a pot, which is then cleaned daily by a sweeper. The *chowkidar* pumps water into a bucket for a morning bath. I bathe by pouring the water over my head with a plastic cup. The worst is that the room is used for a court when the Sub-District Magistrate (SDM) visits on certain days of the month on his rounds. Then I have to pack up all my things and lock them inside my trunk.

The next morning, Pukhar Singh brings my breakfast, three pieces of small, hard toast, two boiled eggs, and two cups of tea in a porcelain tea pot. It is not palatable, but I manage to get it down. The food situation is atrocious. The best option for my other meals for the time being is the so-called "Hotel" across the street. It is just a desi Punjabi *dhaba*. I don't knock them. There are some very good ones, but this one is not, unfortunately. It is a dirty place with crude greasy fly-blown wooden tables and dishes which are never clean. Dinner at the hotel is *bakra* (goat) and allu (potato), boiled eggs and *chapatis*. I buy plums and apples and some biscuits for the Rest House. I think that Banga is the dirtiest, most slimy place that I have seen in India. But then, I have not seen that much of India yet, so maybe such a comment is out of order. I must be polite.

The next day, after lunch at the hotel with Baldev Singh, I go to his house and discuss America. We have tea at the little stall. Feeling a little sick, I take a rest at the Rest House, which is not giving me the kind of rest that I would actually like. Not only that, we are forced to live as *Bhramacharis*, as will be explored further below. The male chastity belt is not a joke here in this neck of the global woods. This price of not killing communists comes with a heavy price for a young man. Perhaps a little like radical circumcision. A perpetual dose of saltpeter. Cultural castration. Noassatol and so on.

The next day I take a tour of the small village of Ladhana Jhaika, near Banga, to visit the house of the VLW. The SDM has come to the rest house and I have to pack up my things for the day. There is a Star Meeting in the block office. Those are seemingly interminable meetings where I get so bored that I start seeing stars at some point, so I come to understand the appropriate designation "Star Meeting." It took a brilliant bureaucrat somewhere to come up with that label. Perhaps he has gone to his reward, which I hope was easy, down-hill all the way.

The room is quite full. Quite full of turbans. The BDO acts as the chair. Part of it is a pep talk and he goes through the agenda, item by item. Get the peasants participating in the programmes. Get some birth control cases. Crank up those crop yields, and so on.

Dee Wolf visits again, after a few days, to check up on our housing arrangements. Unfortunately, they are scarce. The Peace Corps is monitoring the progress to some extent. The block has proposed a place for me, but it is not a very serious proposal.

Nevertheless, I press forward with my work. I have made a programme with Sukhdev Singh in Karnana Village to help him spray three acres of corn for maize borer. If I cannot overcome the bureaucrats, then I will have to take it out on these unfortunate maize borers. They are easier targets, and likely much less harmful too, on balance. At least they die out in winter unlike a bureaucrat who has nine lives. And then some.

The last day of August, and I visit Surgit Singh in Khatkar Kalan and have lunch with him. He is friendly and kind and always has some cold beer, not just the sweet and gooey Punjabi tea. A man after my own heart. Then I go over to Kariha to see Jatinder Singh. I see that his corn is also in need of spraying for maize borer. He is not home, but I write him a note, giving the instructions for what is needed. I will get all of them, far and wide. I am declaring war on them. I will cleanse the block of these pests. Back in the BDO office I get some mail and then visit the house where Balwinder Singh and Baldev Singh, the Agricultural Inspectors, are staying. We have a long friendly talk in their apartment.

In other words, life is busy and somewhat complicated, still divided between two cultures. September arrives without a house and without a cook. I am still limping along without a set place to live but continue to work. I am quite patient, perhaps too much so, as nothing much is happening. Both my house and cook are lacking and always just now coming. At least my bike has arrived.

September brings the promise of cool weather, which is refreshing. Soon the monsoon rains will end. I ride my new bike to Karnana along the kucha road to start the insect control programme with Sukhdev Singh. When I arrive, I see that he has bought a new pump sprayer, which I am familiar with from my work on the farm in Missouri. I work with his young son to spray for corn borer. I spend a good part of the morning assembling the sprayer and getting it ready.

Then they invite me to have lunch. I tie into the food, Punjabi village food. Delicious. And I am hungry after the batching life style in *dhabas* and fruit stands in town. I get good and filled up for the first time in a month on good nourishing village food. It is genuine home cooking, as good in Punjab as anywhere. It is so refreshing after scrounging around for meals from here and there.

After lunch, it is back to the field and we test the sprayer. I have to calibrate the sprayer after taking into account the amount of chemical to use on an acre. I have to know the amount to mix with a litre of water. The chemical is Enderin. After getting started and using one tank, we turn the operation over to the worker and go for some tea. They are also starting to plant potatoes and I see the potential for helping farmers spray for potato bugs or jassid. I used to just pick them off by hand and squash them when I was a kid back in Missouri. A much more ecological way to go, but too slow.

I am encouraged by my work during the day because no one I worked with knew any English. I had to do it all in Punjabi. I realised that there would be many times when one could not say what one wanted to say, but I was able to make out with the words that I knew. I thought that it was a little like teaching a course in insect control and pump spray operation in very minimal Punjabi. Very challenging. Of course, I do not know how much they understood. But I clearly was enjoying doing the work, even though it was quite difficult.

I don't know what the psychology of the peasant in the small village of Karnana was, in a corner of Jalandhar District in Punjab. Providence had sent an American some ten thousand miles to his small plot of three acres of maize to douse it with Enderin. He must have thought that he was either blessed by the Gods, or hit with a curse. Why me? And it was not exactly a Godsend, dousing his land and crop with a dangerous poison. I know that now. I don't know, but I don't think that the maize borers were as dangerous as that Enderin.

But they were quite unlucky sons of bitches. What were the odds that they would get hit by a stray American from ten thousand miles away? Otherwise, they could have carried on a quite easy life style munching down on the Sukhdev Singh's juicy maize. That day I was feeling rather proud of myself that I had accomplished something. I was thinking that they could have a better insect programme the coming year.

Late in the evening, I rode my bike back to Banga through the two inches of dust which had accumulated on the path. I had started to enjoy riding the bike in these small paths in the countryside.

The next morning, I was back to Karnana to talk to Sukhdev Singh. I was busy, very busy with Sukhdev and company. I was maybe starting to feel a little silly, busting my ass, my sorry young ass, for a fucking three acres of Goddam corn half-way around the world. Saving the world in a corn field when humanity was going to hell in a hand basket. The US was bombing the hell out of Vietnam. But at least, I was not killing communists. I wasn't helping to blow the shit out of Vietnam. Things could always be worse.

My new friend Sukhdev Singh rode his bike with me to Banga and invited me for some tea. Karter Sweet Shop again. His head must have been reverberating. Why me, O God, why me? What is the meaning of this kismet?

The next day, the Overseer Sahib takes me in the jeep to see a house in Hapowal village just about a mile northwest of Banga. This is the suggested house for my residence. I go to take a look. It has an abandoned look. Perhaps the family has gone abroad, I don't know. It is huge and seems like it could have been a great place to live. My own rural Punjabi mansion or plantation house with a dozen servants, but now it has been abandoned to the local ghosts. A couple of difficulties are clear at once. First, the village has no electricity. There were still such villages in the block. Also the road leading to the village is very bad, even in this season when most of the roads have dried up. It is difficult to get there and we have to abandon the jeep and walk the last hundred metres due to the impassible ruts and standing water. I tell them that I really think that I do need electricity. There would be no lights and no fan. And it would be terribly dreary in the winter without power. There would be no heat in the cold winter evenings, which would force me to huddle in bed unable to read.

Back in Banga, the BDO comes up with some news, this time with some veracity. He informs me that Surinder Singh, a secretary in the office has found me a place to live. He thinks it will be suitable. It is in a big village called Mahil Gaila a couple of miles from Banga. But there is no latrine. When I tell him that the Peace Corps requires a house with a latrine, he says that they can provide me with one. He clearly wants to get the issue out of his hair. But I know how that works. But never mind. If the place is suitable, I can make it a project to build my own latrine.

I can tell that he is a little impatient with me, being so picky. What is this? Insisting on having a latrine, a place to go to the bathroom. Isn't the country just that? From border to border? From Srinagar to Cape Comoran, just that. Fields, fields, and more fields. Wide open spaces and who could ask for anything more?

9

Impostor

"Even now the paraphernalia of American philanthropy in India, consisting of the American Embassy, the technical and financial missions, and even humanitarian ones, constitute in their impressive assemblage an American East India Company, presided over by Mr. Governor Galbraith."

—Nirad C. Chaudhuri

Every morning, I woke up and found myself ten thousand miles from home, half-way around the world. I was not yet quite used to it, after a couple of months. But I loved it. The question everybody wanted to know was what the hell we were doing there. The Indians couldn't figure it out. I don't think we could either. I think it was mostly an adventure. What were the Peace Corps officers doing in Delhi? It was surely much more interesting to work for the Peace Corps and travel and be stationed in a far away exotic country, than to work at some dull job in America. I cannot think that many in the outfit were very idealistic. I remember one big guy in the Delhi office who had been a corn farmer in Iowa. There was no money in that any more. He worked for the Peace Corps, and his young wife was with him, and I am sure they had a hell of a more exciting life than living in flat dull Iowa and cultivating corn near a small town. And there was no snow and frigid winters. He was the kind of guy who would grab your hand and crush it like hell. He once gave us a party at his elegant house in Delhi to melt our eyes down with some of that good old American Jack Daniels. So they were having a quite nice life. This was Ernie Peterson.

During the 1960 Presidential Campaign, John Kennedy brought the idea of a Peace Corps up during a short speech to a group of students at the University of Michigan. It was at two in the morning when he stopped by the campus on a campaign trip. There were some 5,000 students gathered, waiting for him, and he asked them if they would be willing to go to Ghana or some other developing country and serve in health, agriculture or education. It was October 14, 1960. The idea had been around for a while. Earlier, liberal Senator Hubert Humphrey had introduced a bill in Congress to establish a Peace Corps, but the bill had not gone anywhere.

The University of Michigan students were enthusiastic and some 1000 students signed a petition asking for the establishment of a Peace Corps. Others students sent letters saying they would like to join.

When Kennedy became President, establishing the Peace Corps was one of his first acts. On March 1, 1961 he signed Executive Order number 10924, naming his brother in law, Sargent Shriver, to be the first director of the Peace Corps. Volunteers would serve in Asia, Africa and Latin America in developing countries at the formal request of the country. This was part of Kennedy's "New Frontier" which was based upon Franklin Roosevelt's New Deal in the 1930s.

The Executive Order said: "The Peace Corps shall be responsible for the training and service of men and women of the United States in new programmes of assistance to nations and areas of the world, in conjunction with or in support of existing programmes of the United States and of the United Nations and other international organisations."

Shriver had a lot of work to do to get the programme through Congress and to get the funding. He spent the next few months lobbying some 400 individual members of the US Senate and House of Representatives for support for the programme. Some of them thought it was a bad idea from the start.

The former senator from Pennsylvania, Harris Wofford, worked to establish the programme before he became a senator. It was quite difficult getting the conservative senators and representatives in Congress to vote for the programme. They were afraid that some volunteers might be influenced by foreign ideas and they insisted that it be run strictly by Americans.

However, in September 1961, the 87th Congress passed Public Law 87-293 to fund the Peace Corps with 30 million dollars. Since then about 210,000 people have served in the Peace Corps in 139 countries.

Sargent Shriver initially visited eight countries to get the programme going. By the end of 1961 about 500 volunteers were in nine countries: Chile, Columbia, Ghana, India, Nigeria, the Philippines, St. Lucia, Tanzania, and Pakistan. In 1962, twenty-eight more countries were added to the list and the number of volunteers reached 2816. By June, 1966, the number had reached 15,000. The average age was about 24 years. About two-thirds of them were male. About three-quarters had university degrees. To get volunteers, the countries had to request them. India was one of the countries that Shriver visited shortly after the programme was established. John Kenneth Galbraith, a Harvard University Economics professor, was Kennedy's first Ambassador to India, serving from 1961 to 1963, and was closely associated with President Kennedy and his administration. He had asked to go to India as the US Ambassador.

Galbraith wrote about the establishment of Peace Corps in India in his book, *Ambassador's Journal*. He went with Shriver to meet Prime Minister Jawaharlal Nehru and argued that the programme would be good for India. According to Galbraith, Nehru did not think much of the idea and was not highly in favour of the programme because he did not think that Americans could change much in a short time. Things changed very slowly in India, Nehru pointed out. But Shriver was able to convince him that the first group could work in the Green Revolution in Punjab to increase production of wheat and rice. Later groups were sent in education, nursing, poultry production, dairy, and other projects in India.

On 21 November, 1962, Ambassador Galbraith signed the document and sent it to Nehru establishing the Peace Corps in India. Nehru as Prime Minister was also the Minister of External Affairs. Shortly after that the first group of Volunteers arrived to work in Punjab in an agricultural programme.

By the end of his term as Peace Corps Director in 1966, Shriver had developed programmes in 55 countries and 14,500 volunteers were serving.

There was also the idea of establishing a reverse Peace Corps. People from developing countries would serve in the US. Later a small pilot programme was established for this, and some volunteers came to the US, but Congress was generally so hostile to the idea that it could not succeed to any extent. Especially the conservatives thought that foreign volunteers might spread alien ideas in the US and did not want that to happen. The US can be amazingly parochial in certain aspects.

Richard Nixon, who was elected President in 1968, was quite opposed to the Peace Corps. He considered it a haven for draft dodgers. But it was well established by then. He could do it damage, but could not easily kill it off. The best ideas in any country always come from the Left, and it is not surprising that conservative Republicans would react against a programme for peace and international understanding.

Many are called, but not so many chosen.

Our training in Hemet, California, was contracted out to a private company based in New York City. Development and Resources Corporation provided regional economic development services to governments around the world, with a general focus on water resources and construction of dams. The main project was the development of the Khuzestan region of Iran. Founded and directed by David E. Lilienthal, the company operated from 1955 until 1979.

Several of the training staff had agricultural backgrounds and some were farmers and ranchers themselves. For example, Donald K. Brown, the project director, had degrees from the University of California in soil fertility and plant nutrition. He was operating a farm in Tulare, California. He had spent four years in southwestern Iran working for D and R Corporation. After this, he worked in Peace Corps training programmes.

Another staff member and D and R man was Byron Haderlie, who owned a 300 acre ranch in Idaho. He had studied agronomy at Utah State University. Bruce Kratka, who went with us to India, was from the central valley of California. His specialty was producing vegetables in the desert area of the Palo Verde Valley. He had worked in various Peace Corps training programmes.

The group that I was in was India 53. There were initially 23 people in our group that went to India in 1968. Most of us stayed for the whole two years. Some eighteen of us stayed the full time. We got a living allowance of 75 dollars a month. The Indian

Government, through the development block, was supposed to provide us a place to live and a bicycle.

The Peace Corps in the early years benefited from having a considerable degree of independence from the Government. Shriver tried to keep it away from ideology and perhaps it was about as good a programme as one could expect from the US government focused upon the cold war. None of us wanted to go to war in Vietnam. If the programme did keep some people out of the Vietnam War in the early years, it was a very good thing about the programme in my view.

For most people, it helped them learn something about the world outside the US, which is very important as the US is so far from most developing countries. Perhaps it was a small antidote to American parochialism. One gets a better appreciation of the isolation of most Americans when they live outside the US for an extended period.

The Peace Corps operated in India over a 15-year period from 1961 to 1976. According to John Chromy, who was an early Peace Corps volunteer in India and later an Associate Director in Washington, D.C., the departure of the Peace Corps from India was partly related to the Pakistani-Bangladesh War of 1971. Secretary of State Henry Kissinger met with Prime Minister Indira Gandhi and urged her not to interfere in the Pakistani civil war. He warned that interference would likely result in the suspension of USAID Assistance to India.

The Prime minister ignored the warning, assisting Bangladesh in its secession from Pakistan. US assistance was suspended. The Peace Corps Volunteers remained in India until 1973. The Peace Corps discussed the possible placement of new groups in 1972 and 1973, but the Government of India did not formally request new volunteers.

However, several state governments, including Punjab, did request more volunteers, and the Government of India forwarded the requests without formal endorsement but without objection. New volunteers were placed in India in 1972 and 1973. Following this, the Government of India reviewed the role of volunteers and limited the number of volunteers from a foreign country to fifty. Due to the administrative costs of maintaining the programme, the Peace Corps decided not to continue the programme in India, once the 1973 volunteers completed their terms. The last Peace Corps Volunteer left India in September 1976. So the agreement with India was never canceled, but it just lapsed into "dormancy."

The good thing was that we were pretty much left on our own by the Peace Corps and we didn't have to fight anybody, as we would have had to do if we had gone into the military and been sent to Vietnam. And we didn't have to take orders or follow a plan of the day.

A lot of people got idealistic and bright eyed about the wonderful things the Peace Corps was doing. I suppose that a lot of people could not get away from the ethnocentric idea that the American way of life was, after all, best.

But I think that I was never like that. I always pretty much agreed with the Indians that there was never any real reason for us to be there. We were not doing much harm. But I am not sure that we were doing much good either. We meant well. We were trying to be peaceful and not to hate or harm anybody. We were, after all, part of the sixties generation. Peace, brother, peace. Give peace a chance and all that. We were serious about peace and not the kind you get from having a big war.

We always said that bombing for peace is like fucking for virginity.

We were not lazy. We tried to hit the ground running and work hard as possible. I felt a responsibility to put in my time in a responsible way. We would give it the old college try. To go the extra mile. All the cliches. This is clear from my old journals and I made contacts with a lot of local farmers and started projects with them. But sometimes one just could not face it and would say, fuck it. I will stay here today and read. It is not my job to grow more wheat in this corner of the world. Or let me get out of this place and have a cold beer in Green's Restaurant in Jalandhar or Ludhiana or even Delhi from time to time. Or escape into reading the latest edition of Newsweek International to repoison ones mind with some old familiar western comforting bullshit propaganda.

Probably the most reasonable and logical slots for volunteers were being teachers or nurses. Maybe we were all teachers in a way. At least we could show the locals that not all Americans were crazed monsters shooting their way through the world to promote imperialism and American style capitalism. We were supposed to know something about agriculture. That was mostly window dressing in most cases. Most people in our group had never even lived on a farm or done any farm work at all. I had, of course, because I was raised on a farm and had to do part of the growing of crops. So I knew how to grow corn and soybeans and hay in the Midwest of America, but that didn't mean that I knew anything about farming in India, such as an Indian peasant or the agricultural officers would know. I think it was terribly arrogant to think that one could take an English major from an American university and send him to India to teach Indian peasants how to grow crops. Could anything be more absurd or arrogant? So in that sense, we couldn't do much good there. I could take soil samples for the farmers which told them what kind of fertiliser to use and so on. They appreciated that and used the results. But they could have done it for themselves. Punjabi farmers were doing OK on their own in the Green Revolution era without our help. They needed tractors, good seeds, electricity, water, and capital, and they knew where to get it if it was available and they had the money. Only one person in our group had a degree in agriculture, Bob from Ohio.

While, I think claims about how much help we brought was exaggerated, I do not think that is very important. For me, the cultural exchange and learning on both sides made the programme worth while. It was possibly one of the cheapest programmes ever carried out by the US Government. The money spent for the Peace Corps is not even pennies when it comes to the Pentagon.

Looking at the absurdity of the situation, some people started to think that we must be CIA agents. I don't think that I ever learned anything in India that the CIA wanted to know. Besides, most of us would never have worked for the CIA and we hated the war in Vietnam. The people who really understood the situation were the communists, from what I could see. They had a deeper understanding of social and political dynamics of Indian society.

I think most of the talk about development was poppycock. In my opinion, the Peace Corps never accomplished much in the way of development, but perhaps it accomplished some much more important things like cultural exchange. To some extent we were considered successful just by being there and making a lot of friends. I think this is true, but if so, Indians should have been sent to many of the small towns in America to improve the image of other nations among Americans and make friends there. I truly believe that this would be even more important. Americans would also begin to learn from others, which would not be a bad thing.

This volunteers to America programme was actually tried on a small scale in the late 1960s, but Congress did not like the idea and cancelled it. They would not allow other countries to decide who to send. Not only did it go against the assumption that Americans always knew best and so could not benefit from it. Some Congressmen were afraid that Americans would be influenced by foreign ideas.

We were supposed to be leaders, but I never had any such fire in my gut. I only partially bought it, I guess. But I would give it the old college try. For the first year, at least, I was pretty gung ho. I felt like I ought to be working harder, but many of the programmes were delayed or didn't happen. It was pretty tough going and sometimes discouraging. One had to have a sense of humour. Hard after all the pep talks. People I was supposed to meet sometimes showed up but a lot of times didn't. When I would make a programme with the BDO, I would often end up waiting for him, a good part of the day and then give it up and head back home. This started to take quite a bit of the starch out of my resolve. India was not a country in which to be gung ho, especially when one had to deal with the bureaucracy.

Part of the time, I felt rather more like an impostor, and that people around me knew infinitely more about India and what India needed than me, even if it was not true. But I think it was true, generally. Anyway, who was I to impose my ideas upon them?

I remember getting a memo from the Peace Corps in Delhi. One of the American staff, I think it was Jim Wood, had figured out a way to save the farmers labour in picking up their potatoes from the field. If they bagged them in a certain way and then collected them in this way, then it would take less labour. I figured that each farmer would have to dismiss one or two of their poor landless labourers. They would then be out of a job and maybe then their kids would go hungry. So this was not really what I wanted to do. Let them all eat, even if the operation could have been more efficient. What was it to me? Turn it into a deeper capitalist agriculture? So I had no desire to launch a campaign and lead in that way. Of course, it was just to be taken for granted that the Indians would benefit from doing things the American way, including of course, using fertiliser, insecticides, and so on, which were often very harmful. I thought it was going to be bad enough without any encouragement from me. But in those days, most of us believed in the efficacy of fertilisers and insecticides. It wasn't that simple. The truth was to come later.

I sometimes thought about that.. How things, for example big dams and chemical insecticides, are invented in America and pushed onto the world. Then at some point, America realises that this is doing a lot of damage and starts to get rid of them, but by this time the damage has been spread around the world and the system put into place and things cannot be corrected. The big corporations have the profit machine in place, and their party line that they are helping to save the world from something far worse than cancer. That is hunger. The Americans started it, but then the events are out of phase making it an overall disaster. I think there was a lot of this in the Green Revolution. Chemicals like DDT and Enderin were just dumped on the rest of the world after the US banned them. Many other products too that we were expected to push in India in those days were banned in the US.

I think one should enjoy standing out and enjoy the attention for such a job as the Peace Corps. However, no matter what we did, we were going to stand out. But personally, I always felt self-conscious about standing out. The farmers had their own leaders. I guess the big farmers were the leaders, whether they led in the right direction or not. Who am I to fuck up their country with chemical toxins and deeper capitalism. Doing things the American way. If they do it themselves, then I will not be to blame. It might be better to try to stop it, but that was not in the logic of the situation. I suppose every country has to learn it the hard way.

For the most part, people were kind, terribly kind and hospitable and they put up with me and my ignorance. They even took care of me, even though they might not have always liked me and having me there. Surely, I was a strange and out of place creature in the village. One had to try to find their own niche. I was terribly glad to be there, but I still do not know what the hell we were doing there.

Americans would not put up with it as the reverse Peace Corps was cancelled. But the Indians did. They knew it was just a passing phase and that sooner or later we would go away and they would go on doing things their own way. I have no problem at all with that.

10
Mahail Gaila

"The villages stood still."

—Prakash Tandon

The big political man had washed his hands of me and I was now residing in the Circuit Rest House in Banga. I am eternally thankful for his wonderful hospitality. Putting me up for a month and feeding me as I lived in his beautiful and comfortable house. I was asked to join him for drinks of rum or whiskey with his friends and political colleagues in the evenings out in his pleasant court yard. This was far beyond what should have been expected. Of course, I could not follow the discussion in Punjabi, but they treated me very well. The family had been imposed upon and put in a difficult situation.

It had taken a month but now I had my bicycle. This greatly improved my mobility, but now I was stuck in the Rest House. This was a rather spooky place for living and sleeping. I had to leave most of my things in my trunk and could not really move in. I had to find things to eat on my own. The chowkidar continued to bring me breakfast, but I had to scrounge up the other meals on my own.

I had my transistor radio that I bought in Tokyo. This way I could get some news from Voice of America or BBC. Not always good, unfortunately. While I was in the rest house, the Republican

National Convention was being held in the US. Richard Nixon was going to be the Republican candidate for President. We called him "tricky dick." Mainly because he was tricky and secondly and more to the point, that he was indeed a dick. That was when he chose Spiro Agnew to be his running mate. Nobody had ever heard of this creature, or few, anyway, and it was said that his name sounded like it had been conjured up on an Ouija board. He had been the Governor of Maryland. Nixon won the election, of course. He was said to have a secret plan to end the Vietnam War. That plan turned out to be a secret plan to keep it going for many years to come. Well, that's about as close as any politician can be expected to keep their election promises and the voters who fell for it, probably deserved what they got. Voting for Hubert Humphrey, the Democrat, would not have helped much, however, in regard to Vietnam. That US policy was doomed from day one. And it was the only possible one, given the logic of US imperialism.

While I was staying in the rest house, I was shown another house in Banga, which was not bad, but somehow no action was taken on it. One day Surrinder Singh, a clerk in the BDO office from village Mahil Gaila, told me that there was a place in another village where I might stay. This was a quite big and rich village to the northeast of Banga.

On 10 September, I was asked to pack up my things from the Rest House and was taken to the new village in the Block jeep. There was a new cement Agricultural Cooperative Society building with offices and storerooms. I was given a big upper room in the clean pink compound. Down below was a small cooperative store and the offices of the society, which served as a bank and made small loans to farmers. The Society also sold seed and fertilisers and there was a small store. It was a clean place, with just a mungie for furniture, but it was terribly hot in the day and stayed hot all night after the cement walls had heated up during the day and radiated back the heat all through the night. But one could carry one's mungie upstairs and sleep in the open air on the roof. This was very pleasant in the evening when the cool finally came. There was no arrangement for cooking or getting food. I bought a small kerosene cook stove, the kind used in the villages, to do some cooking myself, but what I could do was very limited, indeed. I could cook eggs and potatoes and warm up some canned goods if I could find them. One had to go to a bigger town such as Jalandhar or Ludhiana to find such canned foods. Across the road in the adjacent compound, also belonging to the society was a hand pump, where one could bathe in the open in the morning and evening and wash up ones pots and pans after cooking. The society had a *chowkidar* and night watchman who looked after the place.

It was all very inconvenient but I did the best I could. I decided to go to Ludhiana and buy some supplies such as canned goods, strawberry and marmalade jam and some Nescafe. It was Friday, September 13, 1968. The secretary of the co-operative society, Madho Singh, gave me breakfast at his house. Then I headed for the tonga to Banga where I could catch the bus. An hour later and I was in heaven. Green's Restaurant in Ludhiana down in the crowded heart of the city. I ordered two mutton hamburgers and a bottle of cold Golden Eagle beer and then topped this off with an American Banana split. There was a band that played Beatles songs for my benefit, I presume. After I entered, they switched from Indian music to Western. I listened to "Ticket to Ride", "All My Loving" and "Then Yesterday." I settled back in the plush air conditioning and guzzled the cold beer. What the hell was I doing out in the fucking Punjabi boondocks any fucking way? Why, not killing Communists, of course! Well, somebody had to do it. Here I was out of station, somewhat illegally, and playing hooky from food production. And getting high on the Mohan Meakan brew. But nobody had a clue where I was, except myself. Whatever I was producing, it was not food, but it sure as hell felt better than the goddamn village.

After pigging out, I went to the Keylan Store and spent 78 rupees for canned goods and jam, enough to fill up my travel bag. It was a struggle to get these things back home by bus and hardly worth it, but I was excited about having a place to live. I can say the place was clean, except for the dust, which was everywhere, but clean by village standards. I existed that way for some time, but it was a rather miserable existence.

After some days, I discovered that across the village lane, in the other compound, was the old building of the cooperative society. It was a nice, pink, one story building with two large rooms separated by an open veranda between them, shady and airy. At that time, these rooms were being used to store bags of fertiliser, but were mostly empty. I asked the head man of the society, Sardar Madho Singh, about staying there. I thought that I could live in one room and the other room would serve as a kitchen and room for my cook. This proposal was kindly accepted and I had a place to live at last, after a couple of months of being shifted around from place to place and sort of living out of my trunk. The remaining bags of fertiliser were shifted from the rooms.

On October 12, the *chowkidar* helped me move my things into the new place. In a way I was again being a nuisance, taking up space and resources that could have been used by the villagers. But there was nothing I could do about that except try to be useful and earn my bread money.

I bought the frame for a big mungie, a charpoy, in Banga, and the *chowkidar* of the society wove the strings for me. It was bigger than the normal *mungie* and would be my bed as long as I was in the village. I wrote to the Peace Corps Office in Delhi asking them to send me a cook. After getting settled, I asked the village mistry or carpenter to make me some furniture for my house. I bought a large desk in Jalandhar and chair and brought them by bus to Banga. They were loaded onto a horse cart and brought to Mahil Gaila.

There was, of course, no arrangement for a toilet, and I was forced to follow the practice of the villagers and use the fields for my nature calls for some time. Concrete toilets in the villages did not exist for all practical purposes, as noted earlier, although Hardev Singh had built one in Kariha. But he was a rich man with many political guests. I built a makeshift latrine until I could build a better one that I could flush with water. Living without a toilet is not something that is normal or easy for a Westerner to get used to very quickly. At that time, in the late summer, most of the crops had been cut and so there was not much cover in the fields. If one wanted some privacy, one had to hide in the sugar cane fields. Sometimes, I had to use the fields at odd hours of the day, and so it was off to the cane fields even in the heat of the day and hope to not be seen. In fact, I stood out like a sore thumb everywhere I went! How could one not, being the only one of my kind around.

But there were some others of us in other blocks. Maybe some of the Indians thought they were being invaded by the Martians. And we were coming there to help them? One cannot blame the Indians for being a little suspicious of America's intentions. Especially, considering what the Americans were doing in Vietnam in those days. And maybe they were a little insulted at the idea that people like us could do a lot to help them. In the event, we were just surviving and had to have a lot of help from them.

But in spite of all this, I was happy. I had a place to live now and there was some potential. There was a place to have a real latrine in future when I could have the time to build it and a place for a garden and place to build a small house for some chickens. Keep busy. Keep on trucking. My house had arrived at last. Cook just now coming.

The weather had cooled and I planted my garden in the compound. *Moolies*, pollock, *mirch* and *sarson*. It could be irrigated with the hand pump. I cleaned the rooms and would paint them when I got the time during the cool of the winter.

I started a project to grow sugar beets. A friendly farmer who owned some land in America, Swaran Singh, provided some land for a sugar beet plot. He was also the head man of the village. I got some seed from the Peace Corps. This was quite successful as a winter crop and I spent quite a bit of time preparing the field, fertilising, irrigating, thinning, and weeding the beets. The small field yielded a large pile of beets (*shalgum*), but I don't know what they were really used for. Madho Singh's son took the ones I thinned out and we planted them in his garden near his house.

After I planted my garden and irrigated it with my hand pump, I would soon have fresh vegetables from my garden. I remember an old and poor man from the village who used to come and take greens from my garden almost every day. I was a curiosity in the village. People would watch what I did and maybe they thought I was nuts. They thought it was strange to see a "rich man" like me working with his hands. I certainly did think, from time to time, that I was nuts, doing what I was doing. You only live once, or maybe not, but anyway, it was fun for the most part. Maybe I was reincarnated from an old soul who had lived in India in the past. At least an Indian professor in Santa Barbara, Raghavan Iyer, thought so, later when I was in graduate school.

I was expected to spend some time in the Block Development Office in Banga, although I don't know what good it did except for socialisation with the staff. It was just protocol, I guess. I attended the Star Meetings, not understanding much of what was going on, and discussed things with the agricultural development officers. The young officers wanted to know about America. Sometimes they wanted to know what I knew about agriculture. I knew quite a bit about agriculture in America, in fact, having been a farmer there, a student in vocational agriculture, and a member of the Future Farmers of America in high school. But I did not know much about agriculture in India. I guess that they did not really understand that I was there, not so much to produce food, as to avoid having to kill communists. Better to raise beets than down communists. Somebody said that the Peace Corps volunteers ate up far more food in India, than they ever produced, which I am quite sure is true. But what the hell. But to the best of our ability, we never intentionally harmed anybody. I even made friends with the communists. Especially I made friends with the communists, who could really inform one about what was really going on in the country as they had taken the trouble to try to understand it. I was learning. Better late than never.

No Phone—No Pool—No Pets.

"Youngsters of this age cannot be expected to take kindly to monastic chastity, however good the purpose", said John Kenneth Galbraith.

In Mahil Gaila, my house was simple. There were two quite big rooms, separated by a veranda. There was a small courtyard surrounded by a wall one and a half metres high with a hand pump in the corner. The compound was entered from the village lane by a double door with a latch that could be closed from the inside at night.

Facing the house, from the garden, the room on the left was mine. The room on the right was the kitchen where my cook, Bachan, and later, Mussie, slept. It may have been more comfortable sleeping outside in the summer, except for the mosquitoes, but I never felt comfortable that way. In my room, there was a string charpoy on one side, my bed, with my sleeping bag which I used as a mattress and a thick *rajai* or quilt stuffed with cotton which I used in the winter. I bought ten kilos of cotton and had the big *rajai* made. There were two windows above with wooden shutters that closed from the inside. At one end was my Peace Corps Trunk, which served as a small table. On the other side was my desk, and short wave transistor radio, under a fluorescent light that seemed to attract all the bugs in the country, in the monsoon season. There were small lizards, we called killys, which came out on the ceiling and walls and helped to cut down on the bug population buzzing around in the light. They were harmless, but a little creepy if they fell down on one from the ceiling. I never minded them much. I went after one once and broke off part of its tail, but this was uncalled for. I felt bad about it. They were really doing me a favour, cutting down on the bug population. So I called a truce and we lived together in harmony after that. In time, I had screen doors made and screens made for my windows, which was necessary, given the mosquito and fly populations in the village.

On the side of the desk was a small stand with a table fan. The Peace Corps paid for an electric fan which cost about 190 rupees ($25) at the time. I had a small cabinet built in Banga, which had a door that folded out. I liked it a lot and called it my bar. If I had a bottle of rum, I would keep it in here and sometimes take a shot in the evenings. It also had a lock so I could keep my money there. The back wall of the room had two *almiras* or cabinets built into the wall with wooden doors. Here, I kept my clothes and books and a few other things. There were a couple of chairs. We did not live quite as austerely as Mahatma Gandhi, but we were close.

The other room, where my cook stayed, had a table for cooking and a small Indian kerosene stove, which one pumped up to make a hot burner. There was a small screened *dolie* for keeping vegetables like potatoes and onions.

I had no refrigerator, so no access to ice, unless I bought it in Banga and brought it to the village. It would not last long in the heat. I had no television and personal computers had not yet been invented. In fact, TV had not yet come to the villages of Punjab and it would be several years before they would appear in the richest homes. The only telephone in the village was located in the Post Office. The fastest correspondence was by telegram, but sometimes the delivery was not so fast.

The only heat was from a small electric space heater. Electricity was quite expensive, so I only used it in the cold season in the evenings. I slept under a heavy quilt which was warm enough without heat. If the electricity was off in the evening, then there was no heat and I would be forced to go to bed early. I always wondered if this was one of the reasons for the increasing population in India. Did this make a very large contribution?

In the hot weather using cold water for a bath was no problem. One pumped the water into a bucket with the hand pump and poured it over one's body with a plastic cup. In the winter it was necessary to heat up some water on the small stove if one wanted a warm bath.

At the other side of the house was my cook's room and the kitchen. I had the village carpenter, Gulzar Singh, make me a big beautiful wooden cabinet that had wooden doors and shelves inside. It was my best piece of furniture. There was a clay jug for keeping water cool. The floor was cement, with just a *duree* on the floor, a sort of thin rug. That was all, but it was adequate.

Until I could build a latrine, I constructed a makeshift bathroom outside in the corner of my compound with reed mats. Inside, I had a sit down toilet with a bucket. The sweeper would come once a day in the morning and clean it. That way I didn't always have to go to the fields. This also served as a place to take a bath in the winter.

In those days, the mail service was quite good in the Indian villages. The village *dak walla* would come just about every day and it was wonderful getting letters. I cannot say that everything always arrived, but just about everything. One time I ordered some protein biscuits from Delhi which the Peace Corps provided. I waited and waited for them and they never came. One day someone in the village asked me if I got my biscuits, which of course, I hadn't. But I was sure that they arrived at the village, but someone else enjoyed them. Perhaps they needed the protein more than me, so it was OK.

Later, I got a Christmas package from the US, in a small box. Some women from the local church had sent it. They had packed some home-baked cookies along with some other packaged goodies. They did not realise the hard knocks of sending it half way around the world to a remote village, and so what I received was mostly a box of cookie crumbs with only some hard candy and chewing gum surviving the transit.

Letters were great to receive and a lifeline back home to family and friends long before the age of internet and the telephone was out of the question, except in a city. So we were pretty much on our own. Such lack of communication is quite inconceivable today in the age of Internet, Face Book, Twitter and so on.

We had new clothes made by the local tailors. This was fun. There were so many types of fabric in the shops to choose from, in India. There was a big cloth shop in Newanshahr run by a big sedougie, called Lal di Hathi. I bought cloth there and had some pants and shirts made. The pants were a sort of rough green thick cloth and I liked wearing them when it got cooler. The shirts we made were called bush shirts in India. It meant that they were to be worn loose outside the pants to be cooler.

Later, I wanted to make myself a Nehru Jacket. These were popular in those days. I bought the cloth from a shop in Ludhiana, a thick light brown corduroy cloth, which was beautiful and had a tailor make it in Banga. I loved the jacket and wore it quite a lot but thought it was a little too flashy to wear in Punjab.

In the bigger towns there were Bata shoe stores, a French company. They had nice and comfortable shoes at reasonable prices. I had several pairs that I bought from them.

I also loved the big crockery shops in Jalandhar which had everything for the kitchen. They had lovely mugs for tea and coffee. I loved doing some shopping there and then going to the book store. There was a big one in Jalandhar, but also a small communist book store that sold some of the books published in Moscow in English. One could find lovely books by Rabindranath Tagore and the classic Russian novels. I was able to read a lot and developed a taste for reading classical Russian novels while in India.

There were many daily newspapers in English. So I always read a daily newspaper. The first, published in Chandigarh, was the Tribune. It is an old newspaper of the Punjab and gave the local news from the state, as well as some national and world news. There was the *Hindustan Times* and the *Indian Express*, national newspapers. And there were many magazines in English. I loved reading the *Illustrated Weekly* of India, which was very informative, and the small communist weekly, *Blitz*. This lovely little newspaper poked a lot of fun at the government and politicians. I loved it and bought it whenever I saw it at a news stand. This was my favourite and I never missed getting it when I saw it on a news stand. It was great to read on the bus if one was headed somewhere. I made friends with the guy who ran the news stand in Banga. Of course, in addition to the English papers, there were many papers in Punjabi, Hindi, and Urdu. All of these were sold at the news stands and on the bus stops.

I would generally leave my bike at the news stand when I caught a bus to another town and take it on the way back. Sometimes, however, I would have to wait, if someone had decided to use my bike for an errand while I was gone. This could happen sometimes.

I collected newspapers, which were very cheap, but one could even get part of the cost back, when one sold them to the shops to make small bags and packaging. The shops in the village would send someone around to buy them from you by the kilogram.

And a few magazines came from the US. Imagine, selling a Sears, Roebuck catalog by kilo for packaging. I would get them free from the US and then sell them to the shopkeepers. They did not pay me much, but the paper got recycled for small bags. Also the propaganda from the American Embassy, the United States Information Service (USIS), was free and made excellent bags for small shopkeepers. This was possibly the best use for it as it was too rough to use as shit paper. I also got some small journals from Moscow, such as *New Times*, I believe. They were also propaganda, of course, but interesting to read or browse through.

In the fall, there were village festivals, such as Diwali and especially Dusehra, when there would be a sort of big celebration in the village in a vacant field at the edge of the village. In Mahail Gaila, I began to settle down to village life with my neighbours.

11
My Cook

"It takes some skill to spoil a breakfast. Even the English can't do it."

—John Kenneth Galbraith, 1961

After getting established in the village in 1968, I opened an account in the State Bank of India in Newanshahr, to deposit my Peace Corps check and get cash. This seemed like a simple thing, but nevertheless, it was time-consuming. Cashing a check was not as simple as it is normally assumed. It involved several processes in those days. One presented the check at a window in the bank and was given a token, a round piece of metal, the size of a big coin. Then one would wait on a wooden bench along with peasants from local villages. Eventually, the payment would come to the cashier's window. But first there was a lot of heaving around of huge ledgers, from clerk to clerk, huge books that everything had to be recorded in, with old fashioned fountain pens, and signed and stamped, and so on up to the director and then the authorisation would finally reach the cashier. A signature with a ball point pen was not considered legitimate, so one had to sign with a fountain pen for anything official. Finally one went to the cashier's window and took their cash. Cash, of course, was the only form of payment I ever used when living in India. Checks were not used widely for paying bills and there were no such thing as credit cards or bank cards.

I started asking for a hundred rupees in one-rupee notes, when I cashed my check, because one always needed small notes, especially when people came to one's house asking for a small donation or when taking buses, tempus, tongas, and rickshaws. Sometimes change would be short. These notes would come in a thick pack stapled together with a very strong staple. If they were new notes, they were impressive because most of the notes circulating were dirty and worn. I think some people thought we had a printing press to make our own money when we gave them these new clean and crisp rupee notes. If a note was torn or too worn, sometimes shopkeepers would not accept it.

Just across the street from the old State Bank of India, there was a small drink and snack shop. It was beautiful, cool, and very clean and painted bright green. It could not have been more different from the terribly dirty fly-blown Kartar Sweet Shop in Banga. I would always go there to have a coke and a snack when I came to the bank. There was a powerful fan running to blast the flies away from one's face. I would have loved to see such a shop in Banga, but there was not a single one. Cleanliness might be next to Godliness, but it was about ten miles from Banga.

When I got settled into my house, I still didn't have a cook. Food was a problem and it took too much time to cook for one's self. I sometimes would eat in a place in Banga or Newanshahr, but these were local *dhabas* and generally not good places to eat. Sometimes it was just sweets at Karter Sweet Shop or that sort of thing. I had to batch it. There were better *dhabas* in Newanshahr. I remember one in particular, where I would sometimes eat *bakra* or goat. A couple of places made great omelets and one could dump a lot of ketchup on it and make a pretty good meal. I loved the omelet place near the bus stop in Newanshahr and never missed the chance to grab a nice big omelet there.

I had now asked the Peace Corps office in Delhi to send me a cook. A small guy arrived in the village from Delhi. His name was Bachan and he claimed to be a Christian, although I never detected any sign of it. It was not long before I would discover evidence that argued positively against that proposition. This little guy would be my cook for a few months. I soon found that these cooks who worked for foreigners knew only two types of food. One, they called English food and the second was Hindustani *khanna* or Indian food. Of course, they generally carried around with them some old and worn letters, yellow from age, references from people they had worked for years before. If they were older, they sometimes even had notes from a Britisher. These could have even been historical items for collection. These references were amusing but would not be of much value in knowing about the person.

I soon found that the so-called English food was bland and tasteless, and so it was better to just forget about that from the very beginning. It didn't work. It was inedible, for all practical purposes. After all, the British cannot even eat it in England when it is genuine. They have gone in for Indian food. It was far better to just eat Indian food with rice or chapaties. Normally, bread was chapatti or roti, made of wheat flour and cooked fresh just before eating. One could also buy western style packaged bread, which was called "double *roti*, to make toast." What is called curry powder, the blend of some fifteen spices, is actually not Indian, originally, but a concoction of spices made by cooks for the British. It did not exist in traditional Indian cooking.

When my cook came, I would often send him on my bicycle to Banga to buy fruits and vegetables. I was trusting him to give me the bills for the food after every trip. This went on until around December after he had worked for me about three months. Now the shopping tabs seemed to keep mounting up higher and higher. I started to be a little suspicious about that. One day when I got locked out of my room, I went into his room and found that he was making two sets of price lists. He was fabricating the price to get more money out of me. I found the real price list from the *subzi walla* and the one he made for me, which he was sort of doubling up on the price. In this way, he was stealing some of my money each time he shopped. I was naïve to trust him, of course. It was no big deal, but being a rather honest person, I was rather outraged that he had been doing this to me.

About the same time, a story started going round the village that he had showed money to the village girls through the window of his room on the road and propositioning them. Some people in the village were upset about this. It should have been clear to me what he was doing. He had made himself a new suit of clothes and had bought a new transistor radio. He was building up a good life for himself and all of this was coming out of my pocket. He was becoming a well-dressed dandy with the local girls.

Now he had carelessly left the two price lists lying around and had been caught. I then started shopping for my own vegetables and learned the real prices of vegetables and fruits, or at least the prices that the *subzi walla* was charging me. This too might have been somewhat inflated as well. There was an old friendly vegetable seller in Banga who had a big beautiful shop on a prominent corner of the main road in Banga. I usually went to his shop to buy fruits and vegetables.

Looking back on it, I probably should have kept my cook and done my own shopping until I could find a more honest person. But I was so outraged about his behaviour that I sacked him and sent him packing back to Delhi. In this way, I just made it hard on myself, of course. I had to go back to batching it and cooking for myself.

It may have been the best thing to do however, since he had started making advances to the young women in the village and this would have caused me trouble at some point. The situation might have gotten worse. He was a big city guy from Delhi and could not easily adapt to village life in Punjab. He wanted to play around with some of the young girls, which was completely taboo in a rural village.

At any rate, I kicked him out and was again faced with cooking my own food, which was not very easy to do. There were not many dishes that I could cook with the little kerosene burner that I had. So I started subsisting on lots of fried potatoes and onions, scrambled eggs, raw vegetables and fruits, bread and jam. Back to the double *roti* and jam. I had not learned to cook Indian food, which I had started to love by this time. And getting a bite to eat in the local *dhabas* didn't do it either as they were quite poor.

Finally, after a few months of trying to rough it on my own, without much success, I got an older cook, who was honest and served me well for the rest of the time that I was in India. His name was Mussie and a friend of Bob's cook, Bhagnath, from Ferozepur in the west of Punjab. He had a wife and two small children, so was more responsible.

Later, I found that Bachan had been recycled by the Peace Corps in Delhi to my friend, Ed Marsh, who was stationed in Phagwara. I think that I suffered more than Bachan in the deal, as he bounced right back with another job, while I suffered without a cook. I warned Ed about him. He may have continued to do the same thing but possibly not to the extent that he was milking me. Some Indians thought that all Americans were rich and so it didn't matter if one took advantage of them. Just get out of them what one can. One can hardly blame them, in their pitiful condition, if one is on the level of a servant in India.

I didn't mind to pay somewhat more for things than Indians. There was no way of avoiding that in India and I accepted it. But there had to be some limit as to how much more I was going to pay. My living allowance was geared to the cost of living in India, not America.

Unfortunately, we did not have much money to pay our servant, just a pitiful one hundred rupees a month or so and some extras for holidays and for new clothes. We could not really give them a big raise because when the cooks got together and compared their salaries this would have caused jealousies and upset things. So we did the best we could. We did not have any money left at the end of the month after we ran our household and paid the expenses.

Some volunteers did resort to getting some money from back home to supplement their income, but I never did that. I lived on the equivalent of 75 US dollars a month which the Peace Corps provided. This was something over 500 Rupees a month and since it was paid out of PL-480 funds in Indian Rupees, it was costing the US Government practically nothing to keep us in India. Under PL-480, the Indian Government paid the US for wheat imports in Indian Rupees. Since these were not convertible to dollars, the US had a surplus of rupees and one way to get rid of them was to dump them on us. A portion of these funds were also used to purchase books from India for university libraries in the US where there were South Asian Studies programmes.

In the mornings, I would listen to the Voice of America propaganda from Washington on my shortwave radio while eating breakfast. The November, 1968 Presidential Election was very disappointing to me when the returns gave it all to Richard Nixon. He won by a big margin. It was already afternoon in India on the day after the election when I got the news in the village that tricky Dick had won. But, nevertheless, I was not in the belly of the beast and I was not in Vietnam. Let freedom ring.

Later, older and wiser, I did not to attach great importance to who won a Presidential election in America. The difference would be only marginal in any event. As the late anarchist, Utah Phillips, used to say, the difference between a conservative and liberal is that the liberal will hang you, but from a lower limb. American foreign policy was steady, in any event, driven primarily by factors other than which party won the presidency. Nixon would keep the war going in Vietnam for another four years and then win the Presidential Election again in 1972, against George McGovern.

That was wild, but typically American. By the time Nixon was forced to resign in 1974, I had returned to America and joined the Navy and gone to Greece.

I was foolish to join the military, but I just couldn't take small town dullsville America and I still had some globe roaming to do before being willing to settle down to graduate school.

I learned of Nixon's resignation one morning in Athens, Greece, in 1974, as I rode around in a local bus. Agnew had already made many enemies and had been forced to resign even a few months earlier.

With the Watergate scandal and all of Nixon's criminal activities from the White House, Nixon resorted drinking and was reportedly drunk most of the time in the White House. This charade was turning into a real comedy show, but not really funny. Never mind, things went on largely as usual. Let America be America. Things only seemed to get worse as the war dragged on in Vietnam and spread to Laos and Cambodia.

The day that Nixon won was a depressing time for me in India, and for almost all Peace Corps Volunteers. There must have been some in those days, but personally, I never met a volunteer who supported a Republican. Again, I was not killing commies. But it looked bleak. With Tricky Dick taking the reins we thought things could only get worse for America. We were not wrong.

12
Halloween

"They adopted modern farming, with tractors, trucks and tube wells, and discarded the bullock cart and the Persian Wheel."

—Prakash Tandon

By late October, 1968, I was starting to get settled in but I still had a lot to do around my house to make it more livable. Most of this would have to wait as I tackled things in steps. I help Surrinder Singh, the clerk who helped me find my house, to irrigate his wheat fields. I take a soil sample for him. I ride my bike and distribute soil sample results to some farmers, Hari Singh and Jagjit Singh in Naura, the next village over.

On October 24, 1968, there is a Peace Corps conference for our group at Jadla village, Chris's house. The weather has turned tolerably cool. Fritz Bachman and Chris Marlow are there when I arrive. We wait for the Peace Corps officials to arrive from Delhi. Frank Rojas shows up and then Blake Willeford, and Larry Young. The officials, Ernie Peterson, Bill O'Conner and Jim Woods, arrive by jeep in the afternoon. They are the real American moguls, sahibs, with their own transportation. Something we proles can only dream about in India. We have come by more humble means, generally the tempu from Newanshahr. Now we have a conference of American men in a small remote Punjabi village. Something very strange, quite strange indeed.

In the evening there is a dinner which is at the house of Rani Mota Singh, a big farmer in the village. The food is wonderful, but it must have cost him dearly for the feast for some twenty hungry Americans. We have a discussion about our training and what should be done to improve it. There is some discussion about agriculture. At this point, I think that I am up to the gills with agriculture and that my eyes are starting to glaze over. I rather hate this kind of meetings and see no need for them. Just let me get on with my work of not killing any communists. Leave the gung-ho saving of Punjabi farmers to somebody else. I think things are progressing quite well in Punjab from what I can see. What the farmers cannot do, we cannot help, it seems to me. There seemed to be a consensus at the Peace Corps meeting that it is important to make a lot of friends and that perhaps just living in the village is enough to make one a good Peace Corps Volunteer. It seems to be that the bar is being set rather low for us. Hell, it is not all that strenuous spending the day drinking tea and it sure as hell beats carrying a gun and killing communists. Here I let them give me a nice hot tea, which seems by far the best approach from my point of view. I return the favour when they come to my place. They are not bothering anyone, after all.

The Peace Corps officials bring my "care package" from Delhi which has come in the mail from my mother. It contains mainly candy and gum, which I distribute to the volunteers and we all enjoy the flavours from back home. I also get a songbook, a hymnal, as I was missing the old songs we used to sing in church. Amazing Grace. What a friend we have in Jesus, or Cheeses as Edward Abbey, the Anarchist said. It has nothing to do with being religious, of course, but there is apparently a little lingering home sickness at this point for the old familiar refrains.

The next day there is a good deal of vulgarity from the officials for my tender virgin mind. Early morning: "Drop your cocks and grab your socks." A suggestion to heave out. There were vulgar suggestions about one overweight female staff member in the Peace Corps Office. "Well, if you fucked her, you would have to tie a two by four on your back so you wouldn't fall in," one staff member remarked. Not having been in the military, I was a little shocked, by this male locker room male talk. One would get used to it in the military.

Then there is a tour to see the maize crop of Rani Mota Singh, as if I had not seen corn before. That boredom out of the way, I bum a ride with Ernie Peterson and the other Peace Corps staff members back to Newanshahr. Then I get back to Mahil Gaila by Boeing 747 horse carriage tonga. Just a little slower, but traveling just the same. Almost air borne from time to time.

Inspired by the Peace Corps morale booster, I try a little harder in the afternoon to communicate with the villagers and joke around with them in the village.

I go down with Swaran Singh and plant fifty gobi (cauliflower) plants just as the darkness is falling in the plot he has provided me. We have a little drink together. I told him that I preferred beer. He has some, but when he mixes it with Binnys, the local whiskey, it becomes worse than either, so the taste was quite bizarre.

The next Monday, October 28, I take a look at my gobi and sugar beet plots. Then I ride my bike to Banga and look for some tools, needing a hammer and a saw. I think I will do some small projects like building shelves, not realising at the time that the best thing is just leave it to the carpenters who know the work and can do a beautiful job of it at reasonable cost. In my case, I can just cobble it up. I also do not know which type of wood to buy in which one can drive nails.

I go the Office and talk with the BDO about my projects. I have a feeling that I should be working harder. I am probably suffering from an overdose of the protestant work ethic, which I brought from America, and which is not terribly appropriate for India, perhaps. But I am determined not to shirk my Peace Corps duty.

On the 29th, after cashing my check, I go to the cooperative store to buy some processed cheese, made by Amul. It is a big milk and cheese company that makes some modern products. My trip is in vain, however, as the shop does not have the price list and they don't know what to charge me for it. It is a government shop, but I don't think it is good enough for government work in this case. This is why the private sector always takes over such enterprises, it seems.

In the afternoon, I plant onions and flowers in my garden. Today Lakshmi appears at my door, around half past eight. This produces mixed feelings. On the one hand, it was nice that she came, but I am afraid that people will be suspicious. I feel like I should tell her that she should not come, but on the other hand, I did a very irrational thing and kissed her. It's a lovely secret memory in my mind and I hope that there will be another chance, in spite of the odds and the male chastity belt.

The next day, a farmer's training camp is to be held, but after waiting in the block office, it is called off and I return to work in my garden. I asked Surrinder Singh to send a carpenter to give me an estimate on the cost of making screens for my windows and doors. I seriously need them as the flies are driving me crazy in the day time and the mosquitoes at night. There is also a problem with electricity as the voltage is inconsistent, plus it comes for five or ten minutes and then goes off again. It is not regular enough to read or study and I have to keep a lantern lighted even when the electricity is on. It is difficult to understand the reason behind the frequent cuts in the evening. Perhaps there is no real reason. It is just part of the system. Tomorrow is Halloween and I get out to find a pumpkin to make a Jack-o-lantern.

Halloween. It is the last day of October. Now I have started to run a mile every day in the morning. One of the joys of being young. Or foolish. I think it will do me good. The locals think I am crazy. Bachan my cook takes the bike in the morning and goes to Banga for shopping. I bust my ass. He filches my money.

After writing letters in the morning, I ride my bike to Banga after lunch to try and buy a pumpkin. I try several shops before I find the right kind of big yellow pumpkin. It weighs three kilos, big enough to make a Jack-O-Lantern. I carve the pumpkin and put it on my wall outside facing the street with a candle in it. Villagers passing by ask what it is and I tell them that it is an American festival day. I thought it was worth-while as a sort of cultural exchange. Is this what the Peace Corps is all about? Am I softening up the locals for a renewed attack of American corporate imperialism? Well, I am doing my best not to.

It is necessary to have a medical examination for one's cook. So on the first day of the month, I take Bachan down to the Christian Medical Centre in Ludhiana. The well-known Miss Brown Hospital. We make good time, getting there around ten in the morning. We see some other Americans around, but there is little time to talk. An American woman is in charge of the department and she tells me that several of the volunteers from our group have been in the hospital here. I am an exception so far. It is news to me. I guess I have been lucky.

The hospital has a small book shop for Christian literature. I buy some Christmas cards that have Indian village scenes on them. Then I go to Chadar Bazaar with Bachan and he buys cloth to make himself a new suit. I buy the corduroy cloth to make myself a Nehru Jacket, of a sort of bright brown-gold colour. I am in love with the colour, but it may be rather wild as a jacket.

Bachan wants to spend the night in Ludhiana with his cousin who works at the medical centre. I told him to go ahead and I would see him tomorrow. I go to Greens Restaurant and have a snack and a beer before getting on the road back to the village. I have to fight for a bus at the Phagwara junction and when I get back to Banga, it is already dark. But the moon is full and bright and I ride my bike out to the village in the dark rather easily.

Dinner, without my cook, is part of a coconut which I buy at Phagwara and some coffee and cake left over from yesterday.

I am starting to depend upon my cook Buchan and do not want to do without a cook. Too much inconvenience. But I wonder what effect two years of having my own personal servant is going to have on me. Can I readjust to American society, where everyone has to do everything for themselves?

US President Lyndon Johnson has called a bombing halt in Vietnam today. A little sop for the American elections coming in a few days. But, unfortunately, I am afraid it will not help the Democrats very much in the election.

13

The Librarian

"Winter was the pleasantest time of year in the Punjab."

—Prakash Tandon

With my cook gone, it is a sparse breakfast of a couple of apples and a piece of left-over cake. It is the second day of November. But Buchan returns at one o'clock in the afternoon. I spend some time with the Sarpanch, Swaran Singh, in the afternoon and we go to his fields and pick some turnip greens. Bachan cooks some of these for dinner. I entertain myself with a Newsweek magazine which I just received and an Indian novel.

The next day I use my new Indian carpenter tools to build a book shelf. After the experience, I am inclined to turn all of that type of work over to the official carpenters. It is difficult to find the type of soft wood that is easy to nail. The hammer is very bad and the nails bend very easy trying to drive them through the hard wood. While I succeed, after a fashion, I find it discouraging and will turn future work over to a carpenter. I work in my garden for a little therapy for my brain and muscles.

I weed my *gobi* and sugar beets early in the morning to enjoy the relative cool. It takes all morning and I head off to Banga by bike in the afternoon. I mail my letters at the post office down the Railway Road and have tea with a friend who works at the New Bank of India which is down in the Banga Grain Market.

Tomorrow, November fifth, is the Presidential Election in the US and I have concluded that it does not matter a lot who wins, as long as it is not George Wallace. That is not possible, in any event. But it is a discouraging prospect whoever wins. The Vietnam War is sure to go on. And the terrible bombing.

I ride down to Kariha to see Jatinder Singh. He had fifty-four acres of maize this year, to produce hybrid seed, but the results were not very good, he tells me. The male maize is Dekalb Hybrid from the US and this is being crossed with the Indian variety Deccan, which is the female. But since the De Kalb maize tasseled several days before the Deccan was ready, about twenty-five per cent of the Deccan did not get properly fertilised.

At Sikh National College in Banga, the next day, I mingle with some students, guys, of course and am able to borrow some books from the library. The election day results are rather demoralising, with Nixon and Agnew the winners, of course, by a big margin. The question now is what will happen in Vietnam. We will watch with foreboding from the sidelines in India. The Indians are becoming more and more anti-American about US policy in the war and inviting delegations from North Vietnam to give programmes.

Nishan Singh, a chemistry professor at the college, invites me to come to his office and to visit his class. Later I have lunch with him.

At the end of the week, there is a Star Meeting at the office, which always bores me and it pretty much killed the day. The next day, I see Ravi, the Block Office secretary, on the way to the College. That is a pleasant treat. There I spend some time in the library and talk to students. The librarian engages me in a conversation about American foreign policy and the Vietnam War. I am getting used to answering a lot of questions along these lines and I am afraid that I am becoming more and more critical of American policy, not that I had ever supported the war in Vietnam. The US should just get out and let the country get on with its own agenda. The old regime in the South has proved to be bankrupt and there is no need to try to prop up the crumbling government, getting more young Americans killed, not to mention the Vietnamese who suffer the most.

On Sunday, November 10, I study Punjabi, but the *chowkidhar* comes at ten in the morning and says the Sarpanch, Swaran Singh, wants to see me. I go over to the other side of the village where he is irrigating his garden. I also irrigate my sugar beets and fullgobi (cauliflower) when the water comes through the canal.

The Sarpanch comes back with me to my house and Madho Singh is also here standing in the street. It then emerges that there is a problem with my cook, Bachan, because it seems that he has been talking with the nurse who works at the family planning centre across the field in the community centre. It seems that there is gossip all over the village about them. The Sarpanch invites me to come over to his place in the afternoon and take a walk in the fields. We walk and I spend the whole afternoon there. When we come back to his house, he asks me to stay longer, but I am really tired and want to go.

When I get back to my house, my cook has gone to Banga to the cinema. Madho Singh's son Sodhy and another boy are standing near my house. We had met this boy's father in the fields while walking in the afternoon and I heard some discussion about my cook, but didn't catch everything. Perhaps he is the one who is launching the complaint against Buchan. Then the man's son asks me to go for a walk with him to the fields for a half mile walk or so. I am wondering if they have set up a trap for my cook to catch him talking with the nurse again and are trying to keep me away from the house. They said they wanted to talk to me. So I invited them into my place if they want to talk. One agreed, but the other one wanted me to go out for the walk. This has a tendency to make me hate all this suspicious behaviour in the conservative village society.

In the evening, I warn my cook that he is getting himself into trouble and if he talks to the nurse again that I will have to send him back to Delhi and that he should just stay away from the family planning centre. It seems that the society is rather sick, where it is considered that one can rape a woman just by looking at her.

On Monday, I go with Balwinder Singh Gill and Ajaib Singh for a crop-cutting experiment at Kaleram village near Banga. Balwinder is the Agricultural Inspector for High Yielding Varieties and Ajaib Singh is the Agricultural Inspector for Maize. This is always a little boring for me, but the trip out to the village is pleasant on bicycle.

Later, back in Banga, a guy on a motorcycle runs into the back wheel of my cycle and bends it over. Fortunately he does not fight with me, like happens sometimes. I don't know if it was my fault, but I got the damage. But no problem. I take it to the small bike shop near where we had the accident and they take the wheel off and straighten the rim. In a little bit, it is good as new.

Another day, I make friends with a more modern and westernised family in Gosal village just south of Banga. I will get to know them over the time that I am here. The son, Karamjit Singh, is a student at Sikh National College and I meet his father. But his questions are like the grand in quisition. I feel like, I am being thoroughly examined. He is living here with his son and his wife lives in England. They have some land in the village and also have a house in London. They seem very proud and rather arrogant to me, as some Sikhs are. There seems to be a lot of pretence. But they are friendly and I enjoy meeting them. The village still does not have electricity but will get electrified the coming year. I asked Karamjit how he manages to study. He says that his kerosene lamp, which can be pumped up, makes as much lighting as if they had electricity so it is no problem. I stay and talk and they make tea rather late. Darkness falls before I can get away so I have to ride my bike back to Mahil Gaila in the dark, which is a little tricky. One has to use the little bell on the handle bar a lot to warn other riders away. And there are the inevitable bullock carts lumbering in the dark. If a big truck comes on the small one lane road, it is off the bike until it passes.

The next day, I visit Karamjit and his father again to see their fields. This time they have produced tea and bananas and biscuits for my visit. I wish they had not gone to that much trouble. There are no women to help. The roads to the fields are really bad over old rutted oxcart trails in their rather poor village. We go to their sugarcane field. Some of the stalks have been felled apparently by rats that have eaten the stalks. Their hired hand is starting to make sugar in the field. Then they showed me the fields they were cultivating to plant wheat. The fields have been plowed and levelled with a *swagha* seven times, dragged down with a heavy, flat board. This seems excessive to me. The device is pulled by bullocks. All old fashioned methods but they work well and big crops of wheat are being produced with the old fashioned methods. I stay until almost dark again today.

The next day I plan to go on tour with the agricultural inspectors, but they have left without me. I guess I am just a nuisance. Being left behind, it is not worth trying to catch up with them, so I return to my place and read "*A Bend in the Ganges*" by Manohar Malgonkar.

The next day I have a programme to meet Karamjit Singh at the college. So I go there at ten in the morning and have tea with some students and get into a big discussion with them. They attack me severely about America's foreign policies, racism in the US, the War in Vietnam, and so on. I thought it was quite heavy, but my views are gradually evolving closer to theirs as I know more about the actual situation. It is a good exercise. They are right for the most part, but sometimes do not scrutinise their own society as severely. I do my duty to give lips service to the good intentions of the US policies, but this is getting more difficult to do as the war in Vietnam drags on. What will Nixon do?

I stick to the principle that it is fine to criticise one's own society, but lay off criticising theirs, which they will naturally be more sensitive to. They can do it themselves, and sometimes do, quite bitterly.

The next day is a Saturday the 16th, and there is a scheduled Star Meeting in the office. I am tempted to skip it, but I go to do my duty and pedal into town. No girls on the way today, unfortunately. But then, there is no meeting after all. I leap at the chance of escape. I leave my bike with my cook and take the bus to Phagwara and then to Ludhiana to get away for a night. I get a room at the Deol hotel, not far from the bus stop and Greens Restaurant. I buy Henry Miller's *Nexus* at Lyall's Book Stall and settle back in bed and read in the hotel. The hell with food production for the weekend. I am the only one in the world who knows where I am. But maybe I do not know that either. But there is no danger from communists as far as I can determine. I let Henry entertain me with his nonsense.

At eight o'clock I go over to Greens and have a beer and listen to the band. An exciting life. Le Dolce Vita! I see one girl in Greens but to no avail, and it is back to the hotel.

On Sunday I check out of the hotel and catch a bitê to eat at Greens. It is a breakfast, a couple of eggs, tea and toast. While I am there, Dave from Simrala, another volunteer comes in. Obviously Greens Restaurants are a little haven for the American Volunteers in Punjab. We sometimes run across each other here.

We decide to go to a film: "How the West was Won." Unfortunately it wasn't this way. The film was cut very extensively by the censors and was not worth the coin. Having lost a good deal of the West, we head back to Greens for lunch and then I bite the bullet and catch the bus back to my humble home. Duty calls.

At Phagwara, while bucking the mob for a ticket, I run across the BDO, Mr Harbans Lal, no less, and he asks me to get him a ticket. So I do the favour. We have a pleasant conversation on the way to Banga out across the kallar waste lands of the near-desert villages to the West of Banga. He invites me to come to his house sometime. I am not sure if he is just being polite. He has to put up with these American pests. It is part of his official duty. He is a bureaucrat.

14

Male Chastity Belt

"Young age and asceticism! What an insult to life!"

—Mirza Ghalib

She still puts a blister on my heart. That beautiful tight red *kamiz* and tight *pyjamas*. Petite, Pretty, beautiful slim body. She was the nice young secretary in the Block Development Office. I guess we were all in love with Ravi. She was the only thing that was really developed in Banga Block, as far as I could tell. A friend, Sant Ram, took me to her house, for a visit. She lived in Banga with her mother. I think he may have also been in love with her. She was a beauty and often on my mind. The only thing that happened was that she made tea for us and offered us some biscuits. The wrong kind, unfortunately.

One time she asked me to take her on my bike to the hotel. It was not as it sounds. She wanted to get some food from the restaurant to take to her home. The restaurant was just a poor local Punjabi *dhaba*. It made my day, however, but it was not to blossom any further than that. We had been strictly warned off from chasing any skirts, or in this case, *pyjamas*.

John Kenneth Galbraith, when he was Ambassador to India, said that "I suspect ... that being Ambassador to India is the nearest thing yet devised to a male chastity belt." Being a Peace Corps Volunteer in a rural village in the Punjab, on the other hand, is not the closest thing to a male chastity belt. It is a male chastity belt. No if, ands or buts. No butts for sure. No matter how pretty and cute those young Punjabi girls are, one is not going to get to have much to do with them. This was the wisdom that would sink quickly into our lusty western heads. Or at least it better if one was going to survive rural Punjab, Depressing, Downright hellish, Shit, No matter how seriously, one might fall in love with one of them, just forget it. That is practically one-hundred per cent certain. But youth are like youth everywhere. They would like to have friends and play around and sometimes even flirt with sex. Girls, of course, are cautious, but they would also like to have a friend and play around. And it is amazing how curious and even daring young girls can be in such a puritanical and sexually repressive society. The affair is not going to go very far, almost certainly not, in most cases, as there are too many constraints. But such flirtations serve mostly as a recreational past time until youths can be roped into the prison of marriage for life.

Perhaps sexual puritanism in modern India is part of the Indian Renaissance as has been suggested by Agahananda Bharati in his book, *The Ochre Robe.* He was a rather wild Sadhu, an Austrian, Leopold Fischer, who became an Indian monk and later taught at Syracuse University in the US. But this sort of sexual puritanism is certainly strong and deep in rural Punjab. It is mainly a tool for social stability. So it is not very encouraging for a young person from the West. We were supposed to be *Brahmacharis*, essentially, for the two years we were there. That's all. We were just expected to accept it. Love marriages were certainly the exception at the time, and still somewhat of a scandal for most families. Everything had to line up, caste and sect and income and profession and village and so on. All such a complicated tapestry. It is a wonder that it worked at all. Sometimes it doesn't. It cannot work, it seems, without a lot of repression. A lot of discretion is called for.

I made many friends in the village. My two best friends were Sant Ram and Prem Kumar. Sant Ram was a young guy who was not going to the university but to a technical school. Prem Kumar, on the other hand, was a student at Sikh National College in Banga and so always going to classes or studying his English and Punjabi classes. From them, I learned something about the activities of youths in the village. They clued me in on some of what was actually going on in the area of social relations among youths.

I found, indeed, that young guys did have girl-friends secretly. They would sometimes refer to pretty girls as "a piece." They wanted to meet them secretly and "enjoy." It was a general event, but this usually meant petting. Sometimes even sex, but how often, I do not know. It is said that illicit sexual relations are more common among married people or between married women and young unmarried men. Sometimes younger brothers of a husband. This generally happens in a sugarcane field or other such secluded location in the village.

For youth, it seemed that it was risky, but fair game if one could do it secretly without getting caught. Early marriage for girls was always the safeguard for such risks, but by the sixties, this tactic was getting more difficult among those young girls who were going to college or the university and were not ready for marriage. They would not put up with early marriage, so enjoyed some period of relative freedom. So the parents were somewhat losing control, or part of their control at that time. I suppose the fantasies brought by the Hindi films, where the boundaries were pushed as far as the censors would allow, had some effect.

A young girl's relationship with an older married guy would be more serious, which would sometimes result in the suicide of the young girl if a pregnancy were to occur. For the college youth, it was usually more flirtatious pitching woo, without very much serious happening, it seems. It would generally be a passing phase and not result in a love marriage as that was generally not accepted by the families. There was little possibility there, unless one could get completely away somehow, such as to a big city or abroad. It was not generally possible. Sometimes the young lovers would be a Hindu girl and a Sikh boy or vice versa, which would certainly not be the ticket for marriage. Certainly not in rural Punjab. Often the point of flirtation during the day or evening was across the roofs of village houses, close to each other, where the young lovers could see each other and catch each other's eye. Another point was in the village lanes, where they would have to pass quite closely, although the girl would be partially covered by her dupatta. A dupatta or chuney is a very sexual garment, at least it seemed so to me, and has a terribly exotic and exciting feel to it, along with the scent of the woman who wears it. A rough scintillating erotic feel. Many young Punjabi girls wore the long pigtails in their hair, dangling down to their young derriere, sometimes real, if they had long hair, but usually the artificial pieces, which were quite sexy and erotic, for me. Real hair was even more sexy, shiny and healthy, and sometimes came down to their feet when loose. Their clothes would bring out the shapes of their lovely young derrieres and young breasts. Very tight pajamas were in style in those days.

The young women would also be seen when they went out to the fields in the evenings. They would go together, usually in twos or threes, on the roads on their bicycles. Here was a chance to pass notes for a secret rendezvous or have a brief clandestine chat along the ripening rice fields. Another location would be in the streets of Banga, as they rode or walked their bikes from the college to the shops. The girls would stray from the school and play after their classes in the afternoon. Girls did not generally go to the sweet shops, which were largely the province of men, as it could be frowned upon, but they were becoming more daring in those days. Perhaps encouraged by Hindi films, which were still very puritanical, but stretching the limits of what the government censors would allow. Finally, the grounds of the college, as Sikh National College was a co-educational institution, girls and guys mingled to some extent, but not freely as in a Western country. This was certainly worrisome for the parents and elders, and the guardians of the morals of the community. An all-girls college was established in the town in the late sixties which would be less risky for parents. But where there is a will, there is a way. Social liaisons would happen.

These usually took the form of a secret meeting in the night, for part of a night, perhaps in a friend's house, if the coast was clear. Perhaps in another village, if there was a chance. There were some liberal parents who would allow such meetings and hide them, even encourage them, usually in another village during the day. Sometimes there was a room where someone could slip in clandestinely. Then a rendezvous could be made. Largely kissing and petting was as far as it went, apparently. The temptation is universal. Sometimes it would result in sex, but I do not know to what extent.

In Punjab, there was largely, but not total segregation of the sexes. Most schools were mixed, such as elementary schools and high schools. So generally, girls and boys mixed in public but had little social relations with each other after they began to develop sexually. They would not be seen in public talking to each other. Girls generally went with girls and boys with boys. In the colleges they might talk but briefly. Of course, it was more liberal in the big cities, depending on socioeconomic status. Sometimes classes of young men and women gathered for mixed pictures. These were somewhat rare and juicy occurrences, where one could see and have some interaction with pretty young women. I do not know how the culture has changed in the last 45 years, but I suspect that there has not been any real revolution in this regard in the rural areas of Punjab. This is in spite of the rather wild direction that Hindi films have taken. Fantasies can be fed, but then there is reality. The real situation is not very easy to discover, it seems, for an outsider. In such an atmosphere, youth were forced to act clandestinely. This was quite strict in rural Punjab in the sixties.

Some believe that there is too much freedom in the West. But I suspect that the maximum of freedom is better than restriction, especially tight restriction. Deprivation merely whets one's appetite and makes the object more desirable.

Then I had a dream:

In a dream you came to me,

I leapt to hold you in my embrace.

It was but fantasy

I could not hold

Arms ached with longing.

—Bhai Vir Singh

I first saw her a few days after I arrived in the village. A cute young Punjabi girl who lived in the village. I was invited to sit and drink tea in the house nearby. I was then just "The English Man." [sic] There were some young people around watching me out of curiosity. A couple of young girls, Lakshmi and her cousin. They were cute young girls and said hello to me. Then they invited me to drink tea. It was a rather bold move to make in the context of village society in a Punjabi village. But perhaps since the situation was so unlikely, it could be more easily overlooked.

Shortly, after this, she exchanged a note with me, addressed to "the English man." She was interested in being friends with me. I was curious about her too, and she was cute, in a stylish Punjabi outfit. We saw each other on the road and she gave me the note just in front of the big iron gate of the village Agricultural Cooperative Society.

That way we began to communicate. I learned her name and then we began to exchange letters by the village post. I couldn't have been more naive. What was I getting myself into? I was quite innocent in the sense that she seemed to be going after me more than I was going after her. But once contact was made, I liked exchanging notes with her. In my view, however, this was a little risky as the letters, however innocent, might be opened. I was afraid of this and thought about devising a simple code to use and write our letters in. It was probably of not much use, I suspect. It would have only caused more suspicion if discovered. But we did communicate. It was something going on secretly and made life more interesting. I thought she was terribly cute, as many young girls were that one saw on their bicycles on the road. She and her cousin were students at the local college in Banga. They usually went to and from the local college together on their bikes.

I suppose that I got hooked more easily due to my lack of experience with women. In the back of my mind, I might have thought about the warnings we received about getting trapped by an Indian woman who was trying to find a way to get to America. But why should one be that cynical about the motivations of young women? Life is not that simple or one dimensional. Could there be a chink in the male chastity belt? I didn't think there was any hope there. I was not rushing in. Being cautious.

This went on for some time after I had moved across the road to my new quarters in the old part of the Cooperative Society. I knew that she wanted to meet me but I did not have any idea about how that would be possible in the village.

It was a coolish evening in late October. Darkness had fallen. It was the time of day when the village women came out to visit the fields for their nature call. They would pass along the village lane by my place on the way. It was 29 October, 1968. I was sitting in my room when all of a sudden I saw her alone at my door. The gate to my compound was open. It was, indeed, a quite bold and risky thing for her to come in that way. I quickly opened the door and asked her to come in. We exchanged some words, of not much significance, I think, just hello. I was terribly sensitive that we would be caught and that it would be bad for us, if we were.... It would probably get me kicked out of the village, I thought, and then out of the country when the word got back to the Peace Corps in Delhi. So I didn't think it was a good idea for her to be there. But what was I to do? I was not going to be cruel and kick her out and put an end to it, which a hard person might have done. I was receptive. I was awfully happy that she had come, in spite of the danger.

When she was about to leave, on an impulse, and perhaps foolishly, I held her and kissed her, not a great kiss. Was it foolish? Who can say? Of course, in many ways, love is foolish and one of the more irrational aspects of life. In fact, it was a very clumsy kiss, not on the lips, but the cheeks. Her scent was enticing. Exotic. Then it was over and she was outside of my compound. I was somewhat afraid that someone might have seen her enter or leave. That was a worry, but the other side was a feeling of happiness that we had made contact, whatever happened. But at the same time, I had in my mind that it was a terribly foolish thing to do. Why had I done that? And what would it lead to? Those were the thoughts in my mind, but what the hell? Was I about to get my ass in a real sling? Probably. But sometimes things just happen. Things just spin out of control. Things just happen unexpectedly in life. After all, that is life.

Things went on with nothing happening. We wrote letters to each other. One evening as I was walking near the fields and darkness had fully fallen, she was there, purely by chance, in the lane between the fields, and I embraced her and we kissed again. This time, I tasted her lips. I felt her softly in my arms. I slipped my inside her kamiz and touched her tender young breasts. I pressed her to me tightly. I enjoyed this encounter more, which was more passionate, however brief. Thoughts of her soft young breasts inflamed my heart. I cherished the taste of her lips. I hurried back home.

Time went on. The cool winter came with cool nights. It was the season that Punjabis call "Pyar ka Mossom." The season of love. Simply, it gets cool enough to make love comfortably. Punjabi is said to be rich in the language of abuse or curses and in the language of love.

One cool night in November, I was reading in my room around eleven and about to turn in when I heard a scratching on the screen of my window. What could that be? I thought. I got my flash light to come outside my compound to take a look. But when I went to the compound doors, she was there. I quickly ushered her in to the courtyard and closed the doors. I invited her into my room and latched the door. The windows had wooden shutters which were closed, so no one could see into the room from outside. It seemed that we were safe as long as no one had seen her come in and no one came to investigate. I didn't think it was likely that anyone would bother us. I invited her to sit down. The meeting was quite awkward. We could not communicate very well and I wondered if she had come for more than just a talk. What did she expect? What should we do?

After a few minutes, I invited her to lay down with me. I lit a candle and turned off the single florescent light. She slipped her shoes off and lay down in her clothes. I took my clothes off and lay down beside her and began to kiss her. I loved her scent and the feel of her *dupatta*. Then she put it aside. She had brought some cardamon seeds to chew. She slipped one into my mouth, as I asked what it was. I chewed it and tasted the pleasant flavour. After a while, she took off her kamiz and let me feel of her soft young breasts and kiss them. It was heavenly to have her with me. I held her and encouraged her to feel of my hard cock. I knew that I was not going make love to her that night but I wanted her to give me pleasure. I was sure that she would not want me that night. She was not even going to take off her pyjamas, which was OK with me. I loved her young breasts and loved kissing and tasting them. We stayed together for quite a long time, until the early morning. It was a lovely night. I helped her get her things together and she left as silently as possible. The night had come as a complete surprise to me, as an event that I never thought would happen. I could only wonder if it had ever happened to any other of our volunteers but thought that surely it had not.

I slept.

15

Bread Basket

"A peasant earns his bread honestly."

—Mahatma Gandhi

In September the monsoon rains end. The cool nights and pleasant autumn days begin. Sleeping is once again pleasant. This begins Pyar ka Mossem, the season of love, as is said in Punjab. The mosquitoes mostly disappear and there are fewer pesky flies. It is pleasant in the fields of Punjab with the clear blue skies. I loved to go to a small village near Banga, Gosal village, and visit my friend, Karamjit Singh. The peasants were preparing the fields for planting wheat. There were a number of plowings with oxen. I set up some wheat crop demonstrations with the farmers there.

In 1968, peasants were planting Mexican wheat varieties such as Senora 308, PV 18, Keylon 227 and Sherbati Senora. These were some of the seeds developed in Mexico by Norman Borlaug (1914-2009). These were dwarf wheat varieties with short, sturdy stalks which generally do not lodge like the older varieties. Each seed produces several long, full heads of high quality grain because of its tillering ability and resistance to rust. This seed was revolutionising wheat production in India, but unfortunately did not have good milling qualities for making *chapaties*. It was being grown as a cash crop for the market.

The yields of Mexican wheat were four to six times as great as the older varieties. Not uncommon were yields of 50 bushels per acre. Yields of 65 to 85 bushels per acre were frequent. The yields at the time were much less in the dry lands in the US. In rain fed land like ours in Missouri, a yield of 40 bushels per acre was considered a good crop. Because of this, Punjab was called the bread basket of India.

At this time, almost all of the wheat was still harvested by hand. This was done by cutting it with a small scythe, the work being done mostly by hired labourers. The wheat stalks were then bound into sheaths and left in the field until they could be loaded onto a bullock cart and taken to the threshing floor.

The old method of threshing the wheat with bullocks and dragging a plank over it, was still seen in these days, but becoming more rare. When this is done, the wheat must be winnowed to separate the wheat from the chaff, a quite labourious process. But increasingly, threshing was being done with small threshers run by electric motors or a diesel engine. The bundles of wheat are unbound and fed into the top of the thresher and the grain falls down at the bottom. These were being widely used, but were quite dangerous and many workers were injured, losing hands and arms in these machines.

The ground-up wheat stalks are blown out one side of the machine. This is then collected as *turie*, or chopped straw, and bound into stacks in the village to be used as cattle feed. It is an essential ingredient in making good dung patties that burn well after passing through the digestive system of the cattle. So nothing here is wasted. The stacks of *turie*, or chopped straw, are held together by long ropes made of rice straw.

Along the roads, in the village streets, the men and children make ropes of rice straw. One man, or boy, twists the rope which is tied to a small piece of wood which he rotates in his hands. At the other end, a man squats beside a pile of water-soaked rice straw. Skillfully he gathers a few straws in his right hand and places them between the straws in the rope. Then he allows the turning rope to twist through his hand until the straws are bound securely. When these straws have been twisted into the rope adding another two feet to its length, he repeats the process. These ropes are then rolled into bundles and used to bind the wheat straw into a stack.

Part of the grain will be kept but most will be taken to the grain market in town and sold. The roads are crowded with bullock carts taking the grain to market in this season.

In September and October, the land is plowed eight to ten times by bullocks with a desi plow. After each plowing, it is levelled down with a plank pulled by bullocks and fertilised.

Then another type of plow is used to make the furrows for planting the seed. Usually, the wife or son walks behind the plow and drops the seed into the furrow as the bullocks are driven round and round the field. After planting, the field is again planked down level, then divided into sections and irrigated to germinate the seed. Irrigation is done usually by a tube well pump run by an electric or diesel motor.

But at this time, there were still many farmers using the Persian wheel pumps, driven with a bullock or a camel. They walk around in a circle, while a small boy sits on the pole and drives them round and round.

The apparatus for raising the water is a long chain with small metal buckets attached. The chain runs over a large wheel about six feet in diameter and down into the well. The wheat grows through the winter and begins to ripen in March.

April 13 is *Baishaki*, the harvest festival, when Sikhs go to the Gurdwara and the rivers to celebrate the harvest. After the harvest, the intense heat has begun and one must take it easy until time for khariff season which is the rainy season beginning in July.

The wheat emerges and grows through the winter, the rabi season. Using a desi plow was the old fashioned way of planting the crop. Now a small wheat drill had been invented and some farmers were beginning to use it to cut down on the physical labour. We tried to make a demonstration with one in Gosal on Karamjit's land. However, there were some technical difficulties such as how to calibrate the proper amount of wheat being planted by the machine.

This fall, I started a project to make a type of swaga for the wheat fields. It would be a heavy flat plank to be pulled behind a tractor, similar to what was already used. But it would have sharp pointed blocks of wood attached to the bottom of it to make small furrows for irrigating the wheat. I believe the method already being used was much better. I did a lot of work to arrange to have this thing built and try it in the field, but in the end, it did not work well when pulled by bullocks. It did not make the furrows even and deep enough because the bullocks did not pull it straight. It probably could have been achieved with repeated work and modification, but I gave it up after that. It seemed to me that the method being used worked fine and the farmers knew how to do it well. But one of the farmers got the idea and said he would try it on his wheat crop the next year. I did enjoy the fall weather and going to the fields to make pictures of the wheat planting and cane harvesting.

Meanwhile, the sugar cane was slowly being harvested. Some of it was pressed and processed in the village, using the dry leaves to feed the fire and boil the sweet green juice.

November to March is the season for making brown sugar from lumps from sugarcane by the peasants. This is similar to the process of making sorghum molasses, the way farmers in the US used to do it at one time.

The peasant first prepares the place for boiling down the juice from the sugarcane stalks. A circular hole is dug in the ground about three feet deep and about five feet in diameter. Then a large boiling pan is placed over the hole.

A tunnel is dug leading out from the hole on one side and connected to a chimney made of bricks and dried mud. On the side opposite the chimney another smaller hole is dug with an opening into the larger hole. This is used to feed fuel to the fire which is built under the pan.

Then a thatched hut is constructed at the site to serve as a shade. The sun can be quite hot even in the winter.

The sugarcane is cut by hand and the leaves trimmed from them. The stalks are then hauled to the site by bullock cart for crushing. The juice mill is driven by a pair of bullocks hitched to a long pole. As they walk round and round, a man sits next to the crusher and feeds the stalks into it. The juice drains into a bucket. The crushed stalks can also be used for feeding the fire after they have dried.

Peasants and their children love to drink the green juice immediately after the stalks are crushed. It is very sweet, green, and gooey, but they like to drink it by the liter. Sometimes it is mixed with buffalo milk as a snack at the mill.

When one visits a peasant who is making *gur*, he always offers the guest some of the freshly crushed juice. One should relish it so as not to offend him. He will also offer some gur for sampling.

After the juice has been extracted, it is boiled in the big pan over the fire. Dry leaves stripped from the cane are used as fuel. The boiling liquid is mixed with soda and water to separate the impurities. A greenish-white foam forms on top of the liquid, which is dipped off and discarded.

After the juice has been boiled down and begins to thicken, it is dipped up and poured into a flat metal pan about three feet in diameter. It then begins to harden as it cools.

Two men sit on either side of the pan and using a utensil similar to a putty knife, scrape up small portions of the soft brown sugar and deposit in lumps on a piece of paper or plastic. When these lumps are hard, they are gathered up and stored in large reed baskets.

The peasant makes enough gur for his own use. It can also be sold to shopkeepers. Most of the sugarcane, however, is sent to the sugar mill for processing.

The brown sugar lumps are fine to just eat as they are but are generally used to sweeten tea as it is made in the village.

One of the most popular uses of gur is to make illicit liquor, known as desi sherab. Punjabi corn liquor, one can say. Punjabi peasants did not need to worry about prohibition. In fact, as time went along, the large consumption of alcohol would become more of a problem in Punjab.

16

Fall Dreaming

"Days were crystal clear, and everyone warmed himself in the benign rays of the golden sun."

—Prakash Tandon

Actually it is still just a dream and will remain so, for some more time to come. The luxury of having one's own shitter. I am not dreaming of a Corvette, or a Porsche, or a yacht. Nor becoming a millionaire. Meeting beautiful women. I just want a place to take a shit in relative comfort. My enterprise is to emulate the famous John Crapper, who supposedly invented the closet. Considerable water must flow down the Ravi and Sutlej before we reach that Promised Land, to cross over Jordan to the El Dorado of having a real place to take a shit, but it is high on my agenda and I am in hot pursuit of that big rock candy mountain. I will scale those heights, although the path is steep and it takes time.

Monday morning, the 18th of November. I hit the ground running again. Well, it is a hell of a lot better than killing commies. Please grant me that! There is some depression and I feel that the day is rather a loss and that I am spinning my wheels, nevertheless, I carry my cross. This being a roving Ambassador at large for America is not easy, but somebody has to do it. I would that they would appreciate it, give me due respect, but who will? To get respect, one must kill a real enemy of America from time to time.

We are just pinko wimps and letting our country down. We are scorned by America. Draft dodgers. Could anything be more disreputable? Perhaps the price of survival in this case.

I get over and stoically thin my sugar beets. Oh the joy of being young. Having come from a farm, I still actually enjoy that shit and do it quite willingly. The old phrase "strong back and a weak mind," as my mother used to say, may cut some ice here. The beet plot is doing good. Kicking ass. A good winter crop for Punjab. I finish by noon and come back to my place and have lunch. I will hoe them in a couple of days.

The mail comes from America. My younger sister has quit the university for the time being and is getting married in a couple of weeks. I get a letter from my old friend, Ken. He is now in the army, after being drafted some ten days ago. He is lucky. They have sent him to Korea. My fate would have been worse, if I had not fought for the freedom I now have half a world away, or a whole world away, perhaps. Eternal vigilance is the price of freedom.

I think back to just one year ago when all three of us, myself and my two sisters, were all in the university and now we are getting quite split up and my one sister is married and the younger one soon will be. My mother is completing a course in practical nursing and wants to work outside the home. It is healthy for her, at least mentally and psychologically. My father is back on the farm, doing what he loves best. Tilling the soil, growing corn, wheat and soybeans. But not making much money. But it keeps him busy, which is what farming is all about, for the small farmer in America. Just a hobby, which the government helps them subsidise.

In the afternoon, I take the tonga to Banga, along with Swaran Singh and Madho Singh. It seems like something out of nineteenth century Russia, perhaps. Hardly in the jet age in a Tonga. Smelling horse farts in the open air in the fields of Punjab is pleasant in the cool fall air. Just lay back and enjoy it. Relax. There are no dangers here in this pleasant back woods of the world.

I plan more projects and the BDO urges me to pursue them. In the evening, the Sarpanch invites me for some *booze*. My immediate project is a shitter, as noted, something very near and dear to my heart, and which I need badly. I am keeping it on the drawing board along with a poultry project. This also means building a chicken house along with the shitter. I am not without ambition.

In the afternoon I meet Karamjit in Banga and invite him out to my place to have tea. The next day I have to go to the Railway Station to pick up the 40 kilograms of Sherbati Sonora wheat seed that I have ordered from Delhi. Now that should boost production! I meet Lakshmi and talk to her on the road back to the village. That is clearly enough to make my day.

The weekend is an excursion with Baldev Singh, one of the Block Agricultural Inspectors who oversee the various government projects in the villages. On Saturday, we take the bus to his village near Amritsar. This is Mahalowala. It is a very remote village a short distance from the Pakistan border and we arrive quite late at in the evening and have to walk some distance through the dusty roads to get to the village. It is a very traditional village, not at all modernised. One does not see pucca houses in the villages here. The peasants are not rich enough for that. The entire village is of the old mud-cow dung construction, where the houses are joined by a single mud wall running continuously around the village. Inside the house the floors are also of earth and the ceilings are brick, held up by heavy timbers. However, I find the old type of house quaint and appealing in a way, although it rather smacks of poverty and the lack of the ability to construct a modern pucca house. Inside there is little privacy as the family sleeps on mungies all in one big room. Baldev Singh has a young wife who stays here in this village and a small daughter one year old.

The meal is simple and good and is late at night. We have arrived rather late, after ten o'clock.

The next morning is a bright fall Indian summer day and his wife and baby sit outside warming themselves in the morning sun. It is the 24th of November. Mahil Gaila is far ahead in terms of development compared to these villages in the western border areas. And the land is dry and sometimes barren.

Baldev Singh takes me to see the Golden Temple in Amritsar, the next day, which also contains a Sikh museum. On Monday and we catch the train from Amritsar. At Jalandhar, we switch to a bus and make it back in time for a Star Meeting.

Thanksgiving has come and on Wednesday, the 28th. I catch the bus to Sangh Desian near Goraya, which is Pete Bakry's place. He has a spacious courtyard, which is appropriate for a larger gathering. We are having a Thanksgiving get together here for our group, India 53. The first night, I tie into some *booze* and get drunked up pretty seriously and have to suffer the hang over the next day, which is Thanksgiving Day. We eat well and enjoy a leisurely day at the party. There is much card playing. I am not a card player, but learn the rules to play when I need to and this takes up the time.

Back in Banga on the weekend, I again plan for the wheat planting demonstration in Gosal with Karamjit Singh and carry on with the construction of the wheat irrigator.

But the next day, I catch my cook who has been stealing money as I mentioned before, and my reaction is to send him back to Delhi. It was probably not the best way to handle the situation. I should have kept him, but watched him, now that I knew what was going on. It is a result of my too great honesty, I think. I was so outraged by his thieving behaviour that I just couldn't tolerate it, when it is quite normal and quite to be expected, I suppose, especially from a guy from the big city, like him.

December arrives. It is now colder. I wear my big thick lined denim jacket from my Peace Corps trunk. I have met Balhara Singh from a small village in Hoshiarpur District. Now I go to his village on his motorcycle and we take some soil samples. After coming back, I fertilise my sugar beet plot. The next day I irrigate them.

I am having the carpenters in Banga construct the wheat furrow irrigator, using my own funds, of course. I will make a demonstration with another farmer at Gosal village on planting wheat.

Without a cook, I whip up my own dinner, but this clearly is not going to be good in the long run.

Besides getting this machine built by the carpenters in Banga, I am starting to work with the Fijian, Major Singh, who is also from Gosal and runs a travel agency in Banga just down Railway Road. It is a little hole in the wall operation, but he must be making some money out of it. Nevertheless, he always seems to be idle in his little hole in the wall office there.

I spend most of the day socialising and talking up projects and not much happens, but I make a lot of friends. The socialising part is necessary and very much a part of the culture everywhere in India.

At the college, I talk to a professor about getting some tutoring in Punjabi.

Now that I am out of a cook, I have to cook my own eggs for

breakfast. I go and see that my sugar beets are doing well, but fear that they still need more thinning. I am still pursuing screens. I attempt to talk to Swaran Singh about it, but he is not home. I ask the chowkidar, Jagdish, at the cooperative society to go with me to engage a carpenter for the task. I feel like it is taking an inordinate amount of time and I want to get it under way without further delay. This "just now coming" business is just not cutting it. At this rate, it will always be "just now coming."

We go down to the sawmill and talk to a couple of carpenters. We find Baba Singh, a carpenter who is working at a house in the village, and he says he will come in the afternoon. The chowkidar, takes me to his house for tea.

I go to the office in Banga but find the BDO "out of station." It neither surprises me not disappoints me. I talk to some of the officers, and more interestingly, to Ravi, beautiful Ravi. I think she is beautiful and also imagine that she likes me. I wonder about her being around the guys in the office all the time. They are all married, of course. But I think that they must fantasise about her. I love her beautiful red dresses, or Punjabi outfits. And she has a beautiful little shapely body inside there that tweaks my heart and causes my balls to start to itch. Surely a sure sign of love or something along that line. She looks beautiful in red, but would look beautiful in anything or perhaps more so without anything. I study those lips. Those moist red lips and wonder if anyone is actually getting a taste of that honey. And I wish that I was. With those thoughts, I am force to divert my attention elsewhere.

This was the day Ravi asked me to take her on the back of my bike to the hotel where I sometimes eat lunch with the guys from the office. It is mainly a Punjabi *dhaba*. She gets some food in a tin to take to her house after saying goodbye to me. It was so pleasant to be with her and she has made my day. She ignores the damned stares of others as we go together by bike. I guess women have to in such a society if they have anything at all to do with a guy. I am glad that she asked me to take her and not one of the other guys.

At first, Ravi had asked me to eat at the hotel. I misunderstood and thought that she was asking me to eat with her, but I should have known better. I will spend some time drooling over those lovely hips, inter alia, inside that bright red kurta.

My Nehru jacket has been made by the tailor in Banga, and I go down and get it, but think it is a little flashy to wear around the town. People generally prefer more conservative dark colours in this society. The bright colour is worn by the young girls and young women. Well, they should surely get to do something colourful.

At the Post Office, I mail my Christmas cards. This is a more complex operation than it appears, as I have first to go to one window and get them weighed, and then go and buy stamps from another window, then take them and get them registered.

I go and check on my wheat irrigating machine. The carpenter says that it will be done by tomorrow.

I shop for fruits and vegetables. I meet the assistant librarian from the college and he asks me to have tea with him. We again discuss politics. Politics, politics, politics. I start to understand that these developing societies, what will be called third world countries, are immersed in, saturated with politics. These guys probably bear some responsibility for turning me into a so-called political scientist. He gives me a run-down of all the major political parties in India and in Punjab. He fills me in on the Naxalites operating in Kerala and elsewhere. It interests me. I would like to know more about these communists. I have no intention of killing any of them. That is not my job.

Then he asks me what the US would do if India fell to the communists. At the time, I did not know the answer. The result of having studied physics and not politics in the university. The obvious answer is exactly what they do when any country falls to the communists. That is to launch a programme right away to get the government overthrown in whatever way it takes. If that does not prove possible, then it puts India in the camp of enemies, such as the USSR, China, or Cuba and they become part of the evil empire. Amen.

Then we met another of my friends from Mahil Gaila as we left the tea stall. He has just come from Jalandhar and here comes another invitation for tea, which I also cannot refuse. It is serial tea drinking, and I suspect that I may be seriously courting the danger of tea poisoning, but what the hell. So it is off to another tea stall, another dirty hole in the wall with, nevertheless, delicious tea. Banga seems to be rife with dirty tea stalls, the dirtiest ones I have seen anywhere and I always seem to be in them for no worse for the wear. So maybe they are what the doctor ordered for a healthy life. Or maybe I am just young enough to buck the filth.

I see another friend from the village. He is the English teacher at the college, the one with an M.A. Degree in English. I ask him to come over to my house in the evening. The carpenter has come and I show him how I want the screens to be made. My tea compatriot accompanies me back to the village by bike as we discuss things along the way.

17

Shoulder to the Plow

"The earth yielded softly to the plow and the clods broke easily."

—Prakash Tandon

I cook dinner. I can do it, sometimes even enjoy it, but feel somewhat lonesome eating alone. I fry potatoes and onions, boil carrots and peas, slice up tomatoes and cucumbers. For dessert, there are bananas and oranges. I have bread and coffee. I wonder if I should be eating some meat, but usually do not have it when my cook is gone and I cook for myself.

The young English professor with the Master of Arts Degree comes and we talk in the evening. He knows quite a lot about literature, but his knowledge seems somewhat narrow beyond that. He has not been out of the country.

I realise that I am enjoying the time. It is now December and I am having a good time meeting all these people and discussing things with them. It is a quite interesting life and so I feel quite good about what I am trying to accomplish at this time. I do feel like I am accomplishing something even if it is just shooting the shit with my friends. I am making social contacts and working on some projects. I am still naive and have a lot to learn. I start to think that it is a good experience for me. On the other hand, I might get discouraged and say the hell with it tomorrow. I hope not. I am trying to get out of the American ruts, but am afraid that they are quite deep. I am a stranger. The only one around like me.

It is a Saturday and since it is starting to get cold in my house at nights, I make the trip down to Ludhiana to buy an electric space heater. That takes the whole day, but I come back with a nice heater that I hope will keep me warm. One must, of course, have power and electricity which is pretty expensive and we have to pay for them.

On Sunday I head for Jadla to see Chris Klose. We have planned a trip to Bombay over Christmas, but in the end we cannot work it out as it happens. Things are not working out due to the Peace Corps bureaucracy, arranging for leave, getting some money. I ride back to the village in the dark after some shopping in Banga.

I am still working on my wheat demonstration plots in Gosal village with Karamjit Singh and Major Singh, my friend from Fiji. I ask the BDO about the possibility of providing a seed cum fertilised drill to use for the demonstration. The carpenter is finishing up my wheat irrigator today and I go to the shop and watch him work. It is a quite big thing. Perhaps a waste. But I guess it keeps me busy.

The next day, the Star Meeting scheduled for ten o'clock gets underway at half past 12 noon. The focus is upon family planning and small savings. The BDO canvases all the gram sevaks, or village level workers, to see how many cases they have recruited for family planning. Poor guys. This is not an easy task. The peasants want sons. They need sons, or think they do. They need hands for their fields and will get old and have to rely on their sons for labour. Their quota was two cases each, but most claim to have only recruited one case. There is no proof that they have even one case and so one wonders if they do in fact.

It is a relief to get away from that drivel and I meet some professors at the college for yet more drivel, although of a somewhat different genre. When I return to the village my home town paper has arrived, the Post Telegraph from Princeton, Missouri, which is indeed professional drivel. What my niece called the Post Telecrap in the paper itself when she was doing a summer internship. Whether it even comes up to that level is somewhat dubious. Still getting the paper is nice. I enjoy seeing it from so far away and get a different perspective on things. It serves the purpose of reminding me that things could be worse. I could be there, rather than in the far more interesting and exotic place where I am. Maybe I am crazy, but at least, I am different. I will see the world from a different angle for better or for worse. It cannot be bad.

There is a letter from my sister Freddie, who has just married. The Princeton, Missouri high school football team has won the state championship, going undefeated this year. That truly astonishes me. I mostly only remember them losing games. Somehow my rejoicing is seriously attenuated, however, being in my current venue. More bluntly, it doesn't mean didly shit to me in my current context when I am half-way around the world. It does tend to put things into a different perspective.

I talk to Madho Singh's son, Sodhy and he goes with me to take some of my clothes to the dhobi, in the village, who will do serious damage to them, in getting them clean, but that's the way it works. He goes with me to my sugar beet plot and I thin them again, giving him the discarded plants, some fifty plants that he will set out elsewhere. I dig up the remainder of my radishes and turnips from Madho Singh's garden, which I planted earlier. There are still many beets, which I have yet not dug up. One of my big white radishes was fifteen inches long and three inches in diameter. I had Sodhy take a picture of me holding it and said that I would send it to the Peace Corps if they accused me of not working.

My tomatoes were not so successful as some of the plants seemed to be diseased. We set out the sugar beets in the empty plot where I have harvested my radishes and turnips. I set out more of the sugar beets in my garden next to my house.

Swaran Singh comes the next morning and lets me know that there is a family planning conference in Naura village, just half a mile away. The government has started pushing family planning harder. It seems that people are, in fact, actually planning them, planning families, but planning to make them quite big enough, not according to the government criteria. That is according to the slogan, on the poster next to the red triangle, "*Do, ya thien bucha, Bus.*" (Two or three children, then stop.) The question is how do you stop at that point. And there is a lot of information out there about those evil French leathers that the government is polluting the country with. They are sometimes seen as Western and immoral.

I do some work in my garden and then head to Naura. Things are slow to get underway, unlike the enterprise of making more babies. The peasants already have a good head start on the nurses, who are rowing against the current, it seems. The BDO arrives about one o'clock for the programme which finally gets underway around two. A bureaucrat, he approaches it stoically, as he himself adds to the population back in his flat in Banga. The block staff is there along with several nurses in the family planning programme. They are ready to roll out the condoms and the IUDs. Are there any takers? There is no problem with tea and pakoras which are readily consumed. Certainly I have no hesitation.

The highlight is the delicious *pollock pakoras* (fried spinach in chickpea flower) which are lovely in this cool weather with tea. God, I can eat those things forever, I think, and it will save me from some cooking. So much more palatable than the rubbers and IUDs on tap today. The tea party is at the cooperative building. I meet the faculty at the Naura school for girls. It is an enjoyable day with some tasty food and tea, but from my American work ethic standpoint, it strikes me as a day when I did not accomplish anything significant. Probably a false concept. So much of life in India is ceremonial.

It is nearing mid-December and I go to the bank to withdraw some money to give the carpenter for constructing screens. I treat my sugar beets with insecticide, BHC.

The Communists are having a meeting over on the north side of the village, which seems to be more their venue. I might have used some of the BHC on the communists, but was all out, and so they continued to flourish, pests or not. For me, the programme was extremely boring, mainly because I could not follow what was being said in the speeches. I am sure it was standard boiler plate, not very interesting, but also not all wrong.

The Patwari or record keeper for this village and Naura lives at Naura Village. He has a little hole in the wall office there. I meet him again today and he strikes me as being sort of cracked in the head and a lot of what he is trying to tell me in English does not make any sense. He invites me to have dinner with him tomorrow night. He has to know four languages and three alphabets just to keep the records, English, Punjabi, Hindi and Urdu. I am amazed at that. I guess it is enough to scramble one's brains.

I was always amazed at the post office, because one sees letters there with addresses in English, in Punjabi, in Hindi and still, there are many people writing in Urdu, with the Arabic script so long after partition. So I always think that it is amazing how efficient the post office is given that language richness. The US is disturbed about a little usage of Spanish, which is, after all, not so far from English.

I get back on the wheat demonstration plot for Karamjit Singh at Gosal village on the 13th. This was the day we were to plant the wheat. Probably not an auspicious day, although I failed to consult the astrologer, there should have been no need. It was Friday the thirteenth of December, 1968. A good day to stay in bed. Peace Corps Volunteers do not stay in bed. I rush out like a fool. Bhagat Singh, the gram sevak for that circle, was supposed to meet me at the block office, but he did not show. So I went to his house and found him there. After having tea, I dragged him out, and we went to Punia village to see about getting the wheat drill. There is a demonstration farm there. A model farm, I guess, with some very nice plots of wheat. This village is the next one over from Gosal. We arranged to have the wheat drill brought at a later date. We go to Karamjit's house and have tea and coffee and then at Major Singh's house, down closer to the fields, he breaks out the desi sherab, sugar cane liquor. I will cave for Binnys, but really draw the line at drinking this sugar cane white lightening stuff. It is the corn whiskey of Punjab. Sometimes it can positively be dangerous.

I am starting to get the feeling that the priorities of the locals differ quite sharply from mine, running to tea, coffee, boiled eggs, biscuits and desi sherab and to hell with wheat drills and demonstrations. But I journey on, shoulder to the plow.

18

Hill Billy from Punjab

"The sun would rise like a big orange in the mist, and as it rose higher and gathered strength the mist would slowly dissolve."

—**Prakash Tandon**

The delicious December cold has arrived. It is the thirteenth day of the month. But that bothersome Patwari, Ram Serup Gupta, gives me a pain in the ass. He can hardly speak English and seems wacky besides. I have promised to have dinner with him and come to his place in Naura village in the evening. I try my best to understand him. I go to his old and dilapidated office. There are only two chairs and a dirty worn-out charpie. The office is terribly dirty with old ledgers piled up and dust everywhere. Years and years of dust. This is truly historical dust.

We leave the office and he takes me to a big new pucca house belonging to a well-healed sedougie. The owner seems to be quite well off. I am starting up the stairs to the second floor when a real pretty Punjabi girl starts to come down from the roof. She says to me in her best English: "Good Morning." Dear Jesus! The way she looked, it didn't matter what the shit she said. I was in love at once. They could be so cute in those tight Punjabi outfits, before they start to have kids and their bodies go to pot and spread out.

This really took me by surprise, not the good morning, but getting that lucky, and it was a pleasant surprise indeed.

The father was there, but I failed to catch his name, his daughter cutting more ice with me at the moment. But I meet her brother, Lashkar Singh, who knows good English. I talk to him while I eat and drool about his sister.

After the meal, the patwari asks me to spend the night with him. I am not really sure if I trust him, so respectably decline that request. He kindly walks me back to Mahil Gaila and I lend him my flashlight for his trip back to Naura, perhaps half a mile.

On Saturday, I take the runners for the wheat irrigator to Gosal, preparing to try the outfit. Sunday, I take a break and go to Ludhiana lugging my soil samples I have collected down to the University for testing. I enjoy a meal and a beer at Greens, and then catch the bus back, but it is a cram job, with at least ninety people sardined into the bus. It should be 55, but I cannot say that is normal. I ride standing all the way up the GT Road to Phagwara clinging to the roof of the rattle trap bus.

In Banga, Major Singh is at the News Stand. He invites me to spend the night with him. My resistance being quite low, I readily agree. My bike is at the bread shop and we buy vegetables and head for Gosal. On Railway Road, we stop to get a soda. Just then there is a collision in the street between a motorcycle and a bicycle. The guys from the motorcycle, who are young well-built Sikhs, jump off and start beating up the small skinny guy that was riding the bicycle. The wheels of the bike are badly bent, but a cycle walla can fix it. I know from experience. There is no damage to the motorcycle, but they want to beat up on this poor son of a bitch. I start to think that these guys in big turbans are sometimes like young roosters who like to fight and think they are the top dogs of the rather macho society.

We ride our bikes down to Gosal and cook curry and drink some Binnys Sherab, the local whiskey. Major Singh is on his bike too. Even though he is running a business, he cannot afford a motorcycle.

Monday morning blues come soon enough and I get out to the office. Middle of the month. Talk to the BDO. Go to Mahil Gaila and get some mail and have tea with Madho Singh, the secretary of the Cooperative Society. Then back to Gosal where we play cards for the evening. Balhera Singh is there. He has lived abroad and thinks somewhat differently from some of the locals and we get along well. He is a little more westernised in his views.

The next day, Tuesday, December 17, is the day we had scheduled for planting the demonstration plot of wheat at Gosal village on Karamjit Singh's land. The gram sevak, Bhagat Singh, comes and we get ready to plant the wheat. Next to the field they are making gur from Karamjit Singh's sugarcane. I take some pictures of the sunny fall scenes. A peasant then brings the three-row bullock drawn seed cum fertiliser drill and we unload it from the cart.

However, one of the peasants informs Karamjit that the drill is not calibrated and it is not measuring the seed correctly. It should have been calibrated previously, as it takes some time to do it properly. Because of this, Karamjit thinks that it is safer to just use the old method of dropping the seed in the furrow behind a bullock drawn plow. I agree that, this is probably the best, at least the safest way to make sure the amount of seed is correct. But we miss being able to use the seed drill as a demonstration.

Looking back on it, I don't see why it was so important to use the drill. It was no imposition on the peasants to do it with bullocks as the fields are quite small and it is not very time consuming or labour intensive. If labour becomes too expensive, then they will simply switch to a better method if the drill can provide that. At this point it is a little difficult for some peasants to learn something new and technological.

After planting the labourers drag the swahga over the field to level it down so it can be irrigated evenly. This is generally done by dividing the field into sections with small ridges throughout the field.

Today I want to try the furrow maker that I have had built as a means of irrigation. The peasants hook two teams of bullocks to it. But pulling it through the field, the bullocks do not go in a straight line. So the furrows are not straight. I can see that it should be pulled with a tractor to make it work reasonably well. The peasants driving the bullocks did not understand the principle of what we were trying to do, using it just like a swagha, and so it was difficult to explain to them how they should drive the bullocks in a straight line across the field. When it was explained to them, they started to become angry. It is probably more difficult than meets the eye. I could see that it would have worked much better with a tractor but that the runners should have been somewhat sharper to cut into the soil. They probably needed to be fitted with a steel point. Just a little tweaking and it would have worked much better.

Since the crooked furrows that they made were useless for irrigation, I said they should just replank the field and forget it this time. The major problem is that the device would have to be pulled straight and for that one needed a tractor. However, Balhera Singh liked the principle of the machine and said that he would like to try the method on his wheat next year. I had made a valiant effort, even though it did not work correctly on the trial run. It could have been made to work. I thought it was a little like the Kitty-Hawk plane flight, in which the plane took a nose dive and crashed in this case.

In the evening, I stay with Major Singh again. We make pork curry and drink some Binnys and I spend the night there. The food was delicious, even though it is rare to eat pork in Punjab. It is not considered to be clean meat as the pigs eat everything. I suspect it has something to do with the Islamic influence historically.

It is a week before Christmas and back in Mahil Gaila I clean house and anticipate the trip to Bombay with Chris. I have to give the carpenter more money for hinges and screen and so am getting low on funds and waiting for my cheque from Delhi.

I have a nice talk with Surinder Singh in the evening. He says he is bored in India and that life is dull here. It is a common lament of young people in the villages, and they are right. Life in a village is dull. We could put up with it as we knew that we would be staying there only for a relatively short time. I said that maybe he should go to England and later he could come to the US and visit me. It is a distant dream for most, however. Still, many families sent one or more of their family to England in those days, and sometimes to America.

The next day, my money was supposed to come for the trip, but there was nothing, so I am stuck for the time being without funds. The cheque for my leave does not arrive until four days later, the 23 of December, just two days before Christmas. But then, it is too late to make the Bombay trip. The chance is gone. So I cash the cheque and head for Jalandhar to spend the night in the Raj Mahal Hotel. I catch the Deluxe Bus to Delhi the next day, Christmas Eve.

I arrive in the late afternoon at old Delhi bus terminal, reading a copy of the old Communist tabloid *Blitz.* I take a horse carriage to the Lodhi Hotel on the other side of the city. I think this is a little unusual, as usually horse carriages do not go to that modern part of Delhi. I am naive or just a county bumpkin. A hillbilly from Punjab. I realise this later. I think I really looked like an old timer, Rip Van Winkle, coming from the sticks of rural Punjab to the big city. It will be my first hot shower for days.

There is a Christmas party in the Lodhi Hotel with a band. However, there is no one there that I know. Some members of other Peace Groups appear who are on their way to West Bengal and Madras. I am invited to Dr Hibbard's house for Christmas dinner. On the 27th, I go to Agra and Fathapur Sikri to see the Taj Mahal and Agra Fort. The next day, I meet staff Clarry and Bob Baker and we go to a place called the cellar. Then to the top of the Oberoi Hotel for a drink, a rare treat.

We shop on Chandni Chowk in old Delhi and to the Khyber Restaurant near Kashmiri Gate. It is a good place to eat. Bob and I go to the Sound and Light programme at the Red Fort. We will soon be back in our villages.

19

Great Leap Forward

> "I would look again at the green of the wheat, the yellow of the mustard, red of the rai, and the blonde plumes of the sugar cane, all waving joyously in the benign and pale winter sun....."
>
> **—Prakash Tandon**

Back from the end of year holiday in Delhi, for a little rest and relaxation, I buy paint, and paint my room and the windows of my veranda. This involves moving my furniture out. I finish it in three days in the second week of January 1969. It is the winter monsoon. The weather has turned cold and rainy. I find a recipe in the Farm Journal which is being sent for free, for doughnuts and make a big batch.

My next projects involve constructing my latrine and chicken house in my compound. I hope to make some progress on that this month. Now that Madho Singh has seen me painting, he takes advantage of it by supplying me with more paint from the co-operative, which he hopes I will use to spruce up more of the building.

The carpenter comes and I give him more money for springs, hinges and screens. I get mail from the family in the US along with the local gossip sheet, the Post-Telegraph. One day I start to dig the pit for my latrine just outside the wall of my compound. Prem Kumar, my friend and college student in the village, comes and helps me in the afternoon. People are wondering why I do not hire a labourer to do it. I will try to do it myself, at least up to a point. But it is certainly not an easy task. It will be March before I finally get this project completed.

I do not have a proper belcha or shovel to dig the pit and look for one in the village, but cannot find it. So I end up buying a new one. In Banga, I give a carpenter the design for a bookcase. I try the doughnut recipe again using crushed gur, or brown sugar for sweetener. It works nicely and is healthier than white sugar. It is a cold and damp night and the power is out. Since my heater is electric, I have to put up with it and I listen to Radio Australia on short wave.

Still plans for the chicken house are not getting off the ground and I fall back to painting my veranda. In the Office, the next day, I begin to talk up my soybean project to the BDO and he is interested. He says that the Block Office can supply the necessary sprayers and insecticide.

After talking to Karimjit Singh, I shop and return to the village to cook up goat curry. Prem Kumar eats with me. I find that there is something wrong with the electric lines coming into my place, which has caused the electric failure. Everyone else has power except me. I have to have someone come and repair the lines.

The next day I meet Major Singh in his office in Banga and Balhera Singh takes us on his motorcycle to Sikandarpur village in Hoshiarpur District. He shows me his house there, which is new and comfortable. We have tea inside. There is a big gathering of men and women along the road. They tell me that a woman has died in the village and they are celebrating her passing. We have to go to Newanshahr and buy some liquor for the party. We have a few pegs of the terrible stuff ourselves before heading back.

On the way back, I take a notion to go to the Rayman Circus which is now in the big open space at Newanshahr next to the bus stop. Major Singh comes with me. Some of the performers are Japanese and some Indian. It is a quite big circus. At six o'clock we get the bus back to Banga, but it is crammed full, apparently because of the circus, some one hundred people packed inside. Darkness has fallen and it is seven o'clock by the time we make it to Banga. Another day, another circus.

I get my bike and do some shopping for vegetables and head out to the village in the dark on a night when there is no moon to drive by. It is somewhat dangerous on a murky evening.

The Sarpanch comes and I show him some American farm magazines. All those big powerful and shiny tractors make it look like a farmer's paradise in America. But it is deceptive. Farming is just a hobby there and few of them could be out there planting if the government did not supply them subsidies on their crops, which are really subsidies to the farm implement companies. Still, they are going under rapidly as corporate farming takes over. The day of the family farm in America is long gone and corporate farming is taking over. Being a "future farmer" is just a figment of a young farm boy's imaginations. We were sort of the last of the Mohicans in that but we survived because, first, we had very fertile bottom land and secondly, we used old cheap equipment and did not go in for the fancy new tractors that would eat up any profit. That way, there was something left over after all the bills were paid. We busted our gut doing it, but sort of made a living.

I make more doughnuts. I am becoming a donutaholic without a cook. But the Sarpanch takes me to his place for a drinking party with Binnys whiskey in the evening. *Le Dolce Vita.* What more could one ask for? It is a dangerous cliff, in fact, in the boredom of Punjab for many. For those in desperation.

More digging for my latrine pit with my new shovel, getting blisters on my hands. Why don't I just hire a coolie? Digging the pit is the pits. A Sears, Roebuck Catalogue comes from the post office. It is very good to sell the paper for shops as they can make small bags from the pages which will be nicely illustrated with women's underwear. That should be exciting in this venue.

It is 21 January. The pit is coming along. Now for the structure, the shit house and chicken house. I talk to Swaran Singh and he says we can have the bricks brought from the brick kiln in nearby, Newanshahr. We need around five hundred bricks for the building, according to the masons. But they are wrong. My bookcase is done in Banga and I bring it to my place by tonga. We go to Naura and buy the bricks, which will be brought by donkey to my place. Swaran Singh helps me find wood in Banga for the forms for the building later in the day. We scout the wood depot places down Railway Road. The last week of the month, the carpenters finally put up my screens on windows and doors. I have accomplished something in my small village castle.

It is Sunday the 26th and Chris Klose has organised a sports tournament in Jadla village over to the east. I arrive to help chaperone and keep order along with Fritz Bachman. There are two kabbaddi matches, followed by some foot races. It is a tall order to keep all the kids and peasants and bicycles off the track so the races can go on. It is a challenge, with all the chaos which marks the beauty of rural India.

Finally, there is a bicycle race. This is the most hectic of all as it is almost impossible to keep people off the track. The racers are speeding quite fast. Then there is the ceremony for giving prizes. There is no semblance of order, with people crowding in from all sides and talking and shouting. Chaos, Lovely chaos.

One peasant had brought a large stone with a handle carved into it like that of a jug. The trick is to lift the stone above one's head with one hand by swinging it between one's legs and then heaving it upwards. The stone weighs about 85 pounds, being about 12 inches in diameter. I try it, but cannot lift it with one hand. After the event, we have some dinner at Chris's place.

I spend the night with Chris and catch a tempu to Newanshahr the next morning. Back in the village, the masons are to start building my shit house and chicken house the following day. And sure enough they do. The initiation of the new building attracts a lot of attention with villagers gathering around to see what is happening. A new addition to the village, I guess, however small.

Well, I cannot say that I knew of another shit house in the village, so perhaps it is a significant innovation. It may also be significant that I would not be the only one to avail themselves of the luxury in future, once it is operational.

Another day, I make an outing with Swaran Singh to Banga to buy bolts and reinforcing rods for my building and "enjoy." I guess, I am rubbing elbows with the ruling class here but really have no choice if I want to get along. Swaran Singh is actually a somewhat Americanised peasant, although quite socially conservative. He owns land in America, in Colorado, and has spent some time there. He takes care of me and helps me out, but also keeps me out of trouble.

I take a walk in the late afternoon with Nishan Singh, the professor from the college in Banga. It is the time when many villagers go out for their late afternoon or evening walk. We walk out to the fields to the east. He begins to discuss the Indian educational system and tells me that it needs to be overhauled.

He believes that students in the high schools need to be taught a vocational subject so that they would be better prepared for work when they graduate. Watchmaking and vocational agriculture, he thinks, would be appropriate.

He gives me a small booklet from which I can study the Punjabi alphabet.

January has almost passed and I have made some progress in getting my projects around the house under way. The next day there is a political rally in Newanshahr for the "Front Party." I am invited. The peasants take their tractors and load their trolleys or wagons full of peasants and prepare to head out. There are four trolleys, heavily loaded with all men, of course.

Almost the end of January. I am about to go with them when the masons call me and tell me they need more bricks and the timbers for the roof. So I go to Naura and order another five-hundred bricks. After lunch, I go with one of the masons to buy the timbers and window frames for my new building. The next day, I go with the carpenter to Banga to buy wood for the cabinet which I am having made.

I feel like I am settling in for the duration, getting my mansion set up for *le dolce vita*. Soon I will settle back as king of my small castle and be living in the lap of luxury.

Latrine, Just Now Coming.

The building is getting done for my chicks in mid-March, but I still have to put in my latrine. I have to finish digging the pit and then go to Jalandhar and buy the bowl and pipe. After that, I will put them in and lay the cement around them and then construct the cement cover for the pit. This takes quite a bit of work over several days. It will be a bucket flush system. That is, after one uses it, one pumps a bucket of water with the hand pump and dumps it into the squat type latrine to flush it down into the pit. This is a perfectly fine system for my purposes and I am going to get it operational just eight months after my arrival in the village. It is going to be a beautiful luxury, compared with the old system of doing without.

It takes me a day to make the trip to Jalandhar to buy the bowl and pipes. I take advantage of the trip to have lunch at Greens and a beer. I load the bowl and pipes onto a rickshaw and take them to the bus stop. I have to get a porter to load them on top of the bus to take them to Banga. Then at Banga, I have to get them off the bus and take them to the Tonga walla stand by rickshaw to bring them out to the village. After all that, now I am set to install them.

A few days later, March 17, I get around to digging the places for the bowl and pipes which is a hot job even though the weather is still fairly cool. It is already mid-March and the heat has come. I install the bowl and pipes and pack the joints with hemp, then mix the cement for the floor. I smooth it out with a board.

I am forced to cave in and hire a labourer for a day to dig the pit. But by the end of the day, it is still only about half done, about a meter deep. So I say the heck with the labourer, and decide to finish the pit myself. However, when I dig, I attract a crowd of villagers around me to watch me work. It is only interesting because it is me that is busting my ass in the hard soil getting the pit down past the first metre. They are surprised to see a rich man like me working to dig the pit and talk about how hot I am and how I am working. I understand most of what they say, although they do not seem to realise this. They stand on the edge of the pit where I am working and sometimes kick dirt back down into the hole while squatting on the edge. I am getting a kick out of it. Up to a point. Till it starts to get on my nerves. There are hoards of flies to bother me as I dig. I wouldn't want to do it for a living.

The next day, I finish making the cement floor and finish putting in the pipes. All that is left now is to make the cement cover for the pit. But for that I have to buy the lumber to make a form for the cement. This I do in a couple of days along with doors for the new building, the chicken house and latrine. A few days later, I mix the cement for the cover for the pit and finish the job.

At the end of March, the chicken house is also finished and I get twenty baby chicks from the poultry farmer who has an incubator on the fifth of April. I run an electrical wire out from my house to the chicken house to give them heat in the night from the bulb.

While there are no latrines in the village except mine, I am surprised at howmuch the guys from the cooperative society across the street start to take advantage and use my latrine. Hell, it is more convenient than the fields. This might produce some change, however subtle, I think.

It seems that the great leap forward in the construction of

latrines in the villages in Punjab was in the late 1980s during the Sikh Akali agitation for Khalistan, a separate Sikh nation. With terrorism on the rise, it was not considered safe to go to the fields, so people were forced to make provisions inside their compound for security reasons. The women had to cut back their evening outings and stay inside the houses. Many villagers decided that it was a good idea to build a flush latrine rather than continue using the fields.

I have made a great leap forward in my living standard.

20
Bus Madness

"The Grand Trunk Road rolls South and South–a broad, smooth river of peace whose waves are unthinking humanity."

—Katherine Mayo, 1927

It is April and the tremendous heat has returned. I take a break to pick up my new Kurta and pajama from *Lal di Hatti Cloth Shop* in Newashahr. Feeling affluent, I buy a turban, a long piece of thin cloth several metres long and have a friend in the village tie it for me. I like the way it looks on me, and it goes nicely with my beard, although it is reddish brown and not black like the Sikhs. I have someone make my picture in it, but am not courageous enough to wear it out in public. It might suggest that I was a Sikh, which I am not, after all. I thought that I was enough of a novelty without pressing my luck further.

The next day, I go with Baldev Singh, the agricultural inspector to visit a farmer, Brajender Singh, in his village. When we return, we eat in a small *dhaba* near the Post Office and then visit the Banga Cooperative Society near the Railway Station. There are piles of grain, mostly wheat and rice, and all types of farm supplies for sale. It is an interesting place and suggests the richness of Punjab from the fertility of the soil.

Back in the BDO Office, I get mail, a letter from my mother. There is also one from my older sister with a picture of her

Chinese fiancé. The BDO informs me that he is going to Maksudpur, a village five miles to the west, on tour. I decline to go today. I stay at the office and trace a copy of the Banga Block map for my use, showing the roughly one-hundred villages and their names. It will be useful in my work.

Over the weekend, I spend a couple of nights in Phillaur with Staff Clarry and Bob Baker and we go to see a film, in Ludhiana. Monday morning blues come soon enough, however, and I find my shoes and I hit the dusty trail back to the wilds of Banga Block. From Phillaur, one has to catch a bus coming up the GT Road from Ludhiana across the Sutlej River. Maybe partly because it is Monday morning, all the buses coming up the GT Road are fully packed. It seems like everyone in India, at least the men, are always on the way somewhere. I used to wonder about that, but put it down to the lack of telephones, so that one is forced to do almost everything in person. India is a very bureaucratic country and the bureaucracy seems never to end. It is a cradle to grave enterprise. A legacy of colonialism, perhaps. The iron framework.

I have to get up to Phagwara junction and catch the bus to Banga on the buses coming down from Jalandhar. These buses too are usually fully loaded. Catching buses at interim points presents such a difficulty.

This morning, it takes an hour to get a bus at Phillaur. There is no bus stand, just a general location along the GT Road where the buses stop. Sometimes, that is. Today, there is a mob. OK, they are people. But in such a situation, people, the people can become a *bona fide* mob. Mob rule in this new Indian democracy. Mob rule rules the bus routes. Along with me, and standing somewhat aloof, is an Indian just arrived from abroad. He has been working in Ireland for some twelve years. One can see from his clothes that he is coming from abroad, now just off the plane, trying to make it to his village, a trip down memory lane, but unfortunately Indians coming from abroad generally cannot take India for very long. Their nostalgia is quickly dampened down.

He is just standing and looking at the mob in astonishment, as the monstrous crowd rushes forward towards every bus that sweeps to a stop in the cloud of dust at the side of the road. The wave of humanity surges forward, and some are lifted into the bus on the sheer momentum of the surge, then the others fall back, when the bottle is full to overflowing and they are crushed against others.

My new friend says that he cannot stand the heat in India and the bus system is terrible. No shit. Too true. But eventually, we manage in the ebb and flow of the waves of humanity, and get swept inside. Punjab Roadways blasts a cloud of black soot and gas into the eyes of the crowd, coughs, roars, and is off up the metaled highway. *Chelloway chel.* (Let's go!)

In Banga, the bus always stopped on the west edge of the town near the BDO office. But to get out to Mahil Gaila, one needed to take a horse drawn tonga. There were no regular buses making the trip in those days. The tonga stand was on the east side of the town, just near Garshankar Road. One has to walk over to the tonga stand. It was a grungy place, with small dirty fly-blown dhabas. The tonga wallas are there with their horses and carriages feeding them clover and hay before the next village run.

A few months later a local business man came from England and built a quite big market on the corner near the Tonga Walla Stand, with small new and clean shops. On the corner, he opened a restaurant, rather western style, with screens and an inside kitchen. It was such a clean and lovely place, and I thought it was great that such a place was being opened in Banga. But it didn't work. It quickly fell into collapse. It was too clean and fly-free for local culture and tastes.

After a little bit, the cooking was brought outside in front of the place, as in traditional *dhabas*. The screen doors had been installed, but were perpetually propped open, for the convenience of the flies. Inside, the tables were partitioned off with curtains to provide privacy for peasants who came in with their wives. It was quickly converted into a traditional *Punjabi dhaba*. I thought that this was interesting and instructive. The western-style restaurant just did not work in the local town. Once converted to a Punjabi *dhaba*, business picked up and the peasants felt at home.

Travel Madness: "In India traveling is a national pastime, undertaken on any pretext." **—Prakash Tandon.**

We were in India before the advent of the family car. This was to come later with Sanjay Gandhi's Maruti and other ventures. A private car was beyond the reach of all but, the most well-off families. Only rich families and officials had cars in the sixties. Cars were practically non-existent in the villages in Punjab in the 1960s. The most common way of travel was by bus. The buses plied the roads in Punjab and ran continuously, early morning until late evening. It seemed like everybody was always going somewhere.

There were two main bus lines for the masses in Punjab at that time. Punjab Roadways was the state company, and there was a private bus company, called Onkar Bus Service. These were green and yellow buses and usually newer and in better shape than the state buses. The buses were always packed from morning until evening. I would grab whichever one I could catch, even when it was terribly crowded. One never knew when another would come. If the sausage machine was jammed, not a single other person could cram into the door. One would be forced to wait for the next bus. If one had luggage, it had to be put on top. Sometimes there was a coolie to put it up. If not, one had to climb up the ladder on the back of the bus and find a place for it. Stealing luggage from the top of the bus did not seem to present any problem in those days.

When waiting for a bus to leave, on the bus stops and sometimes inside the buses, all manner of things were being sold. It was pretty much of a free for all in those days. Not only sellers, but the blind, the lame, the lepers, those with decapitated limbs, all came through the buses soliciting some coins on which to survive. It is simply part of the culture and one starts to take it for granted.

A bus stop in Punjab was a fascinating place. When the bus was loading, hawkers would come selling *Garbhani*, or religious tracts, various types of metal rings, which they claimed would cure pains, snake oil, coconut pieces, and spicy baked lentils. There were foods and snacks, karati dals and coconuts and cuckerbits, cucumber and tara, with salt and red pepper. Drinks too, real Coca Cola and fake Coca Cola, tea and milk, badam, lemon and scungbie drinks. And sweets; jellabie, fried sweet dough that is delicious. I soon started to develop a taste for many of these things.

These are often sold through the windows of the bus. A metal ring or wrist band is guaranteed to cure all manner of aches and pains and illnesses.

Many things were geared to the common uneducated, non-scientific, and superstitious, peasants and villagers who can easily fall for a gimmick, and believe in it. They would pull a couple of wrinkled Rupee notes out of their dirty kurtas and buy some item.

All the newspapers in Punjabi, Hindi, Urdu, and English and magazines were sold too.

Besides the buses, one sometimes had to catch a tempu, from certain towns, a three wheeler, with one wheel in front which steered it, and two behind. With wide running boards, they could be loaded with 15 or more people crammed and jammed. This was truly amazing. Forget seat belts. Forget the seats too, for most of the passengers! They had to have a pretty good suspension system to carry such a load of people. These vehicles were quite small, not bigger than a medium sized car, but designed to take an incredible number of people, depending upon how vigorously they wished to risk their lives hanging onto a small spot. Farmers in tumbas would ride outside on the wide running boards, clinging to something or other or to each other. I thought they were quite funny vehicles, but they saved me quite a number of times when for some reason, the buses turned out to be impossible to find.

To get to villages, besides bikes and motorcycles, sometimes the only regular form of transport was the tonga. This was a two-wheeled horse cart pulled by one horse, usually an underfed, scrawny and miserable creature, terribly abused, whipped and cursed continuously. Abused with vulgar sexual curses even in front of the village women riding. "O Tierre Pan." Fuck your sister. Or I'll do the same to your mother and so on. It is true what they say about the Punjabi language. That, it is rich in abuses and love lingo. Two sides of the coin, perhaps, all having to do with the prick. Or two sides of the prick, perhaps. Not untypical of peasant societies around the world. The driver generally rode on the shank of the tonga to provide one more seat and another 50 paise fare. If one rode up front next to the driver one had a forward view, but if on the back seat, one looked back to the rear. Sometimes two tongas would get into a race with each other and then one wondered if they were going to be wrecked and thrown into the ditch. This never happened to me, but I have been worried. One felt sympathy for the miserable horses, as it looked like they could collapse at any time and just give up the ghost in the road. There was such cruel abuse of animals.

If one could not get a tonga, sometimes it became necessary to take a pedal rickshaw out to a village. This was quite frankly dangerous, on a one lane metaled road meeting a big truck driven by a crazed sedougie, coming on full force, the rickshaw would have to leave the metaled road for the side, and one could be almost blown away or almost not get off on time. The roadside would be dust or in monsoon, mud. The poor driver, had a hell of a struggle and I never felt bad about paying them more because they were risking their lives to haul your ass. Sometimes the wheel a rickshaw would simply collapse, from the too heavy weight, the wheel buckling over, if there were two heavy people. One could be thrown out of the rickshaw. I think I was too heavy for them, but still not as heavy as some. Locals would bargain with the driver for a pitifully small price, when the guy and his family were practically starving the way it was. They always asked me too much, but it was not more than they should get for their labour. Sometimes, as in Ludhiana, where the road went up over the railway track, a flyover, going out to the west, the rickshaw driver could not make it to the top even with a flying run at the hill, and one would have to get out and walk a distance up the hill, then get back in for the run down—the other side at quite a good speed and hope like hell that there was no herd of water buffalos in the street, that, the driver would have to dodge between in getting to the bottom of the hill.

Sometimes the stiff competition between the rickshaw wallas would get to me. Sometimes when one emerged from a railway station carrying one's own bag they would fight over who was going to take you. One often did not need a coolie, but they would approach one and try to pull the bag out of one's hand for some small change. I didn't blame them for needing more money. But sometimes one just did not need to deal with a porter. I was glad they were there when I needed them, however. So many things in India turned out to be an unnecessary hassle, it seemed. And it was so much worse being a westerner as one was seen as fresh meat for a better fare. We were rich and we were stupid and our white meat was to be preyed upon.

Sometimes a fight would break out between two rickshaw pullers over who was going to take you. One just didn't need this when they were tired from being on a train all day or night, and just wanted to get to a hotel with no hassle.

In the bigger cities, there were auto rickshaws. Motorised rickshaws. They are like a motorcycle with a seat behind for two or three and a roof overhead. Lovely vehicles. I love them. These were quick and great for cities and usually metered, although the meters generally are not used for short trips, or faked in some way for longer trips across the city. More exciting than a ride in Disneyland, dodging between busses and trucks and everything else, at the risk of one's life. I would just ask the price and agree on something, then probably give them a little more anyway. The official price, in any event was ludicrously low, and unrealistic. So there had to be some fair market price to even make the system work. I found that these machines have no reverse gear, for some reason, and the driver had to get out and push them back if one got into a dead end lane.

In cities, there were the old work horses of the auto scene, and taxis, Hindustan Ambassadors, black and yellow taxis, the only ones in those days. Morris Minors, a 1940s British model. Great old cars, very clumsy and a little ridiculous, but they were a luxury in India. And used by the Prime Minister of India himself or herself. There were some people who had an old Mercedes and I rode in one back from Nanital once. What a beautiful ride after other vehicles.

And the bread and butter transportation for the common man and women too, mostly young women, was the bicycle. Transport from the village or home to school and work. And while there is one seat, they are not for just one person in India, but for the whole family, up to four or five. I often rode behind, on the metal package carrier, or pedaled with my cook or a friend behind. The average man is going to have to go with his whole family on his bike if he has to take them to town.

And more upscale was the scooter which was popular, and not as costly as a motorcycle. A lot of young guys were starting to get motorcycles in those days. The more well-off university students would sometimes have a scooter which was handy for getting around the city.

Then air-conditioned deluxe buses began to appear for longer distances such from Jalandhar to Delhi. Here was real luxury, with one's own cushioned seat, and even curtains on the windows to block the sun, heat and dust.

"I would not shed a tear if there were no railroads in India."

—Mahatma Gandhi

The old work horse, of course, was the iron roadway, the train. For long distance and lots of local travel too, if ones village happened to be located on a railway line. Third class was pure hell, no doubt, and slow, in many cases, but it was possible to get there that way. One could get a second or third class ticket straight away, but it didn't mean that one was going to find a seat. One sometimes found the cars packed full with no way to get in or out. Sometimes it was through the window. This was sheer rock-bottom misery. Professional misery. I have made the trip from Delhi standing all the way to Jalandhar City more than once. I loved travelling by almost anything, even if it meant misery and could do it when I was young. Sometimes, especially if it meant misery. One could reserve a seat on an air conditioned chair car, and this was pretty nice going to Delhi or on to Bombay.

I loved the old fashioned coal-burning engines that spit coal soot and dust into the air to blow into the windows and settle on one's clothes. This was pure joy in the heat, the rough track, the scenes in the fields and towns and villages along the way. Here one can oversee the entire way of life in Punjab from the window of a train. The ryots bent and toiling in the fields. The villages, the huts, the drying crops, maize and red peppers, the Gurdwaras and temples and sometimes even mosques. The scents of the towns and countryside are glorious. The piles of gober patties and stacks of turrie from the wheat straw. Peasants and tractors, cars and buses and rickshaws at level crossings. Trucks, young cute girls with long artificial pigtails on their bikes, riding side by side, all covered, but looking delicious in their tight pajamas and colourful kamiz. The long bridge crossing the Sutlej or other river, slum colonies, bustees, naked dirty children, clinging to and cared for by other older children, water buffaloes herded to a pond, lounging in the cool water, herds of goats, fields of wheat and rice and sugarcane and clover, and small *bazaars* with rows of shops. All from the windows of the train. When the train stopped at a station, one got tea through the window, but if it was in a glass, one had to finish it before the train started up again.

Ship me somewhere east of Suez, as Kipling said.

And food. Sometimes one gets wonderful tasty food on a train, somehow it tastes better on a train, maybe because one is hungrier from the travel. In India, it was invariably delicious food. I don't know why it is so delicious, sometimes served on a small bowl made of a dry leaf. The porter comes through the train and takes orders for food and then the food comes when the train stops at a station. And one can have the food with *cha* and chapatis or *nan*, beautiful tasty chapatis and spicy vegetable dishes. And one relishes such simple food.

Domestic airlines were not very developed in those days in India and they were largely a businessman's luxury. It was mostly Indian Airlines, the state company in those days. It was an easy way to travel between major cities if one had money, but of course, one would not see the country side, rub elbows with the locals, and get all the spicy food and tea on the railway stations along the way. We were young and foolish enough to want all the local sights and sounds and smells and tastes and enjoy it, at least most of the time. It was an experience and great to enjoy it, when one was young.

I travelled in some pretty miserable circumstances. But the country was far more interesting and fascinating than anything so far in my life and so I always had a very strong desire to go back whenever I could grab the chance. I actually wanted to live long-term in the country again and would gladly have taken up the opportunity if I could have.

There was almost always a way to get where one wanted to go, but sometimes the conditions were quite miserable. I sometimes thought that if one learned to travel in India, then they could surely travel anywhere.

21

Picnic on the Sutlej

"The more underdeveloped the country the more overdeveloped the women."

—John Kenneth Galbraith

In February, 1969, I ask my friend Shiv Nath to go to Phagwara with me to see Indira Gandhi, the Prime Minister. I go to Banga and wait for him for more than an hour, but when he never shows up I take the bus and go alone. On the bus, there is standing room only all the way to Phagwara, some fifteen miles away. I arrive, and people are lined up all along the Grand Trunk Road waiting for the Prime Minister's motorcade to pass. After just three or four minutes, I watch the motorcade pass. I was lucky. I had almost missed it.

There is the lead car and in the next car is Mrs Gandhi, sitting in the front seat. She is making namaskar to people on both sides of the road and smiling. After the motorcade passes, I follow the crowd to the venue where she is to speak. An elevated platform has been constructed. I arrive after the speech in Hindi has begun. It is not possible to get very close because iron barricades have been set up and there is a huge crowd. Police are stationed everywhere. When the speech finishes, I wait to let some of the crowd disperse before leaving. There must have been some thirty to forty thousand, I guess, but it could have been more. When the police leave, young boys begin to climb up the poles and rip down the Congress Party flags.

The days are pleasant in the middle of February. I go with my friend Prem Kumar, a student at Sikh National College, for their class picnic. The class had arranged a big goods truck with side boards to take us to the site near the Sutlej River in Rupar. Most of the students in the truck, all male, are standing, holding to the sides of the truck. Excited, they start singing Hindi songs loudly and telling jokes. In the back of the truck, some stand clinging to the side boards and some sit on the bed. We roar down the road towards Newanshahr and then will take the road on to Rupar. The driver takes us down to the wide bank of the Sutlej River. The girls in the class arrive by bus and jeep in a more civilised fashion.

Then we walk a quite long distance, perhaps two miles down over the sand bank along the river. The students tell me that one 1000 acres of this land along the river belongs to the Birlas, the big Indian industrialists tied up with the Rockefeller Foundation in the US. Some of the land had now been brought under crop production by removing the natural tall grasses from the flood plain. The land was then levelled and irrigated and planted in wheat using American equipment. We arrived at some large barns, and a seed processing plant for corn and wheat, which interested me in my work in crop production.

The students had packed a lunch of chapatis, corn bread, and vegetables like cauliflower. A nice young girl came over to where the boys were seated and gave us some chapatis. We wished for more, at least I did, but that was as much as was forthcoming. We eat curried vegetables and chapattis, filling our stomachs with good home cooked Punjabi food.

After lunch, we go after the bananas and oranges. The boys begin to throw orange and banana peels at each other, horsing around like young guys like to do. Then the students set up a table for the programme. Everyone was supposed to sing a song or tell a funny story to entertain the group. Then, when it came my turn, they asked me to sing a song. They would have been disappointed otherwise.

I hit upon the song about Hijolly the camel driver. I knew some verses of this song by heart. So I sang the best I could which seemed to be appreciated more by the girls than the guys. We had tea and sweets, *burfi*. A young girl who was very cute came over and offered me some papaya. I was ready to take anything she offered me. The girls seemed very shy and I noticed that none of the boys would talk to them in public. Why not break the taboo. The social sanctions of society are exceedingly strong. I am sure some had talked to them in secret. I asked the young girl her name. It was Usha Sharma and then I talked to her. Some other girls were interested and gathered around to join the conversation and observe the foreigner. Unfortunately, this did not last long, as they quickly rushed off to finish their tea, ending this brightest moment of the picnic all too quickly.

The picnic over, the guys climbed in the truck again. I clamoured up inside with them and we headed for a Sikh Museum in a Gurdwara just outside of Rupar. This is the place where Guru Gobind Singh was killed, according to the legend. One removes their shoes and washes their feet before entering and one's head must be covered. This was just a smaller version of the Sikh museum in Amritsar with all the gory and bloody pictures of a Sikh battle. It seemed to be a treat for the young students.

There are five symbols of the Sikh. The five K's. These are the *kanga* or wooden comb, which represents cleanliness; *kesh* or the uncut hair, a symbol of spiritual power; the *kara*, or steel bracelet, a symbol of unity and the process of constant learning; the *kirpan* or sword, a symbol of respect and justice; and *kaccha*, or special pair of shorts, which is a symbol of modesty.

Some of the students and an English teacher asked me if I believed in Guru Nanak and Guru Gobind Singh. They seemed quite shocked when I told them that I didn't. I could have told them I didn't believe in any religion. On the way back, we stopped at a small tea stall near the village Jadla. While I was drinking tea some Indians who had stopped came up and started taking pictures of me, which made me feel uncomfortable. I was an attraction in that neck of the woods. Back in Banga, my friend, Prem went to spend the night with a friend and I headed for Mahil Gaila. But then one of the guys who had been on the picnic, Balbir Singh, asked me to come and spend the night with him in Naura, the village next to Mahil Gaila. I didn't have the fortitude to resist, after the day, and anyway, did not have a cook for food that evening.

At Balbir Singh's place, we had *mucky ki roti* and *sagh* (corn bread and mustard greens), which was delicious. I guess I was hungry after the trip. Balbir had lived in Delhi and knew English well. Their house is right on top of the village, in the highest place. His room was on the second floor right across from the village Gurdwara. It was a very cozy place and being tired from the picnic, I slept very well. They always bring you warm, sweetened milk to drink before going to bed in the winter time. I would have liked it better with some chocolate but that's not the way they drink it. It probably does help one to sleep but I didn't need it after the picnic.

The next morning, we had to wake up at half past six to have tea, two or three cups in bed. I am afraid that I combined a little Western flavour with it and promptly dropped back to sleep after the tea. As an Indian, I would have headed off to the fields for a nature call.

After the nap, I faced the day. Some of the villagers were creeping up the stairs and peeping at me so I asked leave to go back to Mahil Gaila. They then saw me off at the edge of the village and I arrived back at my humble abode.

Primitive Rebels

"Punjabi excels in love and in abuse."

—Prakash Tandon

In Punjab one could come across police brutality, and the police didn't seem to mind to demonstrate it before a foreigner. Once near Jalandhar, in a local town, where I had gone with Jatinder Singh, he took me to the police station. We went inside. I don't know exactly what his business was there that evening. The police had brought in a poor guy who they thought had stolen a bicycle. I don't know whether he was actually guilty. They told him to lay down flat on the floor and then began flogging his rear with a thick strap of leather. He was in pain and yelping, as they kept up administering the hard lashes. That made an impression on me which I never forgot, seeing the poor guy in pain.

Sometimes one saw things that one never expected to see, like the nanga or completely naked man in the street of a local town. One day in Jalandhar, I saw a completely naked, very dark man, a holy man, sadhu, with long beard in the street. Perhaps he was a Jain or *Digambara* or a *sadhu* of some sect who was wandering around the traffic circle with no clothes. Was he one of the "sky clad," as is said of such persons. He was perfectly free to wandering around that way as he was a holy man. No one was going to bother him. It is less likely to see such a saint in Punjab than in a city like Varanasi, but they did appear from time to time.

What is this social mania about always covering up the private parts, which may be either ugly or beautiful, more generally the former, as far as humanity goes, but are part of God's creation. If one is young, then one is naturally beautiful. As one grows old, the opposite is true. Perhaps there is no reason one should be more revolted by the nude body than by looking at a human face, of which the same is true.

When I thought about this, I began to consider how narrow-minded America was in comparison to India in that respect! This is true, even though in some ways, India is a much more conservative society than America. There certain people are free to wander around nude. Americans consider themselves the broadest minded, but they could not put up with that. Perhaps it shows just how narrow minded American society really is. What would they do with the statues of Khajuraho in Iowa? Americans get upset by socialists, communists, anarchists, nudists, and all sorts of ideas they don't like, but why should it bother them? India sometimes just draws the circle wider and takes them in, it seems. Of course, sometimes the narrow minded bigotry comes out there too, but, the scope seems much broader in India.

It was not uncommon in Punjab to see an Akali, a religious oriented Sikh, dressed in a sky blue and yellow outfit with a sword or a sort of long metal lance travelling on the buses. A sort of Don Quixote figure, perhaps tilting at windmills. Still fighting the historical Sikh battles. When travelling by bus, these travellers would sometimes put their long lance on top of the bus. I would not have wanted to be run through with it, so I gave them wide berth when I saw them. A Sikh warrior, one can say, having something to do with being a Sikh, with the militant tradition, but totally dysfunctional in the modern age. Who is he going to run through with that long lance?

There are some politicians who could use it, no doubt about that, and in a number of cases, I would have no regrets, but I suspect those sons of bitches are quite safe.

Another sort of holy man or sadhu could be seen dressed in saffron, orange colour, who would wander with matted hair and dreadlocks. There are all types of wandering mendicants that one comes across in India.

22

Soybeans

"It is the season when the flat Punjab country looks at its best with the rich lush green of the growing crops."

—**Prakash Tandon**

In 2012, India was the fifth largest producer of soybeans in the World. But it was not the case in the 1960s when efforts were being made to increase the prominence of this crop in India. In Punjab, soybeans could be grown in place of rice in the khariff or summer season, using much less water than a rice crop. The crop would be sown in July and harvested in October or November in time to plant wheat on the land for the winter season. However, the crop was virtually unknown in Punjab. Our group was involved in the effort to popularise the growing of soybeans. As of the present time, however, the crop is not yet widely grown in Punjab, the major production taking place in the central Indian state of Madhya Pradesh. However, it might be a successful crop in Punjab in future. A group of non-resident Indians are considering setting up a processing plant in Punjab, which might encourage farmers to grow the crop instead of rice and increase the production of protein needed in the diet.

In February I went with Staff Clarry, another volunteer in our India 53 Group, to the All India Kissan Mela in Pant Nagar in Uttar Pradesh. From Phillaur, we caught the midnight train to

Moradabad, officially known as the Pathankot-Sealdah Express. We got a third-class sleeper, upper bunks, which was not crowded like most third class cars, and bedded down on the steel shelf. One could sleep, but not very comfortably. But in any event, I loved the travel. When the train pulled into a station the next morning, we scrambled out and got some hot tea and boiled eggs from the station platform. The tea was sold in the little clay cups like a small flower pot. After drinking the tea, one just throws them away, usually down on the rocks along the track. This way the tea walla does not have to wait and collect the glasses before the train pulls out.

We made Moradabad at half past ten in the morning. We found a good restaurant in the Mothi Mahal Hotel. After the lunch, we went to the bus station to get the bus to Pant Nagar, but had to wait until half past two. It was a fight for the ticket, but I bucked the line, which is not really a line in India, but more like a mob. I succeeded around two o'clock and we piled onto the bus. Unlike Punjab, they were only selling as many tickets as there were seats on the bus. Very strange for us from Punjab. What is wrong with cramming the bus and standing up? It is pretty normal in Punjab. I slept part of the way up, which took until five in the afternoon. After registering for the fair, we found the hostel where we would stay for free. We talked to some students who gave us information about the university and offered to show us around. The room was a dormitory for two. The dinner of Indian food was delicious after the long trip. There was a puppet show, which provided a cornucopia of boredom and a film for farmers on how to grow better rice, which produced approximately the same result as far as I could tell. At least it was true in my case.

The next day, breakfast was in the Home Science Hostel, ordinarily for girls. It seems that the girls were being prepared for home, however, rather than for science. A tour of the crop station bored me. I was beginning to get bored with this sort of thing. They showed us inter-cropping with sugar cane, triple dwarf varieties of wheat, and sugar beets.

For us the purpose of the tour was to focus on soybean production, which was just then being established in India. But the real objective for staff and me was to come back with a small supply of soybean seeds. The next day, we joined a tour of local farms, and talked to some of the professors about soybeans, one of our hot burning topics. We were able to buy 15 kilograms of soybeans each, for seed for local farmers to experiment with.

The University of Illinois and USAID were working on the soybean project at the university. The local area is called the Terrai, or high planes, where there was a good supply of summer rains. The climate was appropriate for growing soybeans.

Having obtained our quota of soybean seeds, the next day I split off from Staff and got a slow third class train back to Phagwara. I had to wait two hours to get a seat and then arrived at half past five the next morning. I finally made it back to my place a couple of hours later, seeds and all.

I would distribute the seeds to some of the farmers I was working with for the summer crop season. Unfortunately, it was a very small amount of seed, compared to what we really needed for some good crop experiments.

In Missouri, I remembered planting some sixty pounds of soybeans to the acre to produce a good crop. The seeds that we were able to obtain would only plant half an acre.

In the rainy season, I distributed the seed to some of the better farmers who wanted to grow them. At the end of October, I make the rounds to several villages to check up on some of my soybean experiments. Most of the farmers were in the process of cutting and threshing them. First, I rode my bike over to Sujjon village to see Dharam Singh's plot. He had not cut them yet, but they would be ready in a few days.

Then, I rode down to Naura to see Hari Singh's plot. I noticed that he had already cut them. When I went over to his house, I saw the crop spread out on the roof of his house to dry. He had sowed one canal with the seeds and it seems that he had quite a good yield. He was gone to another village and came later and requested that I return at five o'clock to take a soil sample for him.

But my big mistake, in the project, which I did not realise until later, was to distribute the seeds myself as a project, rather than letting the agricultural officers in the Block Office do this. I would have saved myself a lot of work and made them happy, but I guess my idea was to work hard and conduct the project myself. One of the guys told me that I should have given some of the seeds to them. I realised that he was right and that without even realising it, I had been somewhat selfish in the way I used the seed. It was also true that there were many farmers that were anxious to experiment with the crop. So if the production can be made good, the crop could be successful in the state. However, the land must be appropriate with no water logging. That was actually the main difficulty in Punjab.

23

Punjabi Wedding

"Father you have put your daughter in the doli; People shower blessings on you."

—Wedding Song

Attending a wedding in India can be enjoyable and involves much more than just a single ceremony. In March, 1969 I took the bus to Dhinsa village near Ferozepur in the west of Punjab to attend the wedding of Balvinder Singh, the agricultural inspector at the block office. Leaving in the morning, I got to the village around five in the afternoon. While walking from the bus stop, a tractor and wagon came along. It was part of the wedding party and I climbed into the wagon. One of the persons riding in the wagon was another American, Steve Hemenway, a Fulbright scholar who was teaching English at Punjab University in Chandigarh. He had been invited by Prithim Singh, Balvinder Singh's brother, who was in his class and so we met this way. We were on the wagon, so to speak.

After we arrived, we had tea and took a walk in the fields with some of the guys. A few hits of rum were in order, before dinner. Then the Bhangra dancing started. The guests asked Steve and me to sing a song. I suggested "*If I Had a Hammer*," which we sang rather terribly. I am sure we would not have been able to do it without the rum. We joined in the Bhangra dancing, which we found rather easy after a few drinks and fun at our age. Everyone gathers in a circle and someone says a bolie, or kind of dirty rhyme, and then at the punch line, everyone starts dancing around, jumping and lifting the right leg higher than the left. This went on for quite some time until we decided that we had had enough for the night.

The next morning would be the trip to the bride's village for the wedding ceremony. We left the house and went to the building where the guests were to sleep. *Charpoys* were set up with thick rajais as the nights were pretty cold this time of year.

The next morning we were woken up at the ungodly hour of half past five. This is not one of the most pleasant aspects of a Punjabi wedding. After the nature call to the fields and having tea, we all piled into a jeep and headed for the bride's village. The girl's village was some forty miles distant and we were packed into the jeep as only Indians can pack. There was a rendezvous point where all the jeeps would meet. The bridegroom and his father would transfer to a car for the last few miles. This was in the town of Mokstur. The pucca road soon diminished into a rough kucha road and then a narrow canal road. Some kids ran out shouting and trying to tell us that something was wrong ahead. There the canal road had caved off and a jeep, not in our party, was stalled in the road in the soft sand. It seemed that the wheel had been damaged as the driver had taken it off to work on the brake drum.

Some guys attempted to lift the stuck jeep off the road, but this was impossible. So our two jeeps had to go down off the canal road to pass. Some brush and weeds had to be cleared but with everyone pushing the jeeps up the other side, we managed to get around.

We arrived at the Bride's village and waited in a small room until breakfast had been prepared. There were two tables loaded down with an abundance of omelets, toast and butter, liver curry and sweets, and small cakes, all delicious. After eating, we proceeded to the tent where the marriage ceremony would take place. Everyone was seated under the tent. The ceremony began with minstrels singing religious songs. Then the bride was brought in followed by the members of her family and seated at the left of the groom. Then the history of the groom was sung, followed by the history of the bride, including the names of their villages and names of the members of the family. Then the Sikh priest read a passage from the Guru Granth Sahib. Strings were placed around the necks of the bride and groom.

After the ceremony, the men went to another room and waited, some resting on *mungies*. Some sherab was brought and everyone had a drink and some had several. Then we went back with the groom, who received the dowry from members of the girl's family. They came in one by one and placed the money in a towel in his hands and some touched his shoulder and head affectionately.

When the feast was prepared we went in to eat the delicious Indian food, rather stuffing ourselves. We then lounged on mungies. It was extremely hot and I dozed off for a while. I needed to relieve myself, had a toilet been available. But then, it would not have been a wedding in a remote Indian village. One needs an exceptionally strong bladder in India, especially when it comes to weddings. I think that if one needs an extra stomach in Turkey, as is surely the case, with all the good food, then one needs an extra bladder in India, with the lack of latrines. By the same token, one needs an extra wallet in America, given the prices.

A little later, the bride was brought from the house for the trip to the groom's village. We gathered around and watched the lucky girl emerge, although her head and face was covered, all in bright red cloth with golden embroidery. Poor thing, did she know that her troubles were just beginning? I got some pictures as the bride and groom settled in their car. The others piled into the jeeps, but I was lucky enough to get to ride in one of the Hindustan cars in the procession. The front left door would not latch properly and kept swinging open. I was in the back seat, and Balvinder Singh's father was in the front seat ahead of me. I was afraid that he was going to roll out of the car on some corner when the door popped open and be a "long lost daddy," as Hank Williams used to say. The steering wheel is on the right side, of course, in India. The old English system. Finally, he took a piece of string and tied the door closed, which seemed to be a good idea until we stopped in the desert so that everyone could bail out and finally relieve themselves, at long last. The old man couldn't get the door open for his heavenly relief, until somebody could come to his rescue.

At Moktsur Gurdwara, again the rendezvous point, we waited for the other cars to arrive. We toured the Gurdwara and happily, there was a latrine there, which I took full advantage of. Can't get much more lucky than that. I have seldom found my prayers answered, but this was an exception.

Back in Dindsa, Balvinder's village, we rested until dinner, being quite tired from the day.

Steve and I had planned to rise very early on Monday and take the six o'clock train to Ludhiana. The next morning, we overslept, being quite hung over. We were forced to take the bus. We walked the mile out to the road and caught the bus to Moga at half past seven. Steve then got the bus for Chandigarh, and I headed for Ludhiana. The seats were all full when I got on and the conductor insisted on cramming as many people into the bus as possible, mostly standing, and squeezing into the smallest space. By the time we got to Ludhiana, I had an aching back and an overflowing bladder. I then got the bus to Phillaur. Even cattle could not take that kind of abuse and anyway, it would not be allowed, the cattle having some monetary value, unlike humans.

At Phillaur, I stopped to see Staff, and used his latrine generously, finding great relief and satisfaction. Staff was out, but when he came, I had some cake and coffee and happily made it back to Banga by mid-afternoon. I got the tonga out to Mahil Gaila.

Completely fed up with not having a cook, I decided I had to do something about it and soon. That's when I contacted Mussie, who was from Ferozepur in the west of Punjab, as mentioned before. He was an older guy, probably in his fifties. He had a wife and four young kids, two girls and two boys. When I left the country, I would give him most of my furniture. He took it to Banga by tonga and put it on the train and shipped it to his place in Ferozepur. He was an immense help to me and I don't think I could have made it without him. I did not like the idea of having someone work for me, but it was necessary in such a situation. Still, our lifestyle was quite modest. That is an understatement. Even the Spartans lived better.

24
Punjabi Village

"Our Punjab country had five seasons: winter, spring, summer, rains, and autumn."

—Prakash Tandon

When we arrived in Punjab, an *angrez*, or "Englishman" was quite rare in rural north India. The British were long gone. Why were the Americans coming now? The small kids along the street would shout "*angrez*" at the top of their lungs when I rode down the street on my bike. When they would see an "Englishman." It sometimes grated on my nerves to be called an Englishman. I was not an *angrez*, in any event, but an American, but never mind. It was all the same shit, I suppose. We were now the new imperialists in India.

People were, of course, very kind and hospitable. Indians would go out of their way to help a foreigner. Hospitality is a principle, a way of life for a villager in India. It is part of the culture. I made many friends in the villages, both of the elderly and also young farmers. I felt sympathy for the young farmers who were trying to make a living sometimes without very good land, facilities or money. I had done farming myself in America and knew the uncertainties of producing crops. Most of the big farmers were doing quite fine in those days, of course, although they complained bitterly about government policies. It was much more difficult for the smaller peasants in the villages.

The population of Jalandhar District in 1961 was 1,227, 367 with a population density of 353 persons per square kilometer. But due to the bias for boys, there were only 872 females for each 1000 males. Land holdings in 1968 were small in Jalandhar District with 58 per cent of the holdings between five and 15 acres. Some 22 per cent of holdings were between 15 and 30 acres. Only five per cent of holdings exceeded thirty acres.

The big farmers were those with around 20 acres or more. Regardless of size of holdings, the farmers were never satisfied with the amounts of electricity and water they got from the government or the prices of grain set by the government. They complained bitterly about the PL-480 programme of the United States, under which large quantities of wheat was being sold to India and paid for in rupees. This tended to keep the price of wheat low, although the official price was set by the Indian Government. The big farmers in Punjab grew richer while they continued to complain. The smaller farmers were just trying to feed their families and raise their children and keep their land out of the hands of the money lender. This could prove impossible, if they had daughters, instead of sons. Then they would have to mortgage their land to pay for weddings and the dowries. Things had not changed so much since the British Civil Servant Malcolm Lyall Darling wrote his well-known book, *The Punjab Peasant in Prosperity and Debt* back in the 1930s. Punjabi farmers were often in debt, but government programmes and cooperative banks had allowed them to avoid some of the traps set for them by the money-lending banias or shop keepers in the past.

Sometimes, I would come to a farmer's place in the morning for a visit. Then we would go to the fields and take a couple of soil samples. I would bring the result back from Punjab Agricultural University in Ludhiana after a few days. I took many soil samples in the fields in the local villages. The farmers would always invite one to stay and have lunch with them. Of course, the men ate separately from the women. Sometimes I would be given my food alone, usually a vegetable dish with warm chapaties, just off the grill, some pepper or mango pickles and lussie to drink. There would usually not be a sweet, but maybe some fruit, mango or guava, which was cheap in season. Other fruits were simply too expensive for the poorer farmers. Fruits such as apple and banana were quite expensive and mostly out of their reach except on special occasions. Also suntra or tangerines were plentiful in the fall and winter, sweet and very good to eat. I could just about live on them in the fall.

After lunch, the farmer would insist that one take rest in their house especially in the hot season. By noon, the sun would be intensely hot and it was rather unwise to ride out into the blinding sun in the middle of the day. It reminds one of the legend of the Sikhs who go crazy at twelve o'clock. It's no joke in the blinding heat of a Punjabi May or June. The roads would generally be empty of bicycles at this time. So in the hot season, an afternoon rest is absolutely necessary, even if one is young, as we were. The long hot summer can drain one of energy, stamina, drive and generally wear even a young person down before the cool air of the fall. Sometimes the prickly heat comes on one's body in the hot super saturated air once the monsoon starts. Farmers do not generally work out in the hot summer in the hottest part of the day. It is simply intolerable.

When the work for the summer *khariff* season starts after the first rains in July, the farmers go to the fields very early in the morning. The women bring some food later. They plow and plant until mid-morning, when the heat comes, and then break off and go back in the late afternoon and work until the evening. The fields could not be plowed by bullocks for the summer *khariff* season until the monsoon rains had come and softened up the ground.

The traditional village houses constructed of thick mud walls and fortified with layers of cow dung are by far the most comfortable and cool in the hot season. They are lovely for resting in the day. They are also cooler in the night, although the trend and better idea is to sleep outside in the courtyard or on the roof in the hottest season and between the monsoon rains.

I enjoyed staying in these old traditional houses. They were very comfortable. The floors are also of earth, and fortified with layers of cow dung. It sounds rather poor and dirty to a Westerner, but these houses are clean and lovely places. Sometimes these old houses had spacious and lovely old beds, big comfortable *charpoys*. They were very fine for resting up from the summer heat and the rooms were amazingly cool if there was a breeze drifting through the window. But sometimes they were a shelter from the loo, hot winds blowing from outside. The old beds were quite firm, which is actually better than a mattress for resting and sleeping, as one does not sink down inside. The covers and pillows were home made with embroidered patterns. That was cool comfort and one could take an afternoon nap and escape the heat. These houses made one feel very much at home, something like I used to feel when I was a kid in my grandmother's house. These houses were far more comfortable and cooler than the modern pucca or brick-cement houses, like the rich peasants were now building. The modern houses are like hot cement ovens in summer and cold cement tombs in the winter. But when the farmers had cash from the big wheat crops or got money from their relatives abroad, they would often go outside the village and build a modern pucca house. These houses were now replacing the older dwellings as the villages spread out toward the fields. Of course the modern houses were sturdier and did not have to be repaired every year like the old traditional houses. But I loved the far more comfortable houses with cow-dung covered walls and floors. I would have chosen them, if I could for a dwelling. Of course having a new house was also a sign of prestige and prosperity. They were not built on credit, as in the US, but on cash. In those days a big lovely two-story house for a big family could be built for one lakh rupees, 100,000 rupees, which I thought was a lot of money in those days. Of course, some 14,000 US dollars was a very modest amount for one who had a good job abroad, and many farm families had one or more relatives working in England, America, Australia or elsewhere.

One could only get a break from the searing summer heat by retreating to the nearby cooler hill stations up a few 1000 feet from the plains of Punjab. This was what the British would do, of course, for the summer season. There were lovely small towns in the hills such as Simla and Palumpur.

"The invigorating air brought life and vitality back to bodies drained by the desiccating summer." **—Prakash Tandon**

The village level workers, who I sometimes worked with, were assigned to a circle of ten villages each. Some days I accompanied the young village level worker from my area on my bicycle. We would check the crops and visit farmers in the area and drink tea. Continuous drinking of tea all through the day. How one avoids a severe case of tea poisoning, I have no idea.

We were supposed to live at the same living standard as the local Indian population in the village, so as not to appear rich. Actually, I never considered that there was any danger of this, in my case. But I guess I was wrong in the Indian context. The aim of not appearing rich was somewhat unrealistic, because we were going to look rich to Indians whether we had a paisa in our pocket or not. Just our white skin and being from a rich country would give us away. We were paid 75 dollars a month by the Peace Corps, about 560 Indian rupees. But this was a quite good salary for Indians in those days. Out of this, we had to pay our cook and all our living and travel expenses.

The Peace Corps paid for a table fan which was necessary, but there were frequent power cuts during the day when it was needed most. In many villages, the power was off in the hottest parts of the day to provide more power to factories. Load shedding in the villages was a government policy.

Punjab was very much a mixed population of Hindus and Sikhs. There were no Moslems in the villages where I worked in the Doaba. A Punjabi speaking state had been created by the splitting off of Haryana from Punjab in the 1960s and there was also a push for a Sikh state even in those days. Some people confused this division with the creation of a Sikh State, but this is a misconception. Punjabi was spoken by both Sikhs and Hindus in Punjab. Sikhs and Hindus generally knew Hindi as well, especially those who were more educated.

Most of the farmers we worked with were Jat Sikhs, the dominant caste in Punjab. Their houses generally had pictures of Guru Nanak and Guru Gobind Singh. The Sikh tradition is very much infused with the militant ideal. One is invariably told how brave Sikhs are. This used to get slightly on my nerves. I figured that some discretion was also in order. Too much bravery might not be wise at some point. Disproportionate numbers of Sikhs served in the Indian armed forces, and militancy was very much a part of the Sikh culture. The Sikhs had fought the Moghuls and the British, so militancy was just taken for granted. Clearly, the Hindus had lost some of their economic and political power as a result of the Green Revolution, but there was no communal conflict between Sikhs and Hindus at this time.

Almost every village had a village pond, a sort of lagoon or stagnant body of water that would be cleaned after a number of years. There was a very large such pool at the edge of Banga. But I do not remember such a pond in Mahil Gaila. The water in these pools becomes stagnant and breeds mosquitoes. It is also a place where small boys take water buffaloes for washing because they need to be washed and cooled in the water daily.

The big old peeple trees in the village were worshiped by Hindus. There was such a tree near my place. From my window, I could see an old woman come every morning and circle the tree several times, giving it water and saying prayers.

One day, a group of wandering mendicants or Sadhus came to Mahil Gaila village with several huge elephants. The travellers climbed up the peeple tree and began to hack off the small branches and leaves for their elephants. Then they bedded down for the night in a camp in front of the community building, which was in a vacant field right next to my place. They spent the night there and continued the next morning on their journey across India.

There were many wild peacocks in the village. They were very colourful and one would generally see them in the cool months. I would see then near my place spreading their beautiful blue tails and making their calls. They were interesting and colourful big birds.

Khusras would also come to the village. They are eunuchs who dress up like women and dance in the street or at weddings. They are castrated when they are young and are a sort of a caste in India. The new recruits come from other families and are adopted into the community. They are also called *hijras* in Hindi. There are some one and a half million of them in India. When they come to the village, the villagers gather around and watch them perform. This is an old tradition in India.

Around the village there were also many wild dogs and sometimes in the evenings, they would come very close to my house, which was close to the fields. They would start a wild howling and barking. I would sometimes try to drive them away by throwing rocks but they are fully wild and cannot be tamed. Sometimes they become rabid. One day when I was visiting a friend in Gosal, a village near Banga, we encountered a strange acting dog which turned out to be rabid. The dog was killed the same day.

Punjab was a meat-eating part of the country, mainly chicken or goat. There are some places where beef is available, especially in places where there is a Christian population, but the distribution is somewhat secretive. My cook offered to bring me some beef from Ferozepur, but I never really cared for it. There was no place locally where one could buy processed meat. The lack of a reliable source of electricity would preclude such a possibility. Chicken had to be bought and killed by the cook the same day it was to be eaten.

For goat meat, there were local shops in the towns. In Banga, there was a row of meat shops near the bus stop. They struck me as quite fly-blown and were not very clean. While the meat is kept in a small screened place, it is not very effective in keeping the flies away. The animal is killed in the morning and then sold the same day. Sometimes, I would buy goat meat and have my cook curry it, usually when my friend Gulzar Singh, the carpenter wanted to come and eat at my place with his brothers. This was actually very delicious, eaten with rice. It was also delicious with beer, but we would usually have it with the local whiskey, Binnys Sherab. This local whiskey was a terrible drink for me and I could not take very much of it. But I did run across it quite often when my friends would offer it to me in the evenings.

In the summer, the area was quite rich with fruits, but most families were too poor to buy much of this luxury, except perhaps mango in season. In the hot season, the great and plentiful fruit is mango, beautiful in Punjab and quite cheap. And guava is good, plentiful and delicious. There was leechi and grapes too. Apples which come from the hills were more expensive. One could eat a lot of bananas too. The locally produced ones were small but delicious. There were many coconuts too.

In the fall, the beautiful fruit is suntra or tangerines. They are cheap and very nice to eat. There were also nice oranges. Sometimes grapefruits would also appear in the market in the winter. They were cheap but were not of very good quality. Still, I loved to buy and eat them when I saw them in the market.

In the summer, there were also plenty of watermelon and cantaloupes, but I did not eat them much, as there is some danger of eating them in the hot season. Strawberries usually come from the hills only in the early spring.

We did not have Jackfruit in Punjab, which I first saw when I took the train to Bombay. I found it to be delicious, but it was not sold in the markets in Punjab.

In the villages, the diet was quite steady and the rich farmers did not change their diet as they became more affluent. However, more vegetables were being eaten than in the past. Vegetables were plentiful and delicious. In the winter, allu-gobi or potato and cauliflower were delicious.

The growing of potatoes in the fall season in Punjab was a great innovation and produced much food for the market. New varieties of potato had been developed in the hills around Palampur.

In the fall, I loved to see the beautiful irrigated fields of potato and cauliflower. This had greatly improved the diet in the villages.

Among the youth, and villagers, there was a scattering of leftists, some with progressive ideas about social and political change. I made many friends from Sikh National College in Banga. I noticed the pictures of Vladimir Lenin on some of the walls of the college. The men in the village often greeted each other by the name "comrade." I do not know to what extent it was just a joke or whether there were really some political notions behind it. There were clearly some who believed in communism, but I do not know how many. I am sure it was not the progressive farmers who were getting rich with the new wheat and rice seeds. To them it must have been a joke.

There was at least one serious communist in the village, who must have been a member of the party. He had a brilliant son, Jagbadal Singh, who was a student and became one of my best friends in the village. As a brilliant young man, he got a scholarship to study medicine in Moscow. His father was in and out of prison in those days, suspected of being a Naxalite. There was a big crack down on Naxalites in the late sixties. This made me curious and I learned something about the movement.

Jagbadal Singh became a medical doctor and sent me letters from Moscow after I returned to America. It was great to get his letters, sometimes direct from the USSR. Sometimes he would have someone take them out of the country and post them in the US. Some years later, he left Russia and began to work as a doctor in Canada. I do not know if he remained a communist after leaving Russia. I suspect that he was disillusioned by the deteriorating situation in the Soviet Union in the 1970s.

There were others around with leftist views. Sometimes friends would tell me that a friend was hiding in the sugar cane fields to avoid being arrested, as they were suspected of being a communist. There were plenty of small journals circulating that were published in Moscow. They were propaganda, of course, but interesting to read and gave a different perspective on American politics the war in Vietnam. There was much truth in them, but they ignored the problems in the Soviet Union. I subscribed to some of them and got them in the mail. They were practically free.

I also received the propaganda, sent by the US Information Service from the American Embassy in Delhi. Neither could actually be taken very seriously. Socialist ideas always have greater appeal to the masses of course. The peasants, of course, were naturally conservative as they feared losing their land as Lenin understood.

At first, I doubted what my communist friends were saying about America, but found that it was largely true as I learned more about the real situation. It explained the Vietnam War and the world situation in a more understandable way. I was getting a better education on my own than if I had been in a university in America. This would be useful background experience for studying politics in an American university later. It helped my understanding of things better than those American students who had not lived outside the US. Research in a library is useful, but dull and drab. Learning things through experience imparts knowledge that penetrates into ones blood and bones. There are many American academics that teach the world but have never felt the heartbeat of the villages in their minds and bones. Only then can one penetrate into the hearts and minds of the people. In Punjab, in any rural setting, one learns when one comes to feel it in their bones, with all the sweet smell and aura of the setting.

Le Dolce Vita:

"I hate it, yet hug it in love." **—Rabindranath Tagore**

In the winter months, life was sometimes bleak on the cold winter nights. Sometimes a local farmer would invite one to have food and a drink. They would produce a bottle of Binnys Sherab, the locally produced whiskey. The village sarpanch, Swaran Singh, would invite me to come over to the north side of the village for the evening meal. It would usually be *mukhy roti* and *sagh*, corn chapati and mustard greens, quite delicious on a cool night, with a strong shot of Binnys sherab. He was a dear man who looked after me and took care of me. He helped me in a many things. He provided me a plot for sugar beets and cauliflower. He was always kidding me about going to Delhi, "going over there to do giddy, giddy," and he would imitate the motion with his hands and laugh.

In winter, most of the farmers would be making gur, crushing the juice from sugar cane and boiling it down. Gur was delicious, but when one came around, they would take some of the raw green cane juice and mix it with milk and offer it. For me the taste of this concoction was terrible and I could never get used to it. I much preferred scungbie, the peppery lemonade, which was nice on a hot day.

In Banga town, Kartar Sweet Shop was the place to meet, whether with farmers of students from the college. It was a grungy and dirty place that made delicious samosas with hot sauce and all kinds of sweets. I couldn't turn down an invitation to go there and drink a coke and eat samosa. Some shops in Banga bottled their own soft drinks, the old bottles that had a ball in the neck that opened by popping the ball down.

In the fall, when the sugar cane harvest was in progress, big trucks would come through the main road in Banga loaded for the sugar mill in Newanshahr. Small boys would run behind the truck, jump on and pull out stalks to chew. That was a crazy place. After a while, I knew many of the shop keepers in the town and they would invite me to sit down and have tea and want to discuss things with me. There was a druggist who had a strange device that he used to enlarge men's cocks. I don't know if it worked.

Gulzar Singh, my main carpenter became a good friend. He and his brothers did beautiful work by hand. Some members of the family went to the Gulf to work a few years later in the 1970s. He loved to make programmes to come to my place with his two brothers and eat rice and chapati and bakra, or goat meat, and drink Binnys Sherab. My cook would make the food and they would come and eat goat curry and enjoy themselves. It was a way to get away from the women in the house as well. Sometimes their small sons would hang around. They made my screen doors and windows and a large cabinet for my kitchen.

I had several friends in a rather poor village, Sujjon. One was a poor peasant Sham Singh. They were friendly people and I tried to help them as much as possible. They became good friends of mine.

Another friend in a small village, a heavy-set guy, had come from Fiji and brought some money. I would go to his place in his village from time to time and chat with him. One summer, he was preparing for his daughter's wedding almost the entire summer. There was to be a big wedding feast for the whole village, and so there was a vast amount of expense and preparation. One room of his house was being used as a storage godown for the supplies which were being purchased. He was storing bags of sugar, flour and lentils for the coming wedding.

He complained bitterly about the system that required this and the great expense involved. But there was no avoiding it. There was nothing that he could do about it. One can understand it well by reading the old classic by Malcolm Lyall Darling mentioned above. Later in the summer, I attended the wedding.

In the late sixties, the style of Punjabi dress for young girls was very tight *pajamas* and *kurta* or *kamiz* with *chuney*. I thought it was terribly stylish, and cute. It was easy to fall in love with the young girls who were very beautiful as they streamed through the roads on their bicycles. But there was little hope in that, it seemed. All one could do was look, and not much of that either. The joys of being young.

Sometimes, I would meet a young friend by chance, or make a new friend and they would invite me to spend a night at their house. Their houses were much more comfortable than mine and so it was a treat and one could eat some delicious food. I remember spending the night in a beautiful big house in Naura, the village just next to Mahil Gaila. It was in the winter time and the beds were big and cozy with blankets and a big warm rejai. My friend had a pretty young sister who brought me tea and food. It was a rare chance to see a pretty young Punjabi girl in her home and I loved that in the rather strict puritanical social setting of rural Punjab. I hardly ever turned down such invitations.

If the house was near the Gurdwara, I loved hearing the *Japji*, the Sikh prayer, being read early in the morning, while still cozy in bed. One could listen to it and doze off for more dreaming. The farmer's wife or daughter would bring Punjabi tea, with a lot of milk and sugar. Sometimes they would use gūr, which gave the tea a village flavour. Those were pleasant days in Punjab.

The fields would often be sunny and clear in the winter. One could see the snow on the mountains in the hills from my place. I don't know if the air is that clear today. The winter days were much more pleasant than the summer, but the winters were quite short and the heat returned early. Still, there could be some very cold days when it was difficult with only a small electric heater and sometimes no power. Sometimes the cold drizzling rain would come on winter days.

By the time I was ready to return to America, after two years, I had come to love India and Punjab. Two years is a short period, but it seems quite a long time in a young person's life. At the same time, there were some things that were hard to put up with. This acculturation to Indian life happened to many Americans who were in the Peace Corps in India. It is such a very complex country. There are so many difficult, even impossible, things, and yet so many beautiful things. How can one describe it? It was hard to get one's head around it. It was an overwhelming experience in one's life, filled with poignant experiences. It was difficult for one to insert one's self back into American society easily. It was not so much culture shock, as being homesick for India. Sometimes America seemed like dullsville after the chaotic dynamism of Indian society. As time went along, some of the romantic image of India faded, and I could see the picture more realistically. We were very young and impressionable at the time. That's why Peace Corps Volunteers always say that the experience changed their lives.

In this memoir, I have tried to give one a feel for village life in India, rather than give a critical analysis of Indian society. The libraries are full of books crammed with statistics on India, but they do not really come to life if one does not know the real India.

Suppose such an experience could happen to Americans en masse. It would not only change individuals, it would change America. What a disaster for the American empire. What a victory it would be for the American people. That's why the old senators and representatives were so suspicious deep in their guts when they heard about the Peace Corps. To run an empire, it is necessary to use the old tried and true mushroom syndrome. Keep the people in the dark and pile horseshit on them. Keep the wool pulled over their eyes forever. That way you can keep them scared and keep the whole game going and the profits of capitalism and empire roaring.

Romantic as village life was, however, sometimes one would just have to play hooky and get out of the village, head for Jalandhar or Ludhiana and drink a cold Golden Eagle beer in Greens Restaurant. Nothing can taste better than that cold Punjabi beer on a boiling hot day in Punjab with spicy Punjabi chicken and rice. Sometimes there would be a local band in Greens in Ludhiana who would try their hand at an Elvis or Beatles song when an American appeared. That was pure bliss, as they butchered the song and I snorkeled down the cold refreshing brew. The hell with the Jeffersonian ideal. Karl Marx was closer to the truth when he remarked about the idiocy of rural life. Let those peasants irrigate their fields in their tumbas. Let them drink their lussie. I will enjoy my cold beer and forget about the fields of Punjab.

Around Christmas and New Year's holidays, we were able to escape to Delhi and meet some of the other volunteers for a break. This was a big treat after coming from a village in Punjab to stay in a hotel and enjoy hot showers, restaurants, and the urban atmosphere of the city.

25

Duniya

"Sometimes I drink for love of life. It is necessary for one to stagger in order to hold one's self erect."

—Abdul Hai Sahir Ludhianavi

It was April, 1969. Now that the carpenters have completed the work on my house, making the screens and cabinet, they remind me that I owe them a feast and should buy them new Turbans. With an eye to needing them in the future, I followed up on this suggestion and arranged their feast. It was expected, of course, that I would buy them meat and Binnys Sherab, or local whiskey.

The carpenters began to down the wine and get high at once. They are terribly pleased with the party. Gulzar Singh starts getting mellow and telling me what a good man I am and that he is sure that I come from a good family. He had been deceived. He said that I was not like my American friends that he had seen who had come to see me in the village. He could tell by looking at our faces, he said. I hadn't quite expected this much shit. It was getting deeper and deeper.

Then he started telling me that he was first in his class when he was in High School. The other carpenter then left early because Gulzar Singh said that he wanted to go and enjoy with his wife.

Gulzar Singh's young son has also come to watch and to enjoy the feast.

This was just the first of many times they would come to my place to eat and drink, when there was an opportunity. They couldn't do it at home. So they would use my place as their sort of drinking place away from home. Their place for some sinning and grinning.

The next day, I go to the college and borrow a couple of Russian novels. Here I meet up with a real playboy professor named Amrik Singh. He wants me to come and have lunch with him. The English teacher from the village, who is a little wimpy, also comes along. On the way, the professor buys a bottle of whiskey. We go to his place and have a couple of shots, but the English teacher, who is a high caste Brahmin, does not drink. I guess it explains his wimpy looks, compared to the lusty and worldly meat-eating Sikhs.

We gather in a small sitting room of a modern house in what is called Model Town, just near the truck stop on Garshanker Road. The playboy professor has five small kids running around the house while his wife is making the lunch. After each shot, he quickly hides the whiskey bottle behind one of the gaudy framed pictures of Guru Nanak which are propped up on the mantle. We finish the bottle and the lunch.

I mentioned before that my cook Buchan got recycled to Ed Marsh after I fired him. Later, as it turns out, they try to pawn Ed Marsh's old cook, Darshan Singh, whom he had fired, off on me. So it would be a switch, even Steven. One day I met him along the road coming out to my village. I didn't know who he was, but he wanted a job as my cook. I said OK, I would give him a try. That was just before my trip to Pant Nagar, but then he just disappeared. After I got back, I went to ask Ed if he knew what had happened to Darshan Singh. Apparently the two cooks were coordinating their activities rather closely.

On the way to Ed's village, I remembered that it was the Holi Festival Day, when Indians throw coloured water on each other. But it was too late. I was unarmed with any colour to throw. So they plastered me with a coloured powder along the road on the way. There were too many of them and anyway this is fair game for this festival day. As it turned out, Ed was not home, but I ran across Bob Baker riding up on his bike. He had also come to see Ed Marsh.

So I went on down to Bura Pind with Bob to his place and we discussed our plans to go to Kashmir on leave in a few days. The weather was getting hot now and it was time to get some break from the village. We thought the mountains would be ideal and we could stay on a house boat on Dal Lake. I asked Bhagnath, Bob's cook to send me a cook. That is how I got my cook Mussie from Ferozepur after a few days.

The old cooks who remembered the British days, like Mussie, told me that they thought things were better under the British. They said it was easier to get work and things were not so expensive then. Mussie said that the poor too were better off in those days.

In the hot season, I take leave with Bob and we go to Kashmir for a few days. We took the train and bus up to Jammu and then flew the short hop up over the mountains to Srinager. It was an all day trip up to Pathankot and then to Jammu. After a night in a hotel, we took the plane.

In Srinagar, we spent several days in a houseboat on Dal Lake. This was a popular thing to do in Kashmir back in the sixties and it was perfectly safe in those days. Each boat had a cook to make food and tea. In the day we did shopping for silk and other things. I took some silk back to America, although I do not know if it was ever used for anything useful. However, it was beautiful silk. It was popular in India, but not so useful in America.

Unfortunately the weather did not co-operate with our trip that year. It was rainy the whole time that we were there and so we missed the opportunity to go up to the high mountains. After a few days on the house boat, it was rather enough, especially since it kept raining almost continuously and we started to get bored. We shifted to a hotel. It was a classical old hotel with five course meals. Still quite affordable with many tourists from Eastern Europe. The rooms were very old fashioned with bathtubs brought by the British, decades before. We found this to be very quaint. We would have tea in the rooms in the afternoons. It all seemed very British. The weather was pleasantly cool, but sometimes too cold. At the time, Henry Kissinger was negotiating with the North Vietnamese on ending the War in Vietnam. We followed it in the English papers, but not a lot was happening on that front.

It was not a very exciting leave, but we did get the feel of Kashmir, at least the mountains and the rain. Finally, we arranged to take the plane back to Delhi, direct. That is the easy way, if one can get the plane.

Duniya

"Love is a thing which gives no comfort even in union with the beloved."

—Mirza Ghalib

Time went on as usual and we wrote to each other. Then Lakshmi visited me again in the night. This time it was not so much of a surprise and I wanted more of the comfort she had given me the first time. The second night her kisses were hotter. I loved the feel of her in my arms. After a little while, she slipped her pajama off. We were not going to have sex just yet, but we were starting to become lovers.

After the second rendezvous, I thought that it was a rather serious situation and just too risky. So I told her that we should not meet that way again. It was just too risky in the village. There were other safer ways, such as meeting during the day in another village, secretly. For the time being, I wanted to back off and fly straight and not be kicked out of the village in an embarrassing scandal. Kicked back to America, I would end up being drafted for sure.

Somehow, young and foolish as we were, we got the idea that we could go and see a film together. I think that it just happened rather spontaneously and we had no intention of doing it ahead of time. We had not even thought of it. The warm weather came. Soon the hot Punjabi Spring was upon us. It was beyond Piyar ka Mossem, but that had no effect on our hormones, it seems. There was a famous and popular film playing in those days called Duniya or "World," which starred Dev Anand and Vyjaintimala. It was pretty innocent stuff. If one watches it today, it is more boring than anything. It is far from the racy Hindi films that would break out in the 1970s much less those of today. But what the film was about had nothing to do with it. Perhaps it was the daring or flouting of convention.

The strange thing is that it was completely unplanned. On the face of it, it seems so innocent. A young girl and a guy going to a film and sitting together. Not even touching. Not even holding hands. This would have been going too far in those days. This seems perfectly innocent. Yet, inserted into the social atmosphere of rural Punjab, it takes on a completely different complexion. Simply, it is dynamite and one can blow themselves right out of the water with such. Right out of the society. But Lakshmi was a bold and spunky young woman who was capable of going out of her way to do some unconventional things and to hell with it. I think I had underestimated this.

Somehow, we met that day in Banga on our bikes and somehow decided to ride to Nevanshahr and see the film. Now this was a rather wild plan to say the least, because we could be seen anywhere along that long main road, some nine or ten miles. Then we would be seen at the theater, and then seen on the way back, if we came together. Anyway, it did happen and we rode our bikes to Newanshahr. It seems like advertising our relationship and to hell with everything else. We went to the big new film theater near the bus stop and sat together watching Duniya. It was terribly exciting. Not the film, but sitting with Lakshmi.

The film droned on and on, as Hindi films do, but this time, I didn't really mind that. We just enjoyed being close to each other. Then when we came out, we came back together part of the way, although I wanted to go alone from the theater. But then we parted so as not to enter the village together. I took the short cut to the village through the unpaved road to Naura village and arrived back at my place.

It seems that even at that time, the rumours had started flying about us being seen together. It was about to quickly blossom into a full blown scandal. Maybe doing this openly was even less acceptable than the more normal secret meetings in the night. I suspect that is the case. That was done secretly, and while not accepted, was condoned in these villages. But this was done completely open in the broad light of day, which seemed to be flouting the social code, while perhaps a secret liaison was not.

The next day, the rumours had increased. The story quickly travelledback to the officers in the BDO office and I was surely beginning to be seen as a menace to the morality of the Punjab and Punjabi society! One version had it that I had been seen riding on a motorcycle with Lakshmi behind me and that I had a bottle of whiskey in my back pocket. Now that would have been a wild scene even for a Hindi film in those days. In other words, I had quickly become a full-fledged badmash or bad character.

At this point, I decided that it was probably all over for me. I thought that reports would be sent to the Peace Corps office in Delhi and that when they got them, they would call me back and ship me to the US as quickly as they could. Those fears came into my mind. That would not be good because the military draft board would still want me. My deferment would be canceled. At that point, I even considered leaving and just giving it up. I was prepared to do so if necessary. But then, I decided that I would stay as long as I could and see what happened. There was nothing really to lose. In fact, nothing really happened, and while my reputation might have been somewhat tarnished, things went on. I cannot be responsible for God giving me hormones. For putting me into hormonal bondage. My friends came to see me as before and they understood. I went on with my work, visiting farmers and planning crop experiments.

I continued organising a project to have some local farmers grow soybean plots from the seed that I had brought from Pant Nagar as soon as the monsoon rains came and softened the soil. Things settled down, and I continued to stay in the village.

"The record shows, I took the blows, and did it my way."

After this, Lakshmi and I sort of thought to hell with the village. We could make a programme to meet elsewhere. Lakshmi had a friend named Sudarshan who sometimes helped her do things. His mother was very liberal and it was possible to meet in Sudarshan's village near Banga in the afternoons. But in the meantime, we would let things cool off. It was one way to learn about the social boundaries of a traditional society, but perhaps not the safest one.

Our relationship was about to play hell with the family plans for Lakshmi who was slated to go to England, where her uncle lived, and perhaps have a marriage arranged for her there. It would be a typical Punjabi arrangement, but quite boring. I doubt if she would have put up with it, given her rebellious spirit. She would be dependent upon her relatives in England, because the family in India was poor and her father was not living. So it was a household of women.

I take the bus in the morning and go to Chandigarh to buy some rice seed for a farmer. I have 125 rupees in my back pocket, which was a foolish place to carry it. On the way, I have to buy a bus ticket and my pocket is picked. I do not discover it until I am at the seed store and reach for my wallet to pay for the seed. It is embarrassing when I cannot come up with any money. Not only that, all my money was in the wallet, including what I needed for the bus ticket back home.

All I can do is walk to the police station and tell them what happened. The Police give me a chit that allows me to take the Punjab Roadways bus back to Banga. The next day, I have to borrow a few rupees from a friend to get to the bank in Newanshahr and get some money. It is a useful lesson and it is the last time I will carry money in my back pocket.

26

School Partnership

> "Give me strength to never disown the poor or bend my knees before insolent night."
>
> **—Rabindranath Tagore**

A sports tournament is going on in the village. I watch a football match and a couple of *kabbaddi* matches. The BDO is also here along with the Secretary of the Zila Parishad in Jalandhar. Delicious *pakoras* and tea are being made at the high school and I eat my fill. An English and social studies teacher at the Government Secondary School in Banga, Dharam Singh, meets me and tells me that he would like to get some soybean seed if I can acquire them. I tell him that unfortunately I was only able to get a small amount for local farmers this year.

In the evening, the Secretary is anxious to talk to me. He wants to go to America and study nuclear physics. He has an MSC degree in physics from Rajasthan University in Jaipur. I stay talking to the party until almost midnight. The students who have come for the tournament are bedded down on straw on the cement floors of the rooms for the night. The girls are put up in the new co-operative society building across from my place.

The next day, I meet Chris Klose and Jim Farley, who have come to the tournament and they stay the night with me. The next day there is a volleyball match between Jadla Village and

Banga Block. Then we watch the *kabbaddi* matches. There were matches for both boys and girls.

Malah Sodian was a poor village to the west of Banga near the Phagwara-Nevanshahr Road. The population was mostly low-caste. There was no school in the village, so classes were being held in some spare rooms in some buildings in the village. This was very inconvenient for both the teachers and the students.

In early February, 1969, I started a project for the Peace Corps School Partnership Programme to build a school in Malah Sodian. The Peace Corps encouraged us to pursue the building of a school and I am anxious to work on the project. I discuss it with the BDO and he offers his assistance.

Under the School Partnership Programme, the Peace Corps Volunteer and the villagers submit a request to build a school to the country Peace Corps director. Once approved, the request is sent to the Peace Corps Office in Washington for approval and funding. The village supplies the labour, land and teachers. At the same time, schools in the US participate, donating money for the project. Some 239 schools had been constructed under the programme with 187 US schools participating.

A few days later, we make a programme to visit the village with the BDO. It is a dark and foggy February morning. There is some light rain. But the BDO does not come that day, so the visit is off.

A few days later, I finally go to *Mallah* Sodian with the BDO, but there are no village officials around. So we go to the adjacent village, Behram. There we have tea and I make a programme with the VLW of that circle, Man Singh, to meet with the village officials and discuss the programme a couple of days later. But this also doesn't happen.

A few days later, I make the trip to Pant Nager with Staff in the pursuit of some soybeans for seed. When I return, we visit the village *Mallah* Sodhian again with the BDO to discuss the school project. In the afternoon, we go in the Block jeep. When we get there, the known villagers were expecting me and came out in a group to meet me when the block jeep stops at the side of the road. The BDO is on his way to attend a programme where the Chief Minister of Punjab will be the guest.

I go with the villagers including the Sarpanch, Swaran Singh. This head man has the same name as the Sarpanch of Mahil

Gaila. The other village panches also come, along with the village Patwari and the schoolmaster, Mr Satwinder Singh.

First, we go to the building where the primary school is now held. It is a big old pucca building, which seems to have been intended as a house. The village has been using it as a school for the past twelve years. The school has three teachers. Two women, teach grades one to three and Satwinder Singh teaches grades four and five.

Then we see the site where they have started to build the new primary school. A playground and garden is planned. Then we have tea and sweets at the old school. I tell them everything I know about the partnership programme, which links schools in the US with a project in India. Students in the US contribute small amounts of money for the project. I also ask the villagers many questions.

When the programme is finished, I say goodbye and try to catch a bus along the road, going back to Banga. A bus passes, but will not stop as it is already too crammed. Then a guy comes along on a motorcycle and offers me a ride.

The next day, I go to Newanshahr to the Tehsil office to get some information on the village *Mallah* Sodian. They gave me the census book for the village with all the information and I copy down what I need.

I take advantage of the omelet place near the bus stop to get something to eat along with a coke.

A few days later, I go to the BDO office and get the blueprints for the *Mallah* Sodian School. Then I go to the village and take pictures of the school site, the old school building where school is now held, and pictures of the teachers.

A few days later, I get the BDO's recommendation for the School Partnership Programme typed up and signed. I think that I am on my way and all my work will pay off and bear fruit. I am hoping.

However, that same day, I receive a memo from the Peace Corps in Delhi saying that the Partnership Programme has run into trouble with the Indian Government, which is not now in favourof the programme. So the whole thing is called off. I don't have the heart to tell the BDO for a couple of days more. The rug has been pulled out from under me after all the work that I have done. But it is just one of the things that can happen and does happen. One has to roll with the waves. I will be the first to agree that it will be better if the Indians can make the arrangements themselves without help from America, but I was willing to do what I could.

27

Crooked Trail

"May your trails be crooked, winding, lonesome, leading to the most amasing view."

—Edward Abbey

It is a Friday in early October, 1969. Bob baker and I leave Jalandhar for Dharmsala in the hills. We have spent the night in a hotel in the district town. This morning, we take the early train to Pathankot. We had asked the hotel bearer to call a rickshaw which would take us to the station at half past four in the morning and to wake us up at four. But he wakes us up a little late and when we get to the station, the Kashmir Mail is waiting. We hurriedly buy our third-class tickets and rush out to catch the train. We cannot get into the third class carriages, which are absolutely packed. Some of the cars had the doors locked and the passengers inside refused to open them for us. Enough swingin dicks there already. They will not tolerate more. The cars where the doors were open were so packed that it was impossible to climb inside. At the last minute, when the train is about to pull out, and we are stranded on the platform, the railway guard sees us and comes to our rescue. He takes us to the front part of the baggage car, just behind the coal car and the engine and lets us ride there.

The trip to Pathankot from Jalandhar takes about three hours, but this morning it seems shorter. The guard is a very friendly and we have a good talk with him. He has worked on the Northern Railway for some 20 years.

When we get to Pathankot, we take a rickshaw to the Dharmsala bus stand and throw our luggage on top of the bus, which is loading up for the trip. From here to Dharmsala, the ride is about four hours. On the bus are some rather young French hippies, a couple. The ride up is pleasant, but some Indian women start getting sick riding around the sharp hairpin curves in the hills and are constantly thrusting their heads out the windows to vomit.

The road winds up the hills and across small rock-filled streams and riverbeds in the valleys with a ribbon of clear water gushing down. The temperature becomes cooler as the road ascends and gives one the anticipation of the high mountains. To the east a high range of beautiful snow-capped mountains is visible.

The weather in the hills is tricky and when we got up to Dharmsala a shower of rain bursts upon us. As soon as the bus stops, we scramble off and climb to the top of the bus to get our sleeping bags and suitcases down before they get soaked. There is a small one-room bus station where we find shelter until the shower ends. We then walk up to the tourist reception office of the Tourist Bungalow. The Bungalow is on the other side of the town on a hill. We had made reservations beforehand and walk up through Kotwali Bazaar, a very steep incline, to the Tourist Bungalow and register for the rooms.

This is a big sprawling two-story house built of stone blocks carved out of the hills. Small horses pack them down to the construction sites. The Bungalow has a chowkidar to take care of things.

After settling in, we walk down to the bazaar and eat at the Evergreen Restaurant in the town. On the way back, the rain starts pouring and then turns into hail. We hurry to our quarters to avoid the drenching and pelting with ice. This keeps up for something like half an hour until the ground is literally white with the small hail stones. Torrents of water come rushing down the hillside and it appears that the whole place will wash away. It seems that, this is not unusual as there is over 150 inches of rain a year in the foothills of the Himalayas. It becomes so cold that Bob and I go to bed and sleep until time for dinner in the Bungalow.

The dinner is good North Indian food, rice and pollock, *allu-gobi*, and *chapatis*. It is served by a kid of nine or ten years old, probably the most efficient person in the whole operation.

It is Saturday morning. The mountains are beautiful. Bob and I crawl out of bed and cautiously take an icy cold shower, but not together. That might have warmed things up a little better, however. It has been a long time, but we are not at that point yet. After a breakfast of thick omelet, loaded with onions and tomato, and toast and butter on the side, washed down with milky tea, we head up to McLeod Gunge, some one thousand feet above the rest house. It is on the point of the hill with the rest house below. The walk up is a very steep climb. The previous day the rain had washed the road clean, but today it is littered with chewed up leaves which the hail has stripped from the trees.

The early morning sun is pretty hot and the climb up is steep. We begin to sweat. Perhaps three quarters of a mile up from the Tourist Bungalow is the residence and headquarters of the Dali Lama. His compound is on a lane that branches off from the main road.

As one goes up, the trail becomes rockier, and then turns into a foot path. We watched some local people mining big rocks out of the hills. They load these onto the backs of small horses and pack them up and down the hillside. Further up, they were building a house with these stones. After much steep climbing, one suddenly arrives at the top of the hill. Here, there is a small bazaar with Tibetan and Indian shops.

The bazaar is very clean, not at all like Indian towns on the plains. In the centre is a big red and white Buddhist shrine, perhaps fifteen feet tall. At the opposite end is a bus stop for the buses which run down to the centre of town.

There is an old general store, established in 1869, according to the sign in front. Here one can buy all sorts of necessities from liquor to hairpins. Opposite this are vegetable and fruit stands. There are a couple of Tibetan hotels which serve Tibetan food or chow-chow.

We walk down the street and have tea in a little shop served by a pretty Tibetan girl. We watched as she kept flitting in and out of the place while making tea. Bob seemed to be more taken with her than me. Her firm and vibrant young breasts are terribly erotic under her thin shirt. I quickly begin to salivate and felt a slight tickle in my balls. Bob's mother, of course, had precluded any possibilities of a chink in the male chastity belt which she had imposed upon him. One can always dream. I couldn't help myself from dreaming as that vision of her sharp young breasts kept returning for days.

We go shopping. There are carpets, out of our price range, and Tibetan shoes for walking in the snow. Nice items, but I can only buy some incense and incense holders.

The chow-chow is excellent at the Tibetan Hotel. The main dish is fried egg noodles, smothered with small pieces of bukra (goat) and tomato pieces. There was red pepper to sprinkle over the top.

After lunch, we hike down the main road on the other side of the bazaar. Here it is very scenic with the road lined with tall pine trees. Along the sides is lush vegetation with a carpet of moss and grass.

About half a mile down from McLeod Gunj, one comes to an old British church, "The Church of St. John's in the Wilderness." It is set back some fifty meters from the road through a wooden gate hung on stone posts. It looks as if it has been abandoned since the British left in 1947. In front of the church is a huge bell suspended on stone pillars. The church itself is built of native rock carved out of the hills and looks massive and indestructible, but eerie and deserted. I imagined the scene, the British community would have presented around the turn of the century, on a Sunday morning. It is a lovely setting for a church in the cool, damp, forest up from the dry parched plains.

Down from the church is an old British cemetery. We looked at the names of the British buried there and found that many of the dates went back to 1875. They were mostly members of the clergy and missionaries from the church.

The most interesting part of the cemetery is a cluster of graves of people who were killed in the Dharmsala earthquake of 1905. We noticed at least twenty such graves. In one place, a man and his two daughters are buried who had died within five days of each other, perhaps from some epidemic. Biblical passages were engraved on many of the stones. It presented a picture of what life was like in British India. The newest grave we saw was dug in 1947.

We climbed back up to the main road through a briar patch. Further down, perhaps a mile, was another small community and a bazaar. When we arrived, school was just letting out and the road was filled with small children, mostly Tibetan. On the hillside, people were washing woolen sweaters in cold water which gushed out of a pipe. They had spread sweaters out on the hillside to dry in the sun making a colourful scene.

Further down, the road had caved off and Tibetan labourers were repairing the damage. We caught the bus and rode down to Kotwali Bazaar.

The next day, we planned to go up to the Forest Rest House which is an eight kilometre trek from McLeod Gunj. However, we needed to get a permit from the Division Forest Officer of Kangra District, in lower Dharmsala. We take the bus and go to the forest office, but find that the Forest Officer is not there. Fortunately, the aide there was kind enough to give us a permit himself.

We walk back up to Kotwali Bazaar buying some food for the trek because the Rest House does not provide ones food up on the mountain.

It is Sunday, a beautiful morning with the sun reflecting from the snow-capped peaks rising above the small town of Dharmsala. Bob and I hurriedly eat breakfast and pack our food into a back pack. From Kotwali Bazaar, we take the bus up to McLeod Gunj to save us some 1000 feet of the 5000 foot ascent.

At Macleod Gunj, we start the long trek up. The road has been asphalted for some distance and is rather steep. Along the way, there are some old British houses, very nice bungalows. But soon the trail gets much narrower and is unmetalled. Along the road are water hydrants, British style. Further up, there is a storage tank for water. This was apparently built during the British days.

The road begins to wind upward through a pine forest. In a couple of places, the trail had been wiped out by landslides and a huge boulder almost completely blocks the trail. At the edge of the pine forest, we sat down and ate some chocolate bars to give us energy for the climb.

We pass a small temple near a pool of water and some Black Mountain cattle. Soon the trees become small among scrubby bushes. The trail is loose rock, flat, metallic looking, like fool's gold or silver at times. Winding up and up on the edge of high cliffs, the view is fantastic. In the valley a few hundred feet below are small rock houses with golden maize drying on the roofs. Bullocks can be seen plowing in the small terraced fields adjacent to the houses and the peasants are planting wheat in the furrows made by the plows. Occasionally, one sees a mountain goat grazing on the steep, rocky, hillside. Further up, the trail is built from small boulders, going up in steps, like a sort of stairway. Above and below huge boulders cling to the hillsides, threatening to break away and thunder downwards.

We stop to rest and see a pack of little monkeys above us in the rocks and bushes. Some are climbing around on the rocks and looking at us. We see heads peering out at us from a small bush, like a heavily loaded fruit tree. The monkeys start screaming, objecting to our intrusion into their wild habitat.

As we continue on, it starts to become foggy. It is cloudy below. Soon the fog thickens and one can hardly see fifty feet of the trail ahead. Around the edge of the mountain, up a few feet, we see a cave in the rocks, a sort of shelter made by the huge boulder protruding from the hillside. The local sheep herders use it to bed down their flocks of sheep and goats for the night.

Around another couple of turns, the Forest Rest House comes into view, high above on the steep hill. The trail cuts back and zigzags up. Now one seems to be climbing up almost vertically. The trail is extremely rocky here between small trees and bushes. Finally, one emerges into a beautiful, cool, Alpine meadow with lush grass and a small pool of water near the Forest Rest House. Beyond are high snow-capped peaks of 17, 000 feet. It is a different world. One feels that the grueling trek up has been worth the effort.

At the Rest House, the chowkidar brews tea for us. Along with tea, we have some biscuits from our rations. Another party, four Indian men, join us. There are only two rooms for guests, besides a lounge and dining room, and a small kitchen. It is a very cozy little house with fireplaces in the lounge and rooms. The outside is rock with a galvanised steel roof. The interior is made of beautiful wood. And there are barrels at the back to catch water from the frequent rains and snows.

A few minutes after we arrive, it begins to hail little balls of ice until the ground is almost completely white. When it stops, the sun comes out again shining through the clouds. I go out and shoot some pictures of the Rest House and the mountain peaks behind it with the ground covered with hail stones. The air is cool and refreshing.

Later, the chowkidar builds a fire in the fireplace but the wood is very wet and does not burn well, creating a lot of smoke. After the sun goes down, it gets cold very rapidly. Then we have a very good dinner of dal, pea soup, and chapattis, from our food supply. We are hungry after the climb.

After dinner, it was pleasant resting in front of the fireplace with only the fire and a candle for light. The view from the Rest House is beautiful at night, with the stars above very clear and the lights below in the valley. By the clusters of lights, one can make out towns and villages, similar to the view one gets when flying over India. A lovely sight.

Before going to bed, we knew we were going to be short of bedding so we took down the curtains for extra cover. Still, we woke up at four in the morning, too cold to sleep! One needs to bring some very warm clothes for this sort of trek.

We signed the visitors log and saw our fellow India 53 volunteer's signature, Staff Clarry, and his comment: "Efficient, Wow!"

On Monday, after a breakfast of canned sausages, bread, and tea, we start the trek back down the mountain. In the Alpine meadow adjacent to the Rest House, the goat herders, "*Gaddis*" are just starting down the mountain with their herds. Their dress is a sort of heavy coat which flares out around the bottom at their hips. Their legs are bare but they wear heavy shoes. Around their waist, they wear a long brown rope wound round and round. Two brothers are taking a herd of about three hundred goats and sheep down the mountain to graze. The goats are somewhat like Angora with very long hair.

Talking to young men, they tell us that they had no schools and never got any mail. Their diet consists mostly of milk products from the goats, some rice and dal, and chapattis.

The trip down was rather fast, but perhaps just as tiring to ones muscles. When we reached McLeod Gunj, we took the bus down to Dharmsala and repaired to the Evergreen Restaurant. After the strenuous trek, it was good to get back to the Rest house.

The next day, we walked up to the Dali Lama's house and took some pictures. We were generally tired and sore from our trek. In Kotwali Bazaar, I bought a couple of shawls and a pair of shoes made of rope like women wear in the mountains. Bob bought some shawls and cloth. In the afternoon, the pouring rain came again.

It is Wednesday, and we take the eight o'clock bus from Dharmsala to Jalandhar. There was a young guy from the German Volunteer Service on the bus who was teaching at the Gram Sevak Training Centre in Nabha near Patiala.

The ride down, unfortunately, was rather reckless with a wild driver, just a young kid, who was very immature, cocky, and a sort of show off. A Sikh, named Sohan Singh. I was tempted to report his reckless driving, but thought I might be in danger of getting quartered with a kirpan if I did.

Just before we got to Kangra, he hit a guy on a bicycle. He stopped the bus, some hundred meters ahead. The collision had knocked a piece off the old bus. It seemed that the driver intended to just go on, but people on the bus saw what had happened and made him stop.

Then some men came carrying the injured person up the road between them. The poor man was trying to walk, but couldn't support himself. The German volunteer suggested that they put him on the bus and take him to a hospital in Kangra. They did put him on the bus, but just drove to the bus station as if nothing out of the ordinary had happened. I was really disgusted at the attitude of the driver and the whole affair.

Further ahead the road became more winding and dangerous. The driver was trying to make it to Hoshiarpur in record time. Several times, he barely missed colliding with other buses or trucks on the blind curves. He also hit a cow and had a big argument over who should go first at a narrow place in the road. This argument went on for several minutes, while the time for the driver to back up and let the other pass would have been a matter of seconds. It was just a macho contest of egos and neither wanted to yield.

At one point, the road passed through a tunnel which had just been blasted out of the rock with no reinforcements whatsoever. Further down, a bridge was washed out. The river was mostly dry at this season so we drove right across the riverbed through more than a foot of water in the stream. In midstream, the driver stopped to fill the radiator with water using a metal can he carried with him.

Eventually we made it to Hoshiarpur, seemingly by the mercy of God alone. While at the station, we saw that a bus had run over a little dog which was flopping around on the ground. People were standing around watching the poor creature and laughing. Somebody was putting water on the dog in pain. A sad and pitiful scene.

The next stop was at Adampur and there we saw Frank Rojas, another of our volunteers. This was a nice surprise. Finally, we made it to Jalandhar and parted with the German. I got a bus to Banga and Bob headed for Goraya. I got back to Banga fairly fast, but had to take a tonga to Naura village because there were none going to Mahil Gaila. From Naura, some guys helped me carry my baggage up to the village and I was very glad, to be back home. There's no place like home even if it's on the other side of the world.

28

Darshan Singh Pheruman

It is October 28, 1969, and the news has come that Darshan Singh Pheruman has died yesterday. This is significant as he has been on a fast unto death demanding the inclusion of Chandigarh and some Punjabi speaking areas into Punjab since August 15. He has refused food and passed away after 74 days. He was a long-time political leader in Punjab, beginning in the 1920s Akali Movement for gaining control of the management of Sikh Temples from the British. Later, he was active in the *Shiromani Gurdwara Prabandhak Committee* (SGPC), which controls the Sikh Temples.

Today all government offices and schools will be closed. I have to cancel my trip to Ludhiana to take my soil samples down to the Punjab Agricultural University because of this development.

I ride my bike to Naura village to take that soil sample and drink tea with Hari Singh at his place.

It is also a Hindu festival day of sorts, but not an official holiday on that account. The day is called *Tij*. This is the day when the parents of a new bride, within the last year, give her gifts, such as cloth and other things, and bring her sweets. They also give the brothers in law and sisters in law of the bride gifts. It is celebrated on the third day of the new moon. It is celebrated to ensure that one's husband lives a long and wealthy life. The women eat their last meal at four o'clock on the previous day and get up early in the morning and chew the stick of miswak, datun in Hindi, which cleans their teeth and also makes their mouth red. Then they fast, not eating anything until the moon rises at night. It is now about eight in the evening and the moon has not yet risen, but will rise soon in the east, big and full and bright. The women will sing songs. October skies are generally bright and clear in this part of India.

There is also a feast given tonight which is sometimes attended by the parents of the bride, but sometimes only by her brothers. She will get something like 30 to 40 rupees worth of goods. But better off families spend 300 to 400 rupees on gifts.

The next day, while I am eating breakfast, the BDO and one of the agricultural inspectors show up unexpectedly. I usher them in. I thought that perhaps he had come to see me about moving me again, but fortunately he has come to talk to the Sarpanch, Swaran Singh. So I do not actually know if it was about me. Perhaps it was. Is there a plot afloat?

The BDO and the inspector have tea at my place. He tells me that he can supply me with one-hundred tons of gypsum for local farmers. Farmers who need to treat their land for water logging and excess salts can purchase it at fifty per cent subsidy. This is rupees ninety per ton and it takes five tons to reclaim an acre. In other words, three hundred and sixty rupees to treat an acre of land.

One of the young farmers that I am trying to help get gypsum is Mohan Singh at Sujjon. Part of his land has been ruined by the rising salts. I ride down to his place and tell him that the BDO has promised to get some gypsum for me.

Then I visit Dharam Singh who I helped get some gypsum before. I ask him to tell other farmers in Sujjon about this opportunity, who also need to reclaim their land. Kaller soils are a particular problem in Sujjon. I suspect later that I am jumping the gun. One should actually wait until the gypsum actually materialises as it is often just an empty promise and the gypsum will actually end up going somewhere to a place where there is a politician with some political clout. The old gypsum "just now coming" syndrome. I was still naive enough as an American to latch onto promises, which would likely never materialise.

In the afternoon, I irrigate my garden in my compound. This is done by the rather back breaking work of humping and banging at my old hand pump, which is slow and tedious. I probably should just buy my radishes and onions in the market and not bother with all this.

The next day, I make the trip to Ludhiana to take the soil samples which I have collected. I also buy some farm record books in English and Punjabi to distribute to some of the farmers, I am working with.

The last day of the month is a trip to Chandigarh for shots from the Peace Corps physician, Dr Lawrence. By taking the early bus from Banga, I make it to Chandigarh by half past nine. The venue was the Chandigarh Oberoi, called the Mount View Hotel. It is a luxurious son of a bitch, and I feel like a real hick from the sticks after all the time out in the boondocks. I am a country bumpkin goggling at the wonders of a big hotel. It is also way out of our price range. Volunteers do not stay in such places.

When I arrive, I find that the Peace Corps had sent out telegrams at the last moment, canceling the programme for that day, but the telegram did not reach me. I get the shots anyway and have lunch with some volunteers in the India 52 and India 66 groups who are working in family planning and nursing. Back to the village by dark.

The next day is another staff meeting at the BDO Office in Banga. I will be seeing stars again. Always the same at these meetings. The BDO has promised me three tons of gypsum for Mohan Singh for free but predictably there is quite a long bureaucratic process through which one must go to make it happen. Most of the peasants are just not capable of doing that and getting everything in order in all the associated offices.

The next day I inform Mohan Singh in Sujjon of the procedure and give him the necessary paper work which I get from the inspector Baldev Singh. But he is slow to get the paperwork done.

My sweet young friend, Sant Ram, comes in the evening. He likes to kiss me. He sometimes even kisses me on the lips, which makes me feel a little uncomfortable. I think it does not mean anything except that he just likes me a lot. He wants to be a good friend and shoot the shit about the girls that he is keeping an eye on in the village. He is keeping track of some "pieces" that he tells me about.

Early November. I help some of the young guys in the village clean the field next to my house. We have been playing volleyball there but there is a hole that needs to be filled up. We collect the rubble around. We mostly finish it today, but still need to bring more soil to fill in the hole completely and make a level playing field. This is the true meaning of a "level playing field," which the economists are always talking about but have never seen.

After the work, I offer tea to the guys but they want coffee. They can have tea anywhere and it is old fashioned. They are modern young guys. After the work, I sneak off to Banga and buy a couple of bottles of beer and bring a big chunk of ice along to cool it in a bucket. A man needs to lean back and enjoy his humble palace and that surely means a cold beer now and then, if anything.

I have trouble tracking down the Agricultural Inspector, Baldev Singh, for a few days to get the paper work taken care of for the gypsum. A couple of days later, I go to Swaran Singh, the Sarpanch's place. His men have been shelling corn and after it is finished, he invites me to stay and drink some rum with his friends. I cannot refuse him and the six of us finish the bottle.

Still no Baldev Singh the next day but I meet G.S. Bedi, the local small businessman, in Banga. He asks me to test his soil. I then go for the same purpose to Lashkar Singh's village. I don't hesitate since he has a nice young sister who always gives me a big smile when I pass their house. This is terribly unusual for a village and is what drew me to him, in the first place, rather than the noble task of testing his soil. I guess, I probably had my mind on testing her soil. But there is no chance of that. Forget it. Today, I only get a couple of glimpses of her but she gives me another nice smile. I will go back tomorrow to take some more soil samples. I am thinking to get to know him better. Testing her soil would be heavenly.

The next day, Baldev Singh appears at the Block Office. After lunch, I ride down to Naura and take soil sample results to Davinder Singh and to Hari Singh. Also I give the soil reports to Bahader Singh and explain what the various test results mean. He is having a party for the workers today who are working on his new house. There are sweet *jellibies*, which I love, and tea. I join the party, but no chance for smiles from that cute young girl today.

The next day I had a programme to meet G.S. Bedi in Banga. The family is prominent in Banga in several business enterprises. I have tea and sweets in his house. He asks me how he should plant his small plot of Triple Dwarf Wheat, which all the farmers are trying to get these days. I have given him a small amount of seed. I buy some fireworks in town as Diwali Festival is coming up.

The next day I distribute more results of soil samples which I had taken to Ludhiana. My cook Mussie leaves for Ferozepur for a Diwali Holiday and so I take him to Banga by cycle to catch the bus to Jalandhar.

I take soil sample results to Mohan Singh at Sujjon. I am still trying to work through the bureaucracy to get him his free gypsum to treat his kaller soil, but it takes much time. I tell him what papers he needs. He says he can get them filled up and bring them to me at Mahil Gaila. I ask him to do it soon.

The next visit is to Subedhar Dharam Singh who is the Secretary of the Sujjon Co-operative Society. He is a nice old gentleman to visit and he makes me rest in his comfortable house on a big old comfortable mungie, sometimes in the afternoon. If I come early, he gives me lunch. I take a nap and when I wake up he gives me tea and biscuits. That is the kind of hospitality that one gets so often in Punjabi villages.

Today, when I ride my bike up, I find that he has gone to the fields, so I will come back later. I see some peasants sitting around passing time. I talk to some of them and one of them invites me to come to his house for tea. The women in the family are out working in the fields, so he makes some coffee. It was made with real ground coffee. I asked where he had gotten the coffee and he said that his friend sent it to him from England. It was Maxwell House. He gives me some sweets too.

I next visit Mohan Singh down in Sujjon village and bring him the results of the soil samples I took. I had taken them once before for him, but they were somehow lost in the lab at Punjab University and I had to do it all over.

I next visit a young friend Sham Singh in Bhaura village and return the results of his soil samples and explain what each reading meant. He takes me and shows me his fields. Toria and Alfalfa. The Toria is very heavily infested with caterpillars and they are now invading the Alfalfa as well. I tell him that I have medicine for it and will give it to him if he will come to Mahil Gaila and get it. It is a distance of only one mile. He said he would come and that he knew where he could borrow a sprayer.

Back in Mahil Gaila, I have to scrounge up a meal for myself, since my cook is gone. Sant Ram comes, along with a friend from Chandigarh, and we have some coffee. I cook eggs for dinner, heat water and have a bath. After this, I figure I have done enough damage for one day and do some reading before bed.

In the night, a wild dog breaks into my compound and kills several of my chickens. The door of my chicken house was not strong enough to keep out the wild dogs that keep roaming around the edge of the village.

29

Dussehra Festival

"I have had my invitation to this world's festival, and thus my life has been blessed."

—Rabindranath Tagore

Dussehra Festival comes in the pleasantly cool days of October. In 1969, the festival begins on October, 19. My friend Sant Ram comes for lunch. After eating, I go with him along with Sodhy and Darshan Singh, to the Dussehra Festival which is happening in the field, just next to my place. On one side of the field is a huge crowd of women in colourful saris and Punjabi dress of *pajama* and *kurta*. The men are on the other side of the field. There are roving monitors in between, who are supposed to keep the men and women separated and prevent any trouble. Among the men, there is always a lot of drinking at such festivals in Punjab.

My friends make a couple of cautious dashes down through the women's side of the field. I go with them, letting them lead the way. I would not have been brave enough to do this on my own. After all, they cannot condemn me for doing as the Romans do, even if this may be an infraction of the rules of the quite rigid separation of the sexes. But being a young man like them, I don't mind seeing if I can spot some pretty girls in the gathering. The village women, unfortunately, lose their beauty all too soon with the daily grind and heavy load of house work in addition to bearing children.

On one side of the field, some boys from the village are acting out the epic story of Rama and Ravan. As the story goes, Sita, Rama's wife, is kidnapped to Sri Lanka by Ravan. Rama makes a journey to Sri Lanka to bring her back and a three day battle ensues. On the final day of Dussehra, the return of Sita is celebrated. This will be tomorrow.

The whole episode is being acted out by costumed villagers in thousands of villages around the country today. Most of the actors here are young boys.

When the play is over, the women are given a chance to leave the grounds first. This gives them a head start back to their houses, before the men leave.

It seems, from what I have observed while here, that Dussehra is the only time in the year that women can take the privilege of really putting on their best clothes and jewelry and coming out into the open in the village without some social stigma attached. After such rigid confinement, they enjoy the small amount of freedom given them.

In the village, a brigade of volunteers has been organised. These trusted boys of the village keep the woman on one side of the field and the men on the other. At first, this seems unfortunate to me. Before the day is over, I begin to see that it really is necessity to keep order. Some of the big rowdy peasant boys who get a little *desi sherab* inside them may not be able to resist the temptation to grab some girl. This seems strange to me, but it seems to be the case in Punjabi society. I suspect that it is the result of the strict sexual repression in the rural villages and never having the chance to come into contact with females outside the home.

We return to the grounds in the evening. Around eight o'clock, people start to gather for the evening drama. The programme is presented by a team of minstrels. The men sit in front in the open field just outside my residence near the community centre building on the other side of the field.

The women and children are gathered on the nearby rooftops, and watch from there, where it is safer for them. Bamboo ladders are brought so that the women can climb up to my rooftop. Tall poles have been erected in front of the community centre for electric light bulbs to illuminate the stage.

The minstrels begin their performance. There are four men, dressed as women, with heavy make-up. It strikes me that they actually look more attractive than most women in the village, saddled with child bearing and rearing and the endless round of daily drudgery from before sun up until almost midnight every day for years. A middle aged "joker" clowns around and provides the laughs. Another person acts as master of ceremonies and carries on a conversation with the joker. Music is provided by a drummer and a musician playing the harmonium. There is a small keyboard and it works something like an accordion.

The pseudo-women dance, usually one at a time, keeping rhythm with the silver bangles on their feet. At intervals, a skit is acted out and the joker takes his turn entertaining the crowd. This show goes on way past midnight until the women have left. Some of the men remain.

From time to time, one of the minstrels comes back through the audience to collect money. If a person wishes, he can give one or more rupees and have his name and the amount mentioned by the performers.

The show goes on. The joking and singing is very sexually suggestive and quite lewd. The performers make wise cracks and joke about the "loose women of the village." It is, in fact, far from a joke in Indian villages. Perhaps it tempts some of the young guys who are in the process of getting drunk.

The next day is the twentieth of October and the official day of Dussehra. Early in the morning, way too early according to my thinking, the band at the affair strikes up the music and begins to play loud tunes. People are now excited and in a festive mood. The villagers put on their "Sunday best" and prepare for the festival in great anticipation. Some of the men make preparations by stocking up on some local whiskey, either Binnys Sherab, if they can afford it, or the flat out home-made *desi sherab*. Corn liquor, sugar cane in this case. Punjabi white lightening. Some start to down it early in the day, even before the noonday meal.

The BDO has asked me to come to Banga to see the Dussehra Festival with him there. It is rather a pain in the ass for me, as I really want to see the festival in Mahil Gaila, where I can watch without leaving my compound, or go around with a friend. But I cannot refuse his invitation and agree to come. He is my boss, after all. He has probably invited me out of politeness only.

Mahil Gaila, being a big village, is the only centre in the neighbourhood which has the festival, so it draws many people from the surrounding villages.

I hit the road for Banga around one o'clock. When I arrive by bike, the BDO is just eating his lunch and I wait in his place for him to finish. His two-year old daughter is running around almost naked and trying to eat some *allu-gobi* from a dish and smearing it all over herself, over the floor and whatever else she comes into contact with. She totters over to me and I quickly evade being a victim of her campaign to smear everything in sight.

The family discusses me, while eating lunch and I understand much more of what they say than they suspect. They have two guests, a couple, who I have not met before. The BDO has three daughters. The one, who is about eight, becomes all bubbly and giggly at the first sight of me. She thinks that I am some sort of exotic animal, the likes of which she has never laid eyes on before. The oldest one is around 18, strongly built, and not bad looking. Undoubtedly, she will make some man a great child-bearing wife.

Then, typical as the rising sun, the BDO wants me to take a picture of his "little one." After a scrub down and donning a new dress and pants, such as to make a small child as miserable as possible, we proceed to try to photograph, little sweet cheeks. The parents want her picture to be taken alone and I suggest that they put her in a well-lighted place to get a good bright shot. Can't let that little impish beauty go to waste.

There is a small bench against the wall in the inner veranda, which the sun is lighting up. This is surrounded by a gaggle of hideously ugly flower pots where some sickly plants grow, struggling to survive. No sign of flowers.

When the kid is placed on the bench and I start to take her picture, she naturally starts to bawl at once. We make several attempts to mollify the little sweetie and entice her with various trinkets, but have no luck. But her parents cannot miss the opportunity, so a quite rigorous effort is made. Perhaps it would have been more appropriate to have photographed her when she was smearing the *gobi* all over herself in perfect bliss and being her natural self.

As a last resort, I suggest that they let her older sister hold her so that I can take them both together. We finally succeed, although it is not exactly what they had in mind.

Then the BDO informs me that he will not be able to go to the Dussehra Festival with me after all, so he suggests that I skip along and go with the *Mali* or gardener. How unfortunate! I have to feign disappointment, but was happy to be free to get back to the festival in Mahil Gaila.

I pass through Banga on the way back. Here, the Dussehra Festival is being held just up the road from the BDO's house. There is a tremendous crowd of people from the town and surrounding villages. The road is massively flooded with people. The wild confusion is increasing. A big truck has slid off the road into the drain and its back wheels are completely buried in the dirty black slime. Working my way through this mess, my shoe comes apart and I have to find a *chamidar* or shoemaker to get it fixed before heading back to the village.

Back in Mahil Gaila, I head down to the festival. There is a big crowd here also and the drama has started. Many of the men have clearly been drinking and some are staggering or leaning on the shoulders of their friends. I hoped that a feud would not break out because many of the men were carrying *kirpans* and some had guns. But the most common weapon seems to be thick lathis, bamboo sticks to defend themselves if someone comes after them. There are many old unsettled feuds simmering among the parties from various villages. A little alcohol can spark a feud when an old enemy is spotted.

I mingle with the crowd, meeting several of my friends from Mahil Gaila and the surrounding villages. It is a tradition to buy sweets on this day. A university student from Phagwara suggests that we buy some, but when we go to the shop, they are all sold out. But more are being made.

I hang around for the finale which is coming up. Big cardboard and paper effigies of Rama and Ravan are being brought out which have been made by the village youth. These huge images are then set on fire and people enjoy watching them burn. The women begin to retreat back to the houses. I come back to my house which is just nearby, to take a rest.

I see the mistry sahib, Gulzar Singh, who is hanging around my house waiting for me. He is my carpenter who has done the screens and windows of my house. He wants to organise a drinking party at my house for the evening. I decline firmly, saying "no, not tonight." I think that there are too many drunken men around and we need to keep our wits. Then my cook makes dinner for me and some of my friends. Prem Kumar has brought some *bukra*. Sant Ram is here and the *mistry* too. So we stay and eat, but the *bukra* turns out to be tough.

Tonight will be the final night of the festival with another drama and one can sense that it is going to be a big event. For an hour, the women and children have been gathering on the rooftops, establishing their bivouacs to watch the programme. A bamboo ladder is brought and women and children scramble up to my roof from the back side of my house. Every space on the flat roof is soon filled. The big field adjacent to my place is packed with men. It seems that the majority have been drinking. Some are already drunk. Many are sporting their *kirpans* (swords), guns, or sticks. The police stand around eying the crowd, but hardly looking menacing. They are hardly a match for a party of drunken Punjabi peasants.

The drama gets underway. I am satisfied to stay in my compound, where I can watch from my veranda and smoke one of my cigars. I have a fairly good view of the stage and do not consider it safe to be out in the crowd. After some time it starts to bore me and I retreat inside.

Then suddenly all hell breaks loose. My cook, Mussie, yells "A fight! A fight!"

I rush out of my room and sure enough everybody on the field is on their feet. Near the front, dust is boiling up in front of the lights. Men are wielding their lathis flogging the dust laden air and apparently some target. Then things settle down. The show goes on.

I am afraid of what might happen next and prepare to hole up for the night. The show continues peacefully for another fifteen or twenty minutes. Then the fight suddenly breaks out again. Now people are screaming and shouting, egging them on. It is like a huge audience watching someone flogged to death in a ring as a big attraction. I consider the possibility that the crowd actually expected such a thing to happen and that was part of the attraction.

Then the lights suddenly go out and the crowd begins to disperse. Men are running away. The women start scrambling down from my roof. It is bloody hell out there and I hole in for the night. Talking and shouting goes on into the night as I close the wooden shutters of my windows and sleep.

Tragedy in the Village:

"We are too poor to be late." **—Rabindranath Tagore**

The next morning when I wake up, I hear a lot of talking and commotion outside. I take my morning trip out to my latrine, thankful that I do not have to go to the fields. Outside the compound men and boys are sitting and watching. Police are roaming about in front of the community building still looking useless. There is a *charpie* near the wall. A boy of some twelve years is sitting near a still form under a blanket.

At first, I think the man may be dead. Then I learn from Mussie, my cook, that he is not dead, just badly injured. The police have gone to round up the men who were responsible for beating him up. I learn that they are looking for the *lumbardar* and his sons who live on the other side of the village.

The objective of this is to get the men to pay the injured man one hundred rupees and get him to agree not to take revenge with his own party. The police and Madho Singh have decided that this is the best way to settle the dispute. A blood money deal. This is known as "*ragy numy*" in Punjabi, or settling out of court. It is also being said that the police hid in the house of Madho Singh last night during the incident. There were only two police and the man was attacked by ten or twelve men, so the police were afraid to do anything to stop the beating.

It is also said that the man who was beaten was a very poor man of the village. His parents are dead and he has no brothers and sisters, just his wife. He has several small children and now they have no way to eat.

A little later, a group of men come and settle in a group near the *charpie*. They then disperse and a bullock cart is brought and the *charpie*, along with the man, is loaded onto the cart and taken away.

I thought maybe they were going to take the man to the doctor but later found that they were only moving him to his house in the village.

It seems strange and cruel that someone beaten that badly and whose life is in danger has been left there all night with no medical attention. The poor man has not been taken to a hospital to see a doctor. He has no money and it seems that few care anything about him. This is very disturbing to see.

So now the man has been taken to his house and left there for better or worse.

After the incident, I decide to just spend the day at home and not venture out. It seems that people need to settle down after three or four days of celebration. I thought there might be bands roaming the roads seeking revenge for any atrocities of the past few days.

The BDO had asked me to come to a meeting concerning the "small savings programme" and the crop season coming up. But I thought it better to think about my safety. I take the day off. Unofficial leave.

I have started thinking about graduate school when I return to the US, but am not at all motivated for it. I would like to have some time to just relax when I get back. On the other hand, if one does not get into something quickly, then they risk being grabbed up by the draft board. The war still goes on. It seems that the logic is that if one cannot make up their mind to work, then they can kill some communists while they are making up their mind and no time will be lost.

It seems that the US wants to make every person into a machine forcibly. When a guy turns eighteen until the time he reaches 26, every moment must be used constructively or one is packed off to fight and further the domination of the earth by America.

"Work here or work there." One way or another, you will further our goal! We will have no wasted manpower.

It seems that after living in India I have lost my American drive for personal achievement and perhaps I will have to get back to America to get back on that track. The US now seems so far away in many ways.

The next day I go to the BDO office. I am told that some people in the village want to move me to Banga. The BDO sends me with the peon to look at some places in the town where I might find a room. I would be giving up my humble, but lovely, home that I have worked so hard to make livable, and be housed somewhere for the rest of the time. There was only one place available, but it would not be finished for several weeks or maybe months. I thought that they would likely keep delaying, so I just told the BDO to please inform me when some suitable place was found. Meanwhile, I would remain in Mahil Gaila carrying on my work. I did some shopping and returned to the village for lunch. I figured that, this time, the predictable Indian lethargy and stalling would work in my favourand I could remain in my place. New home just now coming, sahib, but never arriving. I hoped it would be just now coming for the duration of my stay.

Concerning the injured man, some people in the village had gone around the village and collected some money for him, asking each household to give five rupees. I understand that a doctor in the village has examined him and it is said that he is very badly injured and it is questionable whether he will live. The next day I cash my cheque and the *mistry* and his brother bring me some sweets.

Baldev Singh Bedi in Banga tells me the Triple Dwarf Wheat we have planted has come up and is looking good. While I am in his shop, a young man enters who was a student at the University of Missouri in Columbia, my old university. He studied business administration there. He says he did not like Missouri and returned to California. He is now working for an Indian oil company and trying to return to the US.

I visit a friend and meet a young man in Naura village who has come from the Philippines with his family. They are building a big new house in the village. The father is trying to control his son, but there is a conflict and he is trying to break out. The young guy wants to go to England to study, while the father wants him to continue to study in Banga. But he is taking no interest in his studies. He is too bored in India.

On Saturday, I go to Kapurthala to the house of Sant Ram. He takes me out for tea. He has arranged a party to eat some meat and drink rum, but the affair has become glutted with too many uninvited guests. There were seven altogether. He was a little disgusted at that but it easily happens here.

Then in the afternoon we go to a place where a basketball tournament is being held. We watch a match between a team from the Western Railways from Bombay and the Uttar Pradesh Police from Lucknow. Western Railways win and we go and have coffee.

The next day Sant Ram and I have breakfast at a small restaurant. We decide to go to the park and take some pictures with two of Sant Ram's friends. The garden is around the old cremation grounds of the Maharaja of Kapurthala. It was here that the Maharaja was cremated. The old palace is now a military college. I am able to go in and make some pictures. In the afternoon, I take the bus back to Banga and catch a rickshaw to the village.

30

Diwali

"Light, oh where is the light?"

—Rabindranath Tagore

It is November, 1969 and today is Diwali, the festival of lights. Half past nine, I ride my bike down to Thandian Village to the house of a retired military officer, Captain Mohan Singh. It is very good to go and shoot the bull with him. He is quite Westernised and British after being in the military. He has a daughter in Houston, Texas, and another daughter and two sons living in India. Tajinderjit Singh is a student at the college in Banga and his other son is studying microbiology at Punjab University in Chandigarh. His other daughter goes to the girl's college in Banga, Guru Nanak College in Banga. Her name is Narinder or something similar to that. She is a nice looking young girl. Strictly off limits to me, of course.

The family has three dogs. One is a small terrier named spotty. Another is a big dog like a German police dog named spot. There is also a mutt named Bobby.

I ask Tajinder if he wants to go to the cinema in Banga with me. I thought the film was "An Evening in Paris," which I imagined would perhaps be a break from things Indian. I suppose I was fantasising, but the film was actually a depiction of a scene from the Mahabharata, with many gods and goddesses. It is about as close to Paris as one can expect to get here, I suppose, so I deserved what I got. I thought the film was somewhat interesting, but pretty boring for the most part.

I have never seen such a variety and quantity of sweets in the shops as there are in Banga today. Literally thousands of rupees worth of them in the shops for Diwali. *Shamianas* had been erected in front of the sweet shops to display the sweets in layered shelves up to eight or ten feet high. The multi-coloured sweets looked very beautiful. Mostly milk and sugar. It seemed to me fantastic. People really do go crazy over sweets in this culture. Perhaps true in all peasant cultures. It seemed that everyone was buying them, and probably spending too much money.

Back to Thandian after the film. Mohan Singh asks me to have a peg of rum with him. He asks his daughter to bring it. It was a treat to get to see her up close and she smiles at me a time or two and now I think she really is quite pretty. It doesn't take much to make me into a true believer.

Back in Mahil Gaila, which is next to this village, the village is lighted up with the lights of Diwali. A lot of fireworks are being shot off. There must have been thousands of rupees worth of fireworks lighted and blown up in the village, and small kids were running around with a bag of fireworks. I began to wonder if people were more affluent than I usually think.

I also bought some fireworks and shot them off inside my compound. I also put the small coloured candles which I bought on the walls of my compound. I had a lot of small firecrackers and a few big ones, a sparkler, a small rocket and some that they call planes. When you light them, the spin around and then take off and go up some 20 feet. There are also clothes line rockets and snakes. Sant Ram stopped in before I went to bed.

November tenth, the day after Diwali, is said to be a Sikh holiday. It is the birthday of Vishvakarma, the Hindu God of carpentry, engineering, and industrial arts. He is believed to be the one that designed the universe and is called the "divine carpenter." It is usually celebrated on September 16th or 17th. Some fairs were being held for Vishvakarma today. The carpenters call it "Diwala." Gulzar Singh, the carpenter came in the morning and asked me to come to Newanshahr with him to see the fair. The day was an official holiday so I went with him.

The fair was held just outside the town on Rahon Road at a Hindu *Mandir* or temple. The place was covered with shamianas or tents put up for the ceremony. There was a stage where people were performing. They asked me to sit on the stage, but I declined since I wanted to see the performance. It is considered a great honour to sit on the stage and it shows on the faces of those sitting up there, who are affected by such vain glory, it seems to me. I really did not want to be a part of that. That grinnin and starin at the crowd.

A collection is taken up for the performers. Then there is a meal at the *lunger* at two o'clock in the afternoon. I am just about starved and anxious to get some food. But there is total confusion trying to sit on the ground and eat in that crowd. The food, however, is delicious and I enjoy it a lot.

At three o'clock we return to the village. I go to the *mistry's* house for tea. Then I ended up staying for dinner, since I thought my cook would not return that day.

When I returned to my place, however, my cook, Mussie had returned from Ferozepur. Still some fireworks are being used, but not as heartily as last evening.

The next day, the Akalis take out a march in Banga starting at the grain market by the Railway Station. They are orthodox Sikhs and are a political party. Many small school boys are marching in it. This is to commemorate Guru Nanak's birthday which is actually on November 23.

It is the twelfth of November. Today I help Baldev Singh Bedi plant some Triple Dwarf Wheat seed which I got from the Peace Corps. After tea and sweets in his shop, we go to the field and plant it. The lines were being made by bullocks and a desi plow, and the seed placed in the furrow. The seed was enough to plant the small plot.

The next day I am back in Sujjon to visit my young farmer Mohan Singh again. But I find that still he has not got the papers needed to get the gypsum, even though he can get it for free if he does the paper work. I asked him to complete them and bring them to my place in a few days.

The next day I am checking in with the BDO in Banga. Baldev Singh, the Agricultural inspector asks me to go with him to a village near Banga to help set up a wheat drill.

We ride our bikes to the village. We meet the peasant who has bought the machine, a small wheat drill designed to be pulled with bullocks. The small machine works fine, but it takes a good deal of work to set it, because it is not very well designed.

To calculate the rate of seed being drilled, one must turn the wheel sixty times, then take this seed and weigh it in grams. Dividing this figure by 10 will give the seed rate in kilograms per acre. This is the first time I actually learn how to calibrate the machine. It seems there should be an easier way of doing it.

After calibrating the drill, we go to the farmer's huge new house to eat lunch. The new house is beautiful and not yet fully furnished. The farmer brings out some desi sherab and asks me to join them. I decline, as it is so strong for me.

After riding our bikes back to Banga, we go to Baldev Singh's flat and talk the rest of the afternoon.

Fall Therapy:

"Do not be so compassionate to me in the night of union."

—Asrar-ul-Haq Majaz

It is mid November 1969. Through the mail, I make a programme with Lakshmi to meet her in a distant village in another district. I cannot let my cook, Mussie, know about the programme. After it is arranged, I told him that I would be going to Ludhiana for the weekend.

I leave early at seven in the morning, riding with Mussie on my bike, and catch a morning bus to Jalandhar. I wait at the bus station and the two girls, Lakshmi and Lakhbir, come later by another bus. We buy tickets for Hoshiarpur and sit on adjacent seats, so as not to be too conspicuous. My fear is that someone might recognise us. We already start to get hostile stares from the other passengers.

At Hoshiarpur, we disembark and take another bus to the last stop near Chakwall village. Here we get down and walk the last two miles to the village hospital. It is a sort of health clinic or primary health centre. It is some distance from the centre of the village in the open.

Lakhbir accompanied Lakshmi and is the girl-friend of a doctor who works there. The doctor comes later to meet Lakhbir. The place seems deserted. It is a Saturday. Being the only ones there, we have a lot of freedom and it is great. We have a lot of fun together and make dinner, *allu gobi*, and tea.

The girls wear Punjabi outfits, which I always thought were somewhat sexy when they are tight and stylish. When they remove their dupatta, or scarf, the dresses reveal the shape of their tight young breasts. I take Lakshmi in my arms and squeeze her to me. I can taste the delicious flesh of her young velvet brown neck and kiss her cheek. I want to taste her lips. She feels so delicious in my arms after so long. I love her eyes. She discusses things in Punjabi with her friend. We wait for the darkness and the pleasure of the night. *Pyar ka Mossem* is again here and it will be a cool night for cuddling up together. I know she wants to make love to me.

A room has been set up for us over in one the hospital rooms. It is just what the doctor has ordered for some Fall therapy. Some tender loving. Some relief from the male chastity belt, I hope. We walk across a sort of field with dry brown grass in the clear moonlight to get to the rooms. The whole place seems absolutely deserted, defunct. To call it a hospital is a stretch of the imagination. But I think it may cure me.

It is late in the evening. There is no heat, but we will heat each other under a thick rajai when we are not warm enough. I am anxious to get my hands on Lakshmi and have her in my arms. I want to feel her soft, warm, brown skin next to me. I will have her tonight. All of her. We have waited long enough.

Lakhbir goes to another room to spend the night with her friend, the doctor.

We spend the night there, our first comfortable night together without seriously worrying about being caught by a chowkidar. We will explore each other. It takes some time. I slip out of my clothes, loving the cool on my body. We spend a long time kissing, and then she takes her clothes off down to her panties and gives me her body. I want it all, everything tonight. I can no longer resist. This night, she will be mine. I love the feel of her warm brown skin. I love the taste of her delicious young breasts. And then she lets me slip her panties off too. Tonight she will be my lady.

We make love, at least half-way, being cautious, but being lovers, none the less. Her sweetness doesn't disappoint me. We love and sleep. Sleep and love through the night. It was just what the doctor ordered. I liked the prescription.

The next day, Lakshmi and Lakhbir go to Chakwall village, to stay in Lakhbir's house and I catch the bus back to Jalandhar with the doctor. It is late in the afternoon when I am back in Mahil Gaila. My neighbours, none the wiser.

The next day I make a visit to check on my young farmer in Bhaura Village. I had suggested that he ought to do something about the hairy caterpillars eating up his forage crops. I had given him the Enderin but he hadn't used it because he is lacking the equipment by which to apply it. He cannot get a sprayer from anyone. It was a rather hairy situation. I told him that I would try to find him one.

Then I ride over to Sujjon to see Mohan Singh, but he is not home. I go to the house of another Mohan Singh, a boy who is in the tenth class in Mahil Gaila High School. We have tea.

Mahil Gaila has started the preparations for the celebration of Guru Nanak Devji's birthday, which is on the 23 of November. It is not a normal celebration, as this happens to be the 500 anniversary of his birth. One has to be born and live at the right time to catch such an auspicious event.

Arches are being erected at the entrances to the villages. They are made of three bamboo ladders lashed together with rope and then covered with colourful cloth. Then posters and calendars with colourful pictures of Sikhs are attached to the cloth. It doesn't get much cheesier than that, I think. But it is a peasant culture. There are programmes in the village this evening with music and speeches.

The next day I ride down to the south of Banga to see Major Singh at Gosal village. He is the travel agency guy from Fiji and has a little hole in the wall shop on Railway Road. He is a nice and friendly guy and we have become good friends.

There is going to be a really big event in the village. I have stayed at his house more than once, eating our evening food by candle light, since the village has no electricity. But today is the day that the village is going to electrified officially. A programme will be held in the evening for that purpose.

The programme is held at the house of Naranjan Singh. I stay for this important event. Some officials come and switch on the current officially. I have dinner with Major Singh in his place and spend the night there.

Most of the time I have been there he has been alone, his young wife spending part of the time at her village. During this year, she has had a young son. He was lucky enough to have a boy and he has bought a cow for milk. He would never have done this, of course, if it had it been a girl.

The next day I set out to solve Sham Singh's caterpillar problem. Actually these sons of bitches hairy caterpillars were giving me a quite hard time and it seems that I have been considerably more concerned about them than Sham Singh. He is rather laid back about the problem and takes whatever comes. Maybe I would have been better off with the same attitude. I clearly had not learned how to live successfully in India. I am not sure, but these hairy caterpillars may well have had something to do with putting me in the hospital. They would have their revenge, the hairy sons of bitches.

Nevertheless, I have lunch after coming from Gosal and then head out to find Jagtar Singh who is the owner of a sprayer, needed by Sham. I want to borrow his sprayer and take it to Sham Singh so he can use the Enderin I gave him for the caterpillars. This errand takes up most of my afternoon.

By the time I get back to my house, my ass is starting to get sore and swell up, perhaps from all the bicycle riding.

31

A Pain in the Ass

"I know not if I shall come back home."

—Rabindranath Tagore

The winter of 1969–70 was a time in Punjab, when there was a rash of people getting boils, in North India. It happened to me too. I was treated by a British doctor who was practicing at the Christian Medical Centre in Ludhiana, known in Punjab as "Miss Brown Hospital." In my case, I do not know the cause, but I would hate to think that it was something that I picked up as a result of all those delicious sweets and snacks at Kartar Sweet Shop. I would not like to give up those, in any event. Perhaps it happened as a result of irritation from riding my bicycle. I started getting a sore ass and then it started swelling up and getting more painful. Finally, I couldn't sleep.

In the last week of November, I set out to go to Ludhiana to the hospital, perhaps a 60 kilometre trip. It was not possible for me to ride my bike into Banga and catch the bus to the hospital. I also didn't want to ride in a rough tonga. Once there in Banga, I would have to catch the bus to Phagwara and then another bus down the GT Road, to Ludhiana.

I wondered whether I could get someone to take me to Banga by car.

An older man who lived down the lane in the village had an old foreign car which was quite a wreck, but Mussie my cook found out that he was going to Banga that morning and when my cook asked, he offered to give me a ride into Banga. So I waited. Some guys had to help him push the old car to get it started. Finally he came up the lane, but he had to pass my house and then turn around at the end of the lane and come back. This proved to be almost impossible because there was something badly wrong with the transmission and also it was difficult to get it started. It sometimes sounded like the gears were stuck solid or jammed. He got it started but the old son of a bitchin car was dying periodically, and then had to be pushed again to start the engine. He finally got turned around and came back past my place. I got in. It appears that the second gear was not working. The transmission was making a terrible rumbling and clinking all the time. After starting and stopping several times, we finally get out of the village onto the main pucca road and he fortunately managed to get it into high gear. Everything looked good and we are sailing right along. Making time. We were driving things off the road, right and left, bicycles, people walking, bullock carts, school children. However, it was not just a straight shot on a clear road, even though it was only about three miles into Banga. On the way one encounters many obstacles. Big trucks rumbling towards one, wild and crazed sedougies ready to run one off the road, lumbering bullock carts, that block ones progress, bicycles, even rickshaws, on the road, so it is tricky without a reliable car that can actually slow down and then pick up speed again. Actually, this day, we make it about half way to Banga, before the old car sputters and dies dead in its tracks. Just past Kamachon village, we came up behind a string of three or four bullock carts and they stop us. Another serious defect was the horn. The horn was out. One cannot drive in India without a horn. Just as well lose the wheels as to lose the horn. A car in India runs on the horn first and the wheels second.

It is doubtful if the bullock carts would have yielded anyway. They are so slow and lumbering. What can the peasants do? Bullocks cannot be manoeuvred at will. We started around the string of carts to the right. But we had lost so much speed and momentum that the engine wouldn't continue to pull the car in high gear and so we had to slow down and try to get back down in first gear. This failed miserably. The old junker came to clinking halt, as the engine sputtered and gave up the ghost. All attempts to start the old son of a bitch proved to be sheer folly. I was stuck. We were stuck.

I suggested to my friend, being a little disgusted and also disappointed, that just maybe it was time to get rid of it because it could only give him more trouble in future. But in India at the time, cars were just not readily available. He quickly came to the defence of his car, saying that it was just out of petrol. This may have been true, I don't know, however, while that would be a fatal problem, it seemed far from being the major one. He would go to Banga to get some petrol but I could not wait for that.

At this point, and being in pain, I was forced to abandon my friend. I started on to Banga on foot. But luckily, a serdar passing on a motorcycle offered me a ride on the back into Banga. Painful as it was, I accepted and made it into Banga that way to the bus stop.

This next step was difficult also as sometimes it is very difficult to get a bus going on to Phagwara. The buses usually came very loaded from Newanshahr and sometimes the crowd just pushes one into the bus as it comes to a halt. Sometimes it was difficult to cram into the bus being crushed by the crowd. But if there is a rush, the surge can lift one right up and into the bus. One cannot really call it standing room, as there is no room to stand. Perhaps crushing room only as one is indeed crushed. Eventually, I make it to Phagwara, on the GT Road. But the same situation presented itself here. Almost all the buses coming down the GT Road from Jalandhar were already full. There is always a crowd of people standing along the road. When a bus does come, there is a mad rush of the thundering herd for it, sometimes women and children being practically trampled underfoot. Women with babies in arms, men, and so on, hit the dust, just madness. For me, that day, being in pain, it is hopeless, and so the alternative was to get a rickshaw to the train station and take the train which comes around noon, for Ludhiana. I get a ticket for the train, but have to stand, in considerable pain from Phagwara station down to Ludhiana, down across the Sutlej River. When I get to Ludhiana station, I get a rickshaw to the hospital, which is painful on the hard rough seat and with all the bumps on the street. It was not so far to the hospital but I was in pain with my ass swollen up. For some reason, there were usually large herds of buffaloes on the streets of Ludhiana, at least on the way to that hospital, and it is an experience to run into a herd of water buffaloes in the street, considerably slowing down one's progress. You can't roller skate in a buffalo herd, but one can rickshaw in a buffalo herd quite well. I know, having done it so many times. Today is no exception.

Eventually I make it to the hospital, thankfully, and was able to see a doctor. I was told that I had an abscess in my anus and would probably need to have surgery. The doctor punched a hole in my boil, cauterised it and relieved my pain, so that I could return in relative comfort. He gave me some medicine, but I would have to return the next week to have an operation to have the abscess removed. He gave me a prescription for some medicine which I could get at the hospital pharmacy and I returned to the village. At least the surgery would be a little holiday from the village.

I spent the weekend in bed in the village, nursing the pain, but things just got worse and I returned to the hospital on Monday.

The Christian Medical Centre or Miss Brown Hospital in Ludhiana had been started as a hospital for women but now is a large establishment and I am awfully glad it is there. I am admitted for my boil and the operation is done to cut out the abscess from my rear. I stayed in the hospital about ten days. I had the surgery on Thanksgiving Day and stayed until the fourth of December. The weather was quite cool and pleasant. I read a couple of novels. It is a quite pleasant stay, except for getting over the surgery, which was not so bad, and I rather enjoyed it. I had to sit in hot water twice a day, to treat the wound.

When I ran out of reading material, one day I abscond from the hospital and took a rickshaw down to the Lyle Book Stall which was not far from the hospital and got some more novels to read. One was *Anna Karenina* by Tolstoy. I also read *Doctor Zhivago*. I don't think they missed me as I was free to wander around in the hospital during the day.

A couple of days later, my cook came from the village and brought my mail, which was wonderful to get. I also got my beloved monthly Peace Corps cheque.

When I am discharged, I take the bus and pass through Newanshahr so that I can cash my cheque on the way. When I get back to the village, it is a chance to rest up and it is a while before I can ride my bicycle again.

Unfortunately, I continue to have some trouble with boils, generally on my legs, for the next six months that I remain in

India. It seems that there was a general infection going around that year and the British doctor thought it could have been from the food. I never took the precaution to boil the water that I drank, which was just out of my hand pump, and there was no such thing as bottled water in India in those days. It would have been difficult to follow the Peace Corps recommendations on boiling water. When I visited farmers, I arrived very thirsty and needed to drink water. So I certainly did have some bugs in my system which needed to be cured. In the last months, I drank water which was pulled from an open well, in the very hot weather. It could not have been free from microbes but I thought what the hell. I will be going for a checkup in Delhi and leaving India soon and will get the bugs out of my system. I would leave a few of them in Europe and America.

Back in the village, I took it easy for a few days. One day I walked down to Naura village for some exercise and bought *bukra* at the meat shop. The *mistry* came in the evening and we ate meat and drank some local whiskey. Binnys, of course. I bought the meat and he bought the whiskey.

By the twentieth of the month, I was healed up enough to get back to riding my bike and visit some shopkeepers in Banga. I remembered that it was the Christmas season, but not any sign of it was seen in rural Punjab.

One day, Sant Ram took me to his house in the village. We sat up on the roof in the sun and could watch the "pieces" the young girls, across the way on other roofs. Lakshmi was on her roof enjoying the warm winter sunshine, one of the nice features of a Punjabi winter. Another friend was Ram Murthi who came to my place from time to time.

One day, just before Christmas, I rode over to Bhaura village and visited my friends, Sham Singh. I am uncertain as to the fate of his hairy caterpillars, as I lost track of them, but they had certainly taken their toll on me. Charanjit Bal was another young and rather well educated modern peasant in the village. Sham Singh insisted that I stay at his place and have lunch. I felt somewhat hesitant eating the food of a poor family in the village. I thought they needed all they had to live.

Charanjit Bal had a copy of Tolstoy's *War and Peace* and I borrowed it from him. In a couple of days, it would be Christmas Day. Bob and I made our plans and reservations for our long journey to the south of India.

32

Indian Journey

"Udaipur is the superb result of major exactions from the local poor over many generations."

—John Kenneth Galbraith

In February, 1970, Bob Baker and I started on a long trip to the south of India from Punjab to Madras. On the ninth of the month, we meet and have lunch at Greens Restaurant in Ludhiana and stay at the Ambassador Hotel to take the train in the morning.

The next day, we take the Amritsar Deluxe Train and reach Delhi about three o'clock. Coming through Haryana, we looked for signs of rioting after the recent disturbances, having to do with the agitation to cede Chandigarh to Punjab State, but everything looked pretty normal for the most part. There were three or four windows on the train which had been broken by stones, however. At Sonepat the godown was charred and black in some places but that's all.

We went to the First Class Booking Office and bought out tickets for our circular tour of India from Delhi to Madras. We stay in the Lodhi Hotel and have dinner at a restaurant in Connaught Place. In the night a couple in the next room keep us awake for some time with their noisy love making, which was a little frustrating.

It is Wednesday, February, 11 and we go to the American Embassy to cash some cheques. Then we go over to Baroda House to talk to the tourist officer. He arranges to have out reservations made for the whole tour. We have to confirm out reservations at each station along the route everywhere we stop.

After lunch we go over to the Peace Corps Office. Roy Bonney, Erwin Reiner, and Fritz Bachman, are here learning how to make dishes with soybeans. We brought in some beer to drink with the fried dal made with the soybeans.

We take the ten o'clock train for Jaipur after dinner from the Old Delhi Railway Station. It is an old narrow gage line which makes the cars swing from side to side.

On Thursday, our train arrives in Jaipur about six o'clock in the morning. We grab breakfast at the station. Our guided tour of the city costs five Rupees. Our first stop is at the Temple of the Winds, Hava Mahal, inside the Old City. This part of Jaipur is surrounded entirely by a high wall. It was planned in rectangular fashion and built by Maharaja Jai Singh in the early 18th Century (1727).

The whole city is either of red rock stone or the buildings are painted pink. Only some buildings are of the genuine red stone.

Hava Mahal was built as a screen for ladies in *purdah* so that they could watch processions on the street from behind it. The street in front is 110 feet wide as are all the streets in this planned part of the city. The wall of the city has eight gateways.

Then we go to the old fortress of Amber which was built around 1100 AD by Maharaja Jai Singh's ancestors. The main town is built in a valley with hills of rugged rock all around. An old wall runs up and down the hills but has crumbled down in some places. The main landmarks in this old city are the three Hindu Temples to Shiva, Krishna, and Kale. They are very beautiful on the inside and have paintings dating back to the Eleventh Century. This was the ancient capital city of the Kachana Rajputs.

The other notable building in the Old City is the Chamber of Mirrors. This is a series of rooms and chambers with small pieces of cut mirrors placed in the walls and ceilings so that one sees many images. In one of the rooms, the reflection of a candle in the ceiling appears as stars in the sky. The Maharaja used to sleep on the roof of this building while his musicians and dancers entertained him.

At Gaitor are marble monuments, cenotaphs, built as memorials to the Maharajas with designs of gods and goddesses, tiger hunts, and so on.

Jaipur Museum and the observatory are owned by the Maharaja. Here there is a nice collection of old clothes and costumes worn by various members of the family for several centuries back. Also displayed are guns, swords, knives, armour, and various instruments of war. Of special interest is a huge *kirpan* or sword used by one of the Maharajas which weighs 12 kilograms.

Maharaja Jai Singh was a mathematician and astronomer and so he designed and built an observatory which we visited. He also assisted in building the observatories at Delhi and Banaras. It was impossible to understand the instruments without someone to explain how they work. We then ran into a problem because there was a strike in the local college so we missed one of the museums.

When we passed a secondary school the students ran out into the street and stopped the bus. They started hitting and pounding on the windows and broke a couple of them but soon scattered out and we went on with no trouble. We got down at a restaurant, but it was closed today because the whole town is observing *hartal*. The word is that they are protesting the visit of a minister. So it was back to the Railway Station by rickshaw for lunch.

We rested up and took the train for Udaipur at half past seven.

It is Friday morning. We get into Udaipur station at half past nine in the morning. We meet another volunteer from India 56 who gave us some advice about the city. We then booked into one of the Railway retiring rooms which are rupees three per night. We freshen up, and start on a tour of the city in late morning. We hire a tonga for the day for eight rupees, and the driver promises to take us to all the important places.

It is very beautiful city, being an oasis in the middle of a dessert of rocks and hills. Coming into the city, one winds through rugged, rocky hills almost completely bare of vegetation. Around the hills, in the flat, there are only small scrubby bushes or a kind of small cactus. The fields are small and generally near a well for irrigation. The population is very sparse and farmers have an almost impossible task of scraping a living off this most barren land.

The city, on the other hand, is an oasis of green towering palms, plush green lawns, and flowering bushes. Large and beautiful trees line the streets which are generally wide and very clean compared to Punjab. The population of the town is only about one lakh, one hundred thousand people, and it is somewhat spread out, so it presents a contrast to the crowded congested cities of fertile Punjab.

The town is surrounded by rugged hills on three sides which present a contrast to the lush surroundings inside the city. The sun bears down relentlessly as one views the barren hills and hazy desert air. One can imagine what kind of hell this desert is in June.

Rajasthani women, wear a full skirt and blouse which comes down below the breasts but the midsection is bare. They are generally poor, but some are very beautiful and loaded down with jewelry. This includes ear rings, nose pins, and bangles, both around the wrists and above the elbows. They also wear silver ornaments on their toes and bangles on their ankles.

The skirts and blouses are very bright and colourful, especially bright yellow and reds.

Our *tongawalla* picks up some clover for his horse in town. We climb a small hill past a lake and then run down to Fateh Sagar lake next to a Maharajah's garden. Atop a hill is a huge statue of a horse and Rajput rider complete with armour, sword, and uniform. Below is a beautiful garden of various kinds of desert vegetation all in bloom. There is a palace at the top of this hill.

Winding on around the edge of the Lake, one passes a small island with a park in memory of Jawaharlal Nehru. One can take a boat out to this park. These lakes are the creation of the Maharaja of Udaipur, Udai Singh, around the Middle of the 16th Century. The *Sahelion-ki-Bari*, or Garden of the Maids consists of a palace surrounded by gardens and fountains. It houses the Udaipur University Library. Carved black stone pillars surround the fountains. It was designed for ladies, who were sent as a peace offering from the Emperor in Delhi.

Nearby, is the Puppet Centre and museum where shows are staged depicting the folklore of Rajasthan. The museum displays the traditional local dress, musical instruments, and jewellery.

After a lunch in the centre of town we go to the bazaar for shopping. There are colourful bangles. We noticed the women selling vegetables, which does not happen in Punjab.

The City Palace of Maharaja Udai Singh is the largest such palace in Rajasthan. It is on the banks of Pichola Lake. In the centre of this lake is Jag Nivas Palace, which is now The Lake Palace Hotel. We toured the palace. There are exquisitely beautiful rooms and courts with intricate inlaid coloured glass. The rooms have mirrors and glass of various colours. The palace has a pool on the roof for the Maharaja and his courtesans. From here, one has a fine view of the entire city.

We cross lake Pichola by boat to the Lake Palace Hotel. The view of the palace, lake and surrounding hills is rather enchanting. We reach the lush green gardens and head back to the Railway Station. The Tongawalla gets a ten rupee note for an unforgettable tour.

It is Saturday and Valentine's Day. At half past nine in the morning, our train is off for Ahmadabad which gets us there by half past ten in the evening. It is a fabulously scenic ride through rocky hills and the dry barren desert land. The hills are covered by fairly large timber but the population is very sparse. The women are colourful in bright-coloured dresses. The guard on the train asks us to come back and talk to him in his compartment. He offers us part of his lunch of delicious sweet carrots with *chapatti*.

There was no food service on the train and not much was available at the small stations along the way. However, women were selling big white radishes and carrots and another vegetable, which I did not know. Around three o'clock we stop at a station where they are selling snacks and tea. We chomp on big white radishes, which the conductor gives us. At Ahmadabad, we get a retiring room at the vast railway station and make a dinner of snacks.

Our time is short on Sunday, as our train will leave in after noon. After a quick breakfast at the station, we take an auto rickshaw to Gandhi's Harijan Ashram. Now Harijans live and work here engaged in such activities as making *Khaddi* cloth and doing leather work. There is also a library with some of Gandhi's original letters and the hand-written manuscript of his autobiography and pictures of important events in his life.

We saw the house where Gandhi lived for some twelve years and the museum. It was from here that he started his famous Dandi March to the sea to protest the tax levied on salt by the British Government. He told the people to mine their own salt from the beach and boycott the taxed salt. At the sea shore he picked up some salt thus violating a British law and was arrested. In Gandhi's hut we saw the spinning wheel which he used to spin thread for *Khaddi* cloth. When Gandhi left the *Ashram*, he swore that he would never return until India had gained Independence from foreign rule. It is a useful visit for anyone interested in Indian history.

The huge Jumma Masjid, the Mosque built by Shah Ahmed in 1411, is the largest mosque in India and took 32 years to complete. It has 256 rock pillars and a huge courtyard. Nearby are the tombs of Shah Ahmad and the next four rulers.

We get back to the station and leave Ahmadabad at half, just past noon, for Surat arriving at 11 in the evening. Then we board the train for Jalgoan, spending the night on the train.

We make Jalgoan station at nine o'clock on Monday morning, get breakfast and take an auto rickshaw to the bus station. We head out to the Ajanta Caves, some thirty miles and get there at about two o'clock in the afternoon. Ajanta has some 30 Buddhist caves carved out of solid rock around the side of a horseshoe shaped canyon. The oldest ones date back to about 200 AD, and continue to about 600 AD. The walls are sculptured, with women, other figures, and images of Buddha. At the back side of each cave is a huge figure of Buddha carved out of solid rock.

Some caves have intricate paintings on the walls, pillars, and ceilings. Others have sculptures, literally hundreds of them covering the pillars, walls, and ceilings. Some of these scenes are quite erotic. In one ceiling painting one sees ram fighting and cock fighting, sports of those days.

Some caves were started but never finished. This reveals how the caves were constructed. For example in the unfinished caves only the tops of the pillars have been carved. They were carved from top to bottom.

We had trouble getting a bus to Aurangabad and it was getting late, but finally we pile onto a very crowded one, along with bags of mail, and arrive at half past ten after a long and dusty ride. We are now feeling very tired from the journey.

It is Tuesday and we miss the tour to Ellora Caves because we oversleep. There was no way to get out to the caves and back in time to catch our train, so we stayed at the Railway Station. My tour of the Ellora Caves would have to wait another nineteen years.

A little after seven in the evening we leave Aurangabad and arrive at Maunmad at half past ten the same evening. There is a three hour wait to catch the Amritsar Express to Bombay. On Wednesday the 18th, we arrive at Bombay, Victoria Memorial Station, at about eight o'clock in the morning. Our sleep on the train was not enough, leaving us feeling tired again.

Accommodations at the Railway Station were not possible here so we have breakfast and get a taxi to look for a hotel. The first one is extremely dirty near a very smelly fish market. The days catch had just arrived and there was all the hubbub and confusion of a lively market.

We were accosted by a group of beggars as we stepped out of the taxi. We end up staying at a boarding house for 40 rupees. This was a very nice place on Marine Drive, overlooking Back Bay and the eight lane freeway which runs around the bay. This is the famous scene from so many Hindi films. Across the Bay is Malabar Hill, home for rich merchants and industrialists.

We freshen up and head for a restaurant. We land in a lovely place called Berry's. It has a patio with tropical vegetation along the walkway. It is shady with a cool breeze from the sea. We feel like we are back in civilisation again after being in the boondocks for almost two years. We eat delicious prawns and lobster. This is tremendously refreshing after our normal fare.

We experience a sort of culture shock watching people pass in such westernised dress including attractive young women. We think it is like being back home, although my home had never been in a major city. I think I will never be able to go back to rural Missouri after seeing some of the world. I cannot bestow the benefits of my travels on the locals in my home town. Later we are sobered by the knowledge that just a small section of Bombay is this westernised.

It is a short walk down to the Gateway of India, a huge arch which was built in 1911 for the visit of King George V. This is right on the sea next to the harbour and the huge Taj Mahal Hotel. We visit the Victoria Gardens Museum on the north side of the city. Other parts of the city are more traditional and dirty with small crowded bazaars. When we arrive at the Gardens, we find that the museum is closed "temporarily to the public." I was never too hot on museums anyway, so it is not a big loss for me. We go to the zoo instead, but it is not much of a zoo, and head for Malabar Hill. We take a taxi to the Hanging Gardens. One passes through the old part of the city with big black horse carriages, which have a touch of class, very much unlike the Punjab.

The Hanging Gardens are at the very crest of Malabar Hill and the road winds around to the top. The streets are lined with tall palms and other lush tropical vegetation. One has a fine view of Back Bay and Marine Drive.

From the Hanging Gardens one also has a nice view of the Sea and can enjoy the cool breeze. There are beds of small flowers and the hedges have been trained to grow in the shapes of bullocks, deer, antelope, kangaroos and other animals. Nearby Kamla Nehru Park has a nice water fountain and flower gardens. The parks are crowded with strollers.

The evening rush has started on Marine Drive when we taxi back to the hotel. Is this a Los Angeles freeway? Not so different, actually. More of the joys of urban development.

For dinner we go to a place called the Volga. Young kids hang out here, apparently from well-off families. This is the real city life. The food is excellent. There is a juke box with all English music. I had not heard most of the songs, perhaps the latest pop, but the place turns me off with its artificial atmosphere. The kids seem to be put-ons trying too hard to be westernised. And so we see what is going on, eat, and move on.

Thursday, we catch the Secunderabad Express for Poona, arriving at five o'clock but we have to wait until eight in the evening for the Vasco da Gamma Express, for Goa. We sleep on the train. The next day, we pass through the Western Ghats, a scenic journey through many tunnels with valleys below. The land is very dry and barren with hardly any crops in this season.

Most of our Friday is spent on the train. We make Londe Junction at eleven in the morning and then head west towards Goa. On the Western side of the Ghats, the yearly rainfall is nearly 200 inches per year, so it is dense tropical jungle here. We pass the Dada Sagar Falls where the water falls almost straight down eight hundred feet. At the border, liquor is being sold through the windows of the train since Maharashtra was a dry state at this time.

We arrive at Vasco da Gamma at four o'clock in the afternoon and check into the Zauri Hotel, within walking distance of the railway station. After freshening up, we look for dinner. The beef for sale in the meat shops catches our attention. We find a restaurant and have roast beef for rupees one and a half a plate. The beer at the hotel costs only three and a half rupees a bottle, very cheap. This is about half of what one pays in Punjab.

The weekend has come. On Saturday, we check out of the hotel and head for Calangute Beach. This is not a very long distance but requires crossing two rivers, so one has to take three bus rides and two ferry boats to reach Calangute from Vasco da Gamma. The trip takes almost four hours and we arrive at half past two in the afternoon. We check into the Tourist Resort and then head for the beach in our swimming trunks. We see a lot of hippies around but not many on the beach. After dinner we go to a boogaloo where all the hippies sit around outside listening to music and smoking pot. This is the little tropical paradise they have found as a retreat from Western civilisation in the sixties. At some point, they will get tired of it and leave and get a job back home. But meanwhile, it is great for a youth adventure on the other side of the world.

Sunday we sleep late. After eating breakfast we have to do laundry as there is no *dhobi*. At least, we did not know how to find one. This takes up the morning and we hang our things out to dry in the breeze from the ocean. Mid-afternoon, we have a beer and go to the beach. This is the time when Indians come down to the sea with their kids and walk on the beach fully dressed. If any hippies are there the Indians stare at the hippies out sunbathing and tend to run them off the beach. We do nothing in the evening. Actually we are beginning to conclude that this is a very dull place in some ways. It is a good place for a hippie retreat and they are doing their own thing.

Monday morning and we go to the beach for sun. Today it is a rough sea with big waves coming in. By noon I am getting a pretty good sunburn on my pale skin. Some Indians come along and look, but go their own way. They are somehow more interested in seeing the girls in their bathing suits.

About two o'clock a large group of Indians, maybe more than a hundred in white shirts and ties come down to the beach. There were about a dozen westerners on the beach including some girls at the time. The Indian guys come running down and gather around a girl who is lying on the beach and begin to take pictures of her as close as possible. The hippie guys then became angry and began to throw sand at the Indians with the cameras. It is really a disgusting situation. The Indians walk on down the beach taking pictures of everyone sunbathing and eventually almost all the Westerners leave. There were also two catholic fathers who accompanied the group, so it seemed to be a little bit of organised harassment. There is the feeling among some that the hippies are bringing moral pollution to Catholic Goa.

Indians in a poor country like this find it difficult to understand why the hippies would come here and live like they do and the hippies cannot stand to live the way the Indians live, with their Catholic puritanical morality. It is unfortunate situation.

Late in the evening, a group of Catholics come and have a meeting besides a little cement cross built on the beach. They sing religious songs and shoot fire crackers. Perhaps they believe the hippies are desecrating the beach and practicing immorality.

This could really be a fun place in the tropical setting, I think, except for the conflict between the hippies and the religious fanatics with their medieval Catholicism. The conflict seems to ruin the atmosphere. Maybe the Goans feel they feel like they are being invaded. But then, they forget that they were ruled for centuries by Portugal and converted to Catholicism.

When Westerners go down to the beach they tend to attract a mob. People stare and take pictures, particularly of the women. Sometimes they are run off the beach because they cannot stand this behaviour. The Indians stare at the Westerners like they were animals. I start to get completely fed up with the situation here. I would have never known about this situation if I had not seen it with my own eyes.

Having had enough of the situation at Calangute Beach, the next day we move down to Panjim for a night, which is across the Mandani River from Calangute. We take a bus from Calangute to Betum where there is a ferry to Panjim. There is a new Tourist Hostel here where we have lunch. The dining hall overlooks the Mandauri River with cool sea breezes.

Walking around town, we sense that people are not so hostile to Westerners here but they still stare thinking that one is a hippie. We are not hippies but their reputation rubs off on us. The town is very quiet as people take an afternoon siesta. We drink beer followed by dinner and a film, *"Captain Richter,"* which is a genuine waste of time. We are getting bored with Goa and I will be glad to leave.

On Wednesday, February, 25, it is back to Vasco da Gamma, which requires a bus ride from Panjim to Agacaim, a ferry ride across the Zauri River from Agacaim to Cartelim, then a bus ride from Cartelim to Vasco da Gamma. Late afternoon, we arrive and search for a hotel. We try the Indira Lodge. A guy who is drunken shows us a room and we are about to stay until we are informed that there will be no water until the next evening. Another hotel is full due to a football match today. So it's the Zauri again for the night.

"The city of Mysore, with its wide shaded avenues, its fine modern public buildings, its parks and gardens, and its floods of electric lights, is a model town, clean and bright."

—Katherine Mayo, 1927

Our train leaves Goa on Thursday morning for Londe Junction. There is then a four hour wait in the afternoon for the train to Arsikere. It is nice to be back on the road and moving again. It is better to travel than to arrive.

We make Arsikere at about five o'clock on Friday morning, where we have to wait in a small, weary, station, until seven for the train to Mysore city. We arrive at two o'clock in the afternoon and get rooms in the railway station for a needed rest. Dinner is also at the railway station. This old bungalow is the epitome of the British Raj right down to the *Mucher Dani*, the mosquito nets, over the beds. The railway station and the rooms with second story verandah are built very much in the British colonial style and one can get a picture of life in British India from these surroundings. We sit on the verandah waiting for a waiter to bring tea. This is my 25th birthday.

It is Saturday and we have tickets for a tour of Mysore City, which we bought at the railway station for eight rupees each. There are no Government tours here but private agencies carry them out. The name is "Rathna Travels."

The tour takes off from the City Art Gallery which is the first visit. It is inside the Jaganmohan Palace. There are many paintings and antiques from the days of the Maharajas. The Government Silk Factory is next. We watch the looms weaving the cloth. Most of the machines are quite modern and imported from Japan.

The tour is too big with some 55 people on the bus and it is getting quite hot already. We see the Maharaja's Palace built in 1897 but it is not open to the public. It is lit up during the Dussehra Festival with thousands of coloured lights. This palace is a synthesis of Hindu and Moslem styles.

At the City Zoological Gardens we take pictures of the unfortunate incarcerated animals. I am starting to have a loathing for zoos. We head for Lalita Mahal, a palace just outside the city on the road to Chamundi Hill. The huge marble staircase is not bad, but anyway, the building has a lift so it's just for show. It beats the hell out of my humble abode. We proles are only to stare and drool, and so it serves its noble purpose.

Chamundi Hill, named after the Royal Family's Patron Goddess, is the site of Sri Chamundeswari Temple, which is 2000 years old. There are only seven layers of carvings of Hindu gods which was disappointing. I was expecting eight, but I guess it was the best they could do. The top layer of carvings is only 300 years. The feudal political and social structure is underpinned by these religious institutions. They justify and gloss over the most appalling poverty and inequality in the face of such splendour and wealth of a decadent ruling class. My thoughts are running towards cynicism.

Another palace on the Hill is the private residence of the Maharaja. Outside the temple hawkers sell flowers and coconuts for a sacrifice or offering to the gods and goddesses doing a brisk business helping themselves if not the gods. First things first.

Just near this temple is the statue of the Monster Mahisasura, who was supposedly killed by the Goddess Chamundi to bring peace to the country. Killing for peace is the ticket. There must be some political symbolism here.

And the huge *Nandi Bull* carved out of solid rock is here. Back in the bus, we start down the Hill, which is quite frightening and dangerous with the driver who never uses either a low gear or his brakes. I feared that the bus was going to get away from him on the steep hill. In the event, the downhill run rendered the bus out of service and we had to switch to an older bus for the afternoon.

Mercifully, there are a couple of hours to rest up for lunch. The tour guides arrive almost an hour late and argue for another half hour over what, I don't know. The tour resumes around four in the afternoon.

This part of the tour is outside the city and the driver, anxious to make up some lost time, drives so recklessly that some luggage comes off the top of the bus. This causes a further delay, because the conductor has to get down and run back down the road in search of the fallen bags. Well, at least we were having an adventure. One can't argue against that. I would like to say "only in India" but I suspect there are other places too where it could happen. Several sites out in the countryside were a blur and I do not have a clue about them, but they were probably not very important.

While visiting one of the sites, I ask the bus conductor and driver why they are driving so fast and endangering the lives of the tourists. I said we have come here to enjoy the trip and it is clearly not enjoyable when our lives are endangered. I tell them that the safety of the tourists is more important than seeing everything scheduled on the tour. This has some effect. After that, the driving went a little more sensibly. The poor guys are probably just trying to do the tour and keep their jobs.

We go to Krishnarajnagar Dam and the nearby Brindavan Gardens some twelve miles from the city. The gardens are beautiful. However, I am not a big fan of dams. This dam was built for irrigation purposes at the confluence of three rivers, a quarter mile long and forms a fifty square mile lake. It is constructed entirely in stone without any cement according to the official information.

Brindavan Gardens are colourful with many kinds of flowers lining the walks, many fountains, pools and cascading water.

It seems that there is a proclivity to construct such show places of fascination for the masses instead of crafting progressive public policies to use public revenues for more practical purposes. Perhaps this serves to give the masses a sort of religious awe of the rulers but does not address their genuine needs. It serves, in fact, as another instrument of oppression, socially and politically, it seems to me.

The many coloured lights in the fountains were turned on in the Garden at half past seven. Very romantic, if there had been the opportunity. Not a chance in hell.

At the upper end of these gardens is a quite pricy hotel. It takes money to really enjoy. We arrive back in Mysore city. The tour has been grueling and we are extremely tired, but have some things to reflect upon.

It may be that our tour guides were under threat if they did not cover the entire itinerary after the bus screw-up. It was unbelievable that the cost of the tour was only about one US dollar. I cannot understand how they can even cover the cost of running the bus and paying these guys.

On Sunday, the first of March we have a glorious late sleep. Breakfast is at the railway station, which I always enjoyed in India. Governments, including the government of India, do not do everything badly, and they do many things quite well. This would be news to political ideologues in America, but it is even true there if they would admit the truth. Moreover, the private sector sometimes does things very badly at a considerable cost.

We have to leave the Railway Rest house at noon and look for a hotel, having exhausted our two nights limit in state-subsidised quarters. With the help of a *tonga-walla*, we find the Modern Hindu Hotel, a nice clean place with vegetarian meals. Shopping in the afternoon for some wood inlay panels, sandalwood body powder, and silver jewelry, we pick up some big carved wooden statues which are too big to carry and we have them shipped to Punjab. The Chamarajendra Technical Institute has a good arts and crafts emporium.

The next day, we go to an exhibition building and see paintings for sale, but they are out of our price range. Our heavy shopping was at the arts and crafts emporium for some big carved wooden elephants and laughing Buddhas.

At half past ten in the evening, our train leaves for Bangalore and we arrive at half past five in the morning. We freshen up at the station and check our baggage. An auto rickshaw takes us to the State Museum where there are many Hindu and Buddhist sculptures dating back about 2000 years. Next to this building is Sri Visveswaraiya's Industrial and Technological museum to show one what engines are made of and how they work. Ambitious exhibits of Physics, including optics, very good and enjoyable if one likes science, I guess. Here one is welcome to bore one's self to their heart's content.

The Kwality Restaurant comes to our rescue for lunch. We check the State Arts and Crafts Emporium but have already done enough damage when it comes to shopping back in Mysore.

Then, it is John Wayne in the afternoon. "*True Grit*" at the Cinema House. Heaven save us! These sorts of films are very useful in reminding one of the blessings of not being back in Western civilisation. Other than that, I have no idea why one should be tortured by them. As far as the grit is concerned, one does truly need some "grit" to endure them.

"The beaches of Madras are wide, and the waves roll in in a stately fashion." **—John Kenneth Galbraith**

We catch the train for Madras City at half past nine in the evening and arrive at the Central Station at about half past five, in the morning. We are fortunate to get a retiring room here and so have breakfast and freshen up. We get tickets from the Indian Airlines Office for the flight to Delhi, on Friday evening.

It is Kwality Restaurant again for lunch. The museum and art gallery take up our time. Of interest, were Hindu and Bronze sculptures dating back to the Second Century AD. Also stone works of Hindu, Buddhist, and Jain religions are there.

On Thursday, we move to Gupta's Estates Hotel. A rickshaw gets us to Fort St. George. Here we go through the Museum seeing relics from the days of the British Raj. St. Mary's Church is inside Fort. St. George. The Aquarium on the beach road has a variety of sea fishes, sea snakes and Turtles. Again, a fine way to bore one's self, if other opportunities are lacking.

We shift our luggage to the Indian airlines office for the Friday evening flight. We spend the afternoon looking at handicrafts in the Government Arts Emporium and the Victoria Technical Institute all on Mount Road. They have some very nice paintings and carvings but they are quite pricy.

Dinner is again at the Kwality Restaurant with a rather sad band. Then we are off to the airport for the flight to Delhi. Our plane, an old propeller job, takes off from Madras at half past ten, but then we have to land at Hyderabad because of bad weather at Nagpur, the scheduled stop. After a considerable wait, they fly us back to Madras and give us a hotel room at half past four in the morning. We are back where we started.

We have a glorious late sleep on Saturday morning, after the hectic night flights in the old rough birds. After lunch, the airlines bus takes us to the airport for the flight to Delhi by the small French Caravelle jet. This is a much better deal. Three hours later, we land in Delhi and check into the Lodhi hotel. It is nice to be back in Delhi.

We have a Sunday to relax. On Monday, we will take the Amritsar Deluxe to Punjab. We have lunch at the Rambler Restaurant in Connaught Place and see a film *"Hard Contract."* More boredom. Our learning curve is not very steep.

At half past eleven, we board the Amritsar Deluxe for Ludhiana. A pleasant ride up, arriving at around five o'clock in the afternoon. We check into the Embassy Hotel. The contrast after being in the south is striking. Ludhiana is definitely the dirtiest place we've seen on the whole trip and the stench is almost unbearable upon first arriving. Coming into the city, both sides of the track right of way are literally covered with feces and there are various coloured stagnant pools of putrid water. Pea-green and pink-red liquid stands along the track breeding mosquitoes and various another vermin. There are many wastes from industries. Paper and trash litter every place and the air is filled with coal dust from factories. Today it is cloudy and the air is filled with moisture adding to the dinginess of the place.

Upon arriving at the station we are hit by a mob of beggars and hungry rickshaw-wallas who want to take us to the hotel. We literally had to fight them off because they forcefully try to take one's baggage out of one's hands. It is hard enough to struggle and carry one's things without this.

Then two rickshaw-wallas got into an argument over who was going to take us to the hotel. They decided among themselves to each take one of us and get two fares out of us. But we insisted and took one rickshaw. What a hassle. It seems that it is easier to get killed in a rickshaw in Ludhiana than any other place in India.

On the tenth of March, I am back to my house about noon after taking a rickshaw from Banga. Bob took another bus to his place. Today it is cloudy and raining at times. Then, I got my mail from the Post Office. I also got a "care package" from the Princeton Church of toffees and raisins for Christmas. So that was a small treat.

I spend the rest of the day reading my mail. Home, sweet home.

33

Kissan Mela

"What if the sky pants and trembles with the heat of the midday sun..."

—Rabindranath Tagore

The heat of March has arrived and our long trip is over. I catch up on writing letters, get a haircut in Banga, and talk to the Agricultural officers. Everything rolls along as usual, since I have been gone. I get Lakshmi's letter. I have written to her a few times on the trip and I want to get together with her soon.

Friday March 13, 1970. It is Friday the 13th again. I go with Avtar Singh to the sports tournament in Aur and see Fritz Bachman.

The next day, Sunday, I meet Lakshmi's friend Sudarshan. He says that I can meet Lakshmi at their house in Sotran village in the next week. We go to see the film at Banga, "*The Prince*," but it is so hot inside the tent where the film is being shown that we have to leave at half time. The theater is being rebuilt and the building is closed down.

In the village, I look for Lakshmi, but girls are usually not seen on the street on Sunday. So I will wait till Wednesday at Sudarshan's house. I am very worried about my decision and my judgement but I think I love her and forge ahead.

I shop for vegetables and vitamins. I wonder if they are more than a placebo from the Indian chemist's shops. In the afternoon, Prem Kumar comes. We go to the High School where they are giving matriculation examinations. There are a lot of "helpers" there who have come to "help" the students pass. They devise ways to slip answers in to them, which is said to be part of the system. Sometime the monitors are part of this system for some consideration.

Now I feel that I am getting totally disillusioned with this job and losing my motivation. I just don't care anymore. Perhaps it is because the time is so short. I will pursue my interests here in the best way possible for the duration of my stay. But I feel I need more activities. I have been too inactive since returning from the trip. It is difficult in the heat, even for a young man.

On Wednesday, I meet Sudarshan's brother in Banga and we go to their house in Sotram, very close to Banga. Lakshmi comes with her friend, Ranjit Kaur and we meet in a private room with wooden doors that have a latch.

It is nice to meet her again and I am clearly in love or lust or something along those lines. We lie together and kiss and pet but that is all. I tell her that I want to marry her and we stay till nearly dark. Am I a fool? Of course, all men are, but what kind of fool, I really do not know.

On the nineteenth of March, I leave for Phillaur and reach Staff's place about eleven in the morning. Most of the guys in our group are already there. They are playing tapes of popular American songs most of which I have not heard before and really do not have much interest in hearing. I guess, I have probably become too much Indianised. Is it a little bit of reverse culture shock?

I meet a guy named "Chip" from Williams College, who is here with some other students travelling in India for one semester credit for their B.A. Degree. He is a nice young guy who is learning a few things about India and will stay with Fritz for a couple of weeks. Still wet behind the ears. Poor guy. Can he make it out in these Punjabi boondocks?

We have lunch at the local *dhaba* and then head down to Ludhiana to set up the tent for our soybean booth at the *Kissan Mela* or farmers fair. The next day is the first day of the Mela, which is being held at Punjab Agricultural University (PAU). We load everything into a truck for the demonstration. I take the bus along with some others. Along with some bottles of Golden Eagle beer.

There are three parts to our booth. In one big part we are showing an eighteen minute film in Punjabi on the cultivation and uses of soybeans. There is quite a lot of interest. In another section, we distribute information and literature on the crop. In the third section, we are making and selling foods made of soybeans, such as *dal, puris, ladu,* and *pakoras*.

It is difficult just keeping the people out of the movie house once it is filled up, until the next showing. It takes two or three people to control and regulate the film traffic. Finally, we get people to form up in a line. This works pretty well, because just about enough people form up while the show is running to fill up the tent for the next showing. In the two days we figured about 4000 people saw the film.

The India 91 Dairy wallas have their booth just next to ours and the Punjab Dairy Corporation is selling cold milk here so we keep ourselves refreshed on that. I love the sweet drink called milk badam and steal a chance to get a bottle of it quite often.

On the second and last day of the *Mela*, we sell all the food we make as well as all the soybean *ata* or flour that we have.We were really tired after two days of it.

After the fair we head back up the GT Road and have dinner at the Phillaur *dhaba* and then head over to the Beer Bar for some relaxation. While at the *dhaba* we see a really bloody fight, two men on one. One guy is beating another with a long club. The victim got away but then the other guys got an ice pick and went after him on a motorcycle. I don't know what happened after that.

It was on November 3, 1969 that the President of the United States, Richard Nixon was speaking.

"And so tonight-to you, the great silent majority of my fellow Americans-I ask for your support."

Our group is at the beer bar, which was just next to the GT Road. There is a big sign there that one could see as one rode up the GT Road on a bus, "Beer Bar." There are big cold bottles of Golden Eagle beer, 650 ml bottles. They were great in the hot Punjab and we enjoyed them immensely. Unfortunately, alcoholism has become a serious problem in recent years in Punjab, with so much poverty and unemployment. But in those days, it was very nice to enjoy a cold beer and I did not want to live in a dry state, some of which did exist in India. In that sense, I was thankful that I was in Punjab. Those days, the beer was Golden Eagle. After some years, a number of brands appeared.

The discussion turned to the war and American politics. I had ideas as strong as anyone on these issues, but perhaps was not very articulate on them at the time. At least, my nature, still at the time was quiet. I guess I was one of the rather quiet volunteers, along with Bob Baker, the volunteer who I usually got together and travelledwith. We were not very vocal in giving our opinion on things, even though we had them. In terms of loudness and making his strong opinions stick, I have to hand it to Chris Klose, who was from Detroit. Yes, we mid-westerners were rather the quiet bunch. That is how some others started poking fun at us and labelling us "the silent majority." I resented, because it totally misrepresented my views. I was probably more radical than them, but did not articulate my views very fully in those days. The term "silent majority" was the label being used by Nixon for all the rural and middle class Americans who he claimed supported his policies in Vietnam but did not get out in the street and protest like the radical students. It was, of course, phony, and probably most Americans that he referred to did not really support his policies and wanted to end the war by that time. It showed Nixon's values and of Republicans in general in the sense of democratic values. They looked down on those who practiced democracy by exercising their democratic freedoms of speech. The silent majority was a myth. There was no indication that the majority of Americans supported Nixon's policies. I greatly enjoyed the beer there.

The next day, we sleep rather late and have breakfast at Staff's. I head for Banga. At Kartar Singh's sweet shop, I meet Sudarshan and have *samosas* and tea.

At Sikh National College the annual function is being held in the afternoon. Degrees and prizes are being awarded to students. I am invited and it is a nice function. Afterwards, there is tea and sweets and I again meet Usha Sharma, who I had met at the picnic on the Sutlej. I also meet several farmers who I know from the local villages. I arrive back in Mahil Gaila by tonga.

Gulzar Singh, the carpenter, has asked me to go to the Hola Fair at Anandpur Sahib, a Sikh shrine, the next day, but I cancel the programme because I am so tired from the *Kissan Mela*. Prem Kumar came and studied for his exams at my place. It is a Government holiday.

My wood carvings arrive which I shipped from Mysore. I will pack them in my trunk for shipment to the US.

I have planned a meeting with Bob at Jalandhar with Lakshmi and Lakhbir. This is something exciting and somewhat daring.

Back in the village, I sometimes listened to Radio Peking. In those days, the Chinese were still interested in teaching people how to do guerrilla warfare. Now it is a different world, where they make computers. In fact, in the late sixties, the Indian Government was very worried about the increase of Naxalites, the brand of Maoist Communists who were trying to stir up revolution and would sometimes burn down the houses of rich peasants. But this was generally happening in West Bengal or the southern states.

Some of the students around the village had obtained the small journal "*Liberation*" which was brought clandestinely from Calcutta. They would pass it around among themselves. They loaned me some copies to read and told me not to show it to anybody. It was associated with the Maoist aligned Communist Party, the Communist Party of India, Marxist-Leninist.

34

New York Restaurant

"Drunkenness is better far than soberness,

For it keeps you ever in sanity.

—Bhia Vir Singh

One day in March 1970, I conceived another mischievous scheme. Why not meet Lakshmi in Jalandhar for a lunch in a rather clandestine place. I guess I was willing to take a little more risk, partly because the time was growing shorter. It was now only a few months until the end of the two years of Peace Corps service. Anyway, I had already shot my reputation to hell. There were other options as well. In a restrictive society, there are ways to get around the social barriers when the drives are strong in youth. A possibility was to meet in another village at Lakhbir's house. Her village was small and remote near Hoshiapur, called Chakwal, and we could make a programme to meet there in future.

But for the time being, everything was on hold and I concentrated on my soybean project and visiting farmers. Bringing them literature and providing them seed. I wanted things to cool down and be forgotten. However, the time was short and we had already let the deal go down, so to speak, as Hank Williams used to say, and I was not ready to take a chance. And this time I would take a bolder step by involving my fellow Volunteer, Bob, in the quite risqué plans.

So I worked on a programme to meet for a lunch in Jalandhar. It was a rather daring venue, actually a sort of cabaret or club that had belly dancers and where big bellied sedougies came in and drank whiskey over lunch. This was the New York Restaurant on the G.T. Road. Perhaps the restrictive Punjabi society had really pushed me into becoming a full-fledged *badmash* and going with this crowd. I started to feel that way, even though the things that we were doing were so terribly innocent. Lakshmi would come with her friend Lakhbir. I would arrive from Banga and meet Bob at the bus station in Jalandhar. But first I had to make a trip to Bob's village, Budapind, near Goraya, to make the arrangements. Bob was skeptical, but perhaps by that time thought that the adventure could be launched without too much of a risk. He seemed to be interested, and was willing, in spite of the fact that his mother had sternly warned him about mixing up with Indian women. Under no circumstances was he to bring one of those Indian women back to America. That was a proposition up with which she could not put. If it had been my mother, I would have just laughed and told her to bug off. There are certain times in life when one just has to revolt, regardless of the outcome.

March 25, 1970 and I arrive at the Jalandhar bus station about ten o'clock in the morning. I had made an early start. Bob was already there waiting for me. But the girls had trouble getting a bus from Banga and we had to wait for them until around one o'clock. When they came, we took separate rickshaws, Bob and myself in one and the girls in the other and went to the New York Restaurant on the G.T. Road. They were in the lead and we were in the chase, like young roosters. There was already blazing heat in the mid-day inferno.

The New York Restaurant cabaret was very much out of mainstream society, largely a stag joint. Such places are not frequented by the average Punjabi. The restaurant had a small balcony overlooking the tables below. There was only one table in this small loft. We were able to get that table, which would be somewhat more private and discreet. Of course, we were the only two couples there. The place was mostly set up to cater to stag parties. Hard drinking Sikhs, generally.

I thought it was delightful. A little strange, but lovely if one could get by with such socially subversive activities in the sexually repressive Punjabi society. India is a very conservative society, socially. Punjab was largely a peasant society.

Down below our perch, a couple of sadougies were drinking pegs of whiskey and flirting around with one of the belly dancers, laughing and cracking jokes. They would certainly not have approved of our party with young Punjabi girls.

We ordered up some bottles of cold Golden Eagle beer for me and Bob. We were having a good time. I sat next to Lakshmi and Bob was with Lakhbir on the other side of the table. I thought they were not hitting if off very well together, but it was their first meeting, and last, as far as I know. But he was game. It seemed that they could not get a conversation going. At the time, I did not realise that Bob's mother had clasped a male virginity belt on him for his time in India, as if she had needed to. Perhaps, he did not think it was worth the try. But I didn't see what there was to lose. If he got something going with her, then he could always break it off later on. Nothing would be lost. And I never figured that my friend would remain a life-long bachelor. Perhaps he valued his freedom too much.

We ordered food and had a nice lunch of delicious Punjabi food. There was a band and the cabaret dance started down below with belly dancing. It was a rare chance for the young Punjabi girls. We very much enjoyed the beer and food.

After the meal, Lakshmi began to cry and then we headed back out into the blazing heat, got a rickshaw and arrived back at the bus station. I insisted that we return to Banga on separate buses. That would have certainly been more discrete. However, Lakshmi wanted to go on the same bus with me, although we did not sit together. I was afraid of trouble. However, nothing came of our little outing together and Jalandhar was a big enough city to be largely anonymous. If the BDO had somehow walked into the place, either I would have been in a world of shit, or we would have become the best of drinking buddies and things would have picked up for the better. But he struck me as being a quite socially conservative Hindu bureaucrat. There was no chance of that.

It would be the last of such a programme that we managed to pull off. I was about ready to hang up the Peace Corps gig, anyway, at that point. So I didn't mind living a little dangerously.

There had been a suggestion from the BDO that I move from the village to Banga some weeks before, but I did not take it very seriously. I thought if they could find me a decent place, better than mine, then fine, but I did not think it was going to happen. So I just told him that I was ready to move as soon as they had a suitable place for me. But nothing ever happened. They knew I was going to be leaving in a few months anyway and probably just decided to wait it out. Also I had put a lot of hard work and expence into making my place livable. But I was ready to leave if the villagers demanded it. In this case, the Indian bureaucratic lethargy was working in my favour, and I was pretty sure nothing was going to happen.

I am not sure why some people wanted me to move. It might have just been that I was taking up room needed to store seed and fertiliser for the cooperative. Or maybe they thought I was corrupting the village youth. They didn't know that it was actually the other way around. I had been raised in such a puritanical setting that socially conservative India had nothing on me. Now the wild ways of the Punjabi youth were rubbing off on me.

In The heat:

> "Even after living in the country for thousands of years the Hindus have not got used to the heat."
>
> **—Nirad C. Chaudhuri**

The heat had become unbearable by the end of March. Two more months of this hellish heat and I would be getting out of India. The next day after the New York Restaurant cabaret, I decide to go to Jalandhar and talk to a travel agent about getting a passport for Lakshmi. Hari Singh and Sons Travel Agency was a big company and a good place to get information. An agent there told me that it would probably take only about five or six weeks to get her a passport. But I would have to check with the American Embassy concerning the visa. That would certainly involve a commitment to marriage.

On the way back to the village, I see Lakshmi on the street in Banga just from a distance and write her a love letter when I get to my place.

I return to Kariha the next day to visit Jatinder Singh. He is not there, but I talk to his father, Hardev Singh. He is sitting in the courtyard under the big trees and talking with some of his political cronies. Gurnam Singh, the Chief Minister of Punjab had just been ousted from office two days before on March, 25th and this is the hot topic of conversation around the state.

Hardev Singh invites me to have lunch, *dal* and *curd* and *chapati*. The rich eat like the poor. It is good food, but none too fancy. I am thankful. The curds sooth one's stomach in the searing heat. The spices get rid of the bacteria, or so it is said. On the way back to Mahil Gaila, I meet Jatinder on the road, driving his Hindustan Ambassador. I promise to return the next week and spend the night at the big house. Back in the village, I receive a lovely letter from Lakshmi.

Monday, March 30, 1970, and I ride my bike down to visit my old friend Kishin Singh at Khatkar Kalan. His place is relatively cool, sheltered by large Eucalyptus trees. I see that he is reading "*Ambassador's Journal*" by John Kenneth Galbraith. I want to read it as soon as possible also, but this will have to wait until I am back in the US. He also has some Time-Life series coffee table books, one on Michelangelo which is very nice. Also a nice picture book on the Kennedys. He is a quite well-off farmer making good money.

He tells me he will take in about sixty thousand rupees this year from his land of 34 acres, growing wheat, bajra, and potatoes. He is aiming for seventy thousand next year, clean profit, or one hundred thousand total sales. This year the profit was 45 thousand rupees out of sixty thousand rupees income. Not bad. Some farmers are clearly doing OK in the Green Revolution. Perhaps green in Rupees, if not dollars. A man after my own heart, he always breaks out some cold beer and we have lunch.

I get another letter from Lakshmi. She loves me. She really does. I know she is not just out to milk me for a passage to America. Am I a fool? Maybe, but no one could convince me. That dread disease called love. Only age can cure the perennial virus.

Another letter comes from Bob concerning the programme in Jalandhar last week. He sounds as if he is interested in Lakhbir, in spite of his mother. But the prospects of a get together are practically nil.

Now April has come and I reflect that it is exactly two years since we arrived in Hemet, California, for Peace Corps training. I have faithfully stuck with it for a period of two years. I was sweating the draft then and now the draft board is still breathing down my neck. That is life. I am not clear of that danger yet. Eternal vigilance is the price of freedom.

I decide to go to the Superintendent of Police in Jalandhar, on the 7th and get a visa extension. I am all mixed up. The "love sick blues" are taking their toll. There were no girl's heart strings holding me in America when I bolted from that country, but now I am being pulled in by Punjab, by lovely Lakshmi. Punjab has sunk into my bones. I am pussy whipped. No cure for this filthy disease, not soon, anyway. I meet up with my fellow India 53 Volunteer, Al-Barone, who has also come to get his visa extended. But somehow I suspect it is not about a girl.

Al, a good friend. I remembered our main escapade together, that great trip to Nainital where we drank a lot of beer, ate boiled chestnuts and raised hell on the road back to the hotel above the lake, singing *Chantilly Lace* like drunken fools. Although, I don't know it at the time, Al's kismet is to return to Ohio and become a preacher. He was much better than me at the language, but I was always a little embarrassed by his silly and childish antics in speaking with Punjabis. One has to be a little childish to practice a new language, and I was always a little too contemplative. There is no way one can express deep thoughts in a new language. Just trivial shit. He fell in love with a girl in the registration line for divinity school in Ohio and married her. Being silly can get one into trouble. No shit.

The next day I see a looming crisis on the horizon. I make a quick trip to Barapind to see Bob and do something about it. Lakhbir and Lakshmi have made a programme to invite Bob come to Sotran village near Banga where he can meet Lakhbir. I think that this is not a good idea and warn Bob that he shouldn't come. I am being cautious. I am in enough trouble already. If another American shows up chasing the local girls, I might be run through with a *Kirpan* this time. Maybe Bob would like to meet Lakhbir again, but I didn't think it was a good idea for it to happen on my venue in Banga Block. He should try Ludhiana down his way.

The thirteenth of April is Baisakhi, the harvest festival. I go to Banga and have a beer. Although there is no beer bar there one could drink sitting near the shop. It was just a local wine and beer shop. Then I go to Thandian Village to see Tajinder Singh. I have dinner there and spend the night. I like talking to Mahan Singh, the retired military officer. He likes to shoot the shit about America and politics. We can have some fun with it. Just as well, when one cannot improve matters anyway.

I donate my old American magazines to Baldev Singh Bedi in Banga and take a trip to Bhaura village to meet the young farmer, Charanjit Singh Bal. I take some soil samples for Sadhu Singh, meeting him for the first time. Charanjit Singh invites me to have lunch and then I see Sham Singh, the hairy caterpillar guy. I go over to the other side of the village and visit Swaran Singh, the

Sarpanch in the afternoon. I ask him for some of the soybeans he raised on his plot, so that I can make them into soy flour. The next day I take them. I will give it a try. My cook and his wife and son, Raju, arrive back from Ferozepur in the evening.

At Newanshahr on Monday April 20, I cash my last cheques and close my account. I am finished with the bank. One rupee gets me a cheap lunch at the *dhaba* while the puncture in my cycle tire is being fixed. The heat starts to burn while riding a bike. Prickly heat is breaking out on my back. It is simply too hot to be out in the heat of the day. Back in the village, I get mail from America.

The next day, Mussie, my cook is off again with his family to Ambala for a wedding. He needs money so I give him some extra. I go into Banga and take some soil samples to the BDO office. Then I have my picture taken for passport photos. I may need them if I need to extend my visa. The heat is starting to take its toll and an afternoon siesta is becoming necessary. One simply cannot stay awake. If one lays down for rest there is no staying awake. I wilt down and sack out for part of the afternoon. Then I have coffee to revive myself and cook eggs and potatoes. I eat them with tomatoes and finish off with ripe mangoes.

Jagbadal Singh, the young communist comes, and we have a good discussion about politics, poverty, India. He understands the situation and teaches me a lot. He is clearly the brightest and most promising young man in the village, but his father is being continuously hauled off to jail for being a communist, accused of being a Naxalite. Gulzar Singh, the carpenter, comes along with Ram Moti, another young student at the college. I take a cold bath under the hand pump, and now feel somewhat refreshed after the incredible heat of the day.

The next day, April 22, I get up feeling very tired. The heat is reaching over a hundred degrees every day now and wearing me down. It seems that only two years has taken a toll on me. One has to get tough and wiry like the Indians. I am not made of the right stuff for this country.

I have eggs for breakfast and then go to Sotran village to see Sudarshan. Now he is sort of serving as an agent for Lakshmi, to help her arrange things. At the same time, his mother is liberal and we can meet secretly at their place in the small village. We had arranged a programme for Jalandhar, to meet with Lakshmi, but later decided to cancel it. I get some food at the hotel in Banga, come back to the village and try to read. It was 103 degrees at Chandigarh today. I don't think I could take this heat for another hot season. It takes its toll, even on a young person. This heat, coupled with no cook, makes me weak and I feel like I can hardly survive these village conditions. There are now 39 more days to termination and I'm counting down the days.

Today, I am up fairly early and cook some eggs for breakfast. I ride into Banga, get a tempu to Newanshahr, and then another tempu to Jadla. I walk down to Chris Klose's house and meet his cook. Chris has gone to Jalandhar but I return his coat that I borrowed and get four kilograms of Pusa Basakhi Moong for planting. I eat at a small *dhaba* in Newanshahr. In Banga, I meet Sudarshan and have a coke with him. Then ride my bike home in the grueling heat. I just don't like to be out riding a cycle in this heat in these days. The hot part of the day is for taking rest. That's all.

The carpenter's brother brings me some food for dinner. I am grateful for this kindness when I have no cook here. I don't like to cook anything when it is this hot. It is really too much trouble without a cook in these hot days.

It is Friday. I cook breakfast early and get my photos at Banga. Sudarshan is at Kartar Singh's sweet shop. I buy feed for my chickens and fruit. Back at the village I poison my mind with Time Magazine.

Jasbir Singh comes in the evening for a talk. He is bored here and wants to go abroad. It is a common condition of young males in Punjabi villages. One cannot blame them. Opportunities in the West are brighter in the 60 . It is very hot tonight even here in the room the walls and ceiling have absorbed the heat of the day and are now re-emitting it. It was 109 degrees today at Chandigarh.

I get up fairly early and try to boil an egg, but my stove runs out of fuel. I give it up and ride my cycle into Banga. I catch the bus to Jalandhar. There I meet Frank Rojas and have an Omelet and some coffee in Green's. We take in a film called the "*The Ambushers*" starring Dean Martin. It is a break from the monotony in air conditioned comfort. We get lunch at Moti Mahal Restaurant. Today was another hot one. That is an understatement.

The next day is Saturday, April 26. I boil eggs for breakfast. Prem Kumar comes and we discuss (cuss and discuss) the political and economic situation in India.

I fry potatoes for lunch and the carpenter's son brings me

some food for dinner, but now diarrhoea has set in seriously tonight. My food supply leaves a lot to be desired in this hot weather. I take a cold bath and get to bed, feeling another pain, like a boil, on my rear. I hope that I do not develop another abscess that will need another operation. I am happy to see Mussie and his wife and son arrive just after I get to bed.

On Monday, Mussie cleans up the house. It is almost the end of April, the temperature running around 110 degrees every day. But I lie down and nurse the swelling on my ass, hoping that it will not be serious this time. Today the air is dusty and the horizons are gray-brown. I read in the paper that Punjab, Harayana, and Rajasthan are in the grip of a severe heat wave because of the absence of the "Western Effect." This refers to the wind from the west, which is usual at this time of year. But today we get some of the Western Effect. Tonight there is a breeze and it is somewhat cooler. The relief will be short. May is decidedly a hot month and the heat bears down relentlessly hotter each day up until the unbearable scorching dust-laden stifling days of the hell, called June. Fortunately, I'm not planning to bear the whole of that month here. I hope, to be in more northerly latitude by then.

Tuesday, the 28th, I am suffering from a boil on my rear, so I stay and start reading "*The Guns of August*" by Barbara Tuchman. I don't like to be tied down here but there's nothing else to do until this boil gets sufficiently well that I can move out and ride a cycle. Such a thing is aggravating because it is so small yet it is impossible to do anything till it gets better.

I think, I may have contracted an infection in the food or water last week when my cook was gone to cause this. It is quite common around these villages now, I understand. If I stay here, drink boiled water and eat food here, then there's not so much danger but last week I had a case of diarrhoea at the same time. So that may be how I contracted this infection.

It is 110 degrees today. Mussie's wife left today with their son Raju. I advance them some pay for May. Their expences have been heavy with the wedding. I would give them more if I could.

The last day of the month, April 30, and I am still plagued with the boil on my rear but will wait a while longer before going to the hospital to see if it will break open and clear up. Today I have an unfortunate accident. Mussie and I are boiling some soybeans to make some soy flour. After boiling them about ten minutes in an attempt to remove the big tin from the fire, I try to lift it but am unable to hold on to it. It slips from my hand and some of the boiling water splashes up into my face. Fortunately I wasn't burned too badly. I sent Mussie to Banga to get some cream for it. Fortunately it wasn't a bad burn.

It is the first day of May. Prem Kumar comes to my place, as a quiet place to study for his exams. He is with me most of the day. I am still nursing my wounds and reading *Exodus* by Leon Uris. I think that I am recovering and hope to be well enough to ride a cycle by Monday the 4th. I need to do several things before going to Delhi. The date I leave is just three weeks away. The Peace Corps office said we should be in Delhi by the 25 of May. The heat continues. Sant Ram comes and brings a bottle of rum.

35

Final Days

"The night darkened. Our day's works had been done."

—Rabindranath Tagore

One week of May has almost passed. There is a big dust storm today but about dusk a refreshing rain comes through and clears the air. It is cooler tonight. I have to wash my eyes which feel like they are filled with dust.

The next day I go to Banga with Prem Kumar to visit a family of one of his classmates Krishna Sharma. They have a modern house in Model Town. I stay there most of the day and talk to Krishna and her two sisters. It is a treat to have lunch with them. One can seldom enjoy any female company in rural Punjab.

I see the wife of Sat Pal Singh Bedi, who also lives in Model Town. She told me she had made some foods with soybeans, such as *ata* (flour) and *chola* (fried chickpeas). Sat Pal Singh was one of the farmers who grew soybeans from my seed supply last year.

It is Friday, the eighth of May, 1970. A swelling has developed over my right eye. It had been swelling before and now there are two small boils from the burns. My eye is also swollen. So I make a trip down to the Christian Medical College in Ludhiana. I meet Staff Clarry. At the medical centre, I see Dr Franken, a Dutch Doctor, and get some medicine for my eye. I talk to a Catholic priest from Goa of the Franciscan Order with a beard and long white frock. He seems very kind and gentle and understanding. I enjoy talking to him. I then go over to Greens Restaurant to eat with Staff. Nixon has started bombing Cambodia, the newspapers say. Not a good sign. When will this damned war end? I set off in the blinding heat to battle the buses back home.

Over the weekend I nurse my eye and get a Time Magazine in the mail. I don't know if that will nurse my mind. Not likely. I go to Thandi village to take some books and magazines to Tajinderjit Singh and we have a good talk about India.

Now only, two more weeks and I will be heading for Delhi and beyond the *kali pani.* I am glad in a way. I have come to love India, but now need a break. Mussie asks the village shopkeeper to come and I sell him 20 kilograms of magazines and newspapers. They will go for small shopping bags. I have been giving away quite a few things, some to Mussie. Yesterday, I gave my agricultural books to Shokane Singh, a young neighbour farmer across the road, and today several books to my friend Sham Sunder.

It is Monday and we take some of my furniture to the Railway Station in Banga to ship to Ferozepur for Mussie. I talk to the BDO in Banga. He asks for my transistor radio or camera. He says they are going to bring the jeep out to my place to visit before I leave, presumably to load up what he wants. He hinted that I should give him something. "Surely you are going to leave some things in India," he says. Everybody wants something, so they are all chasing after me now, even though what I have is quite pitiful. We may be Sahibs, but we are not rich. The Peace Corps and Uncle Sam has seen to that.

I burn my old letters. The carpenter asks for my luggage, an old brown Samsonite suitcase, but I only have one, and I really need it to travel. The Peace Corps has kept us pretty darned austere. That's the way it's supposed to be, of course.

It is Tuesday, May 12. Mussie asks for leave to go to Ferozepur because his eye is bad. I wanted him to be gone for the last of the week anyway as I will be off myself to an undisclosed destination, namely to see Lakshmi secretly in Chakwal. By the time he left, it was too hot to make a trip out on the road. The sun is just unbearable in the afternoons nowadays.

Without a cook, I think I will have to go out and visit a farmer to get something to eat tomorrow. I have now been reduced to begging for my food. I take some pictures in Banga. Perhaps it will provide me with some memories. I give my sleeping bag to the carpenter.

The next day, I boil eggs for breakfast and ride my cycle to Khatkar Kalan village and take a photo of the famous statue of Bhaghat Singh along the road. In Thandi village, wheat is being threshed the old fashioned way by driving a bullock and plank across it. Now it is almost historical with new harvesting equipment that is starting to be used. I talk to Mahan Singh and also see Hari Singh in Khatkar Kalan. This village is the birthplace of Bhagat Singh, the Indian Freedom Fighter. I had visited his house where he was born. About a year ago, when I went with a friend, his mother was still living there.

I take more pictures in Banga of the *subzi walla* where I always bought my vegetables and fruits and some of the Banga grain Mundi or market. This is the time farmers are threshing their wheat and bringing it in, so the market is in full swing, with bullock carts, tractors, trolleys and high piles of ripe grain.

Swaran Singh, the Sarpanch, and some other farmers from Mahil Gaila are sitting in a tea stall in the grain market, having tea and sweets. They invite me to join them and have tea and pakoras. Swaran Singh had brought 3500 rupees worth of wheat to the market that day. He is a rich farmer, after all.

I pick up my clothes from the cleaning shop and return to the village. Jagbadal Singh comes and we talk a lot about India's problems. Today he asks me to be "his brother" which really means a lot to me. The communists have thought about the solutions to India's problems, whether right or wrong. Whether they would work in India, is a historical question no one knows. The only certainty is that the present system is failing. But this is not true just in India, but around the world. Unfortunately, the vast majority of the villagers are quite ignorant and they continue to be exploited by the ruling class of landlords.

Tonight Gulzar Singh brings me food. I give him my turban.

Thursday, May 14, I boil eggs for breakfast again and go to Khatkar Kalan to see Kishin Singh and say goodbye. He has gone to Banga but I talk to his father. He has a cute granddaughter, about five. I tell the old man that I will be returning to "America" soon. He complained about the heat and asked if the weather was the same in America. Only in Death Valley, perhaps.

Kishin Singh returns around noon. The heat is intense. I knew this would be my last chance to see him. He asks me to stay for lunch. While we eat, he asks me again what I now think about India. I tell him that I don't think the social system is going to change very soon without some kind of revolution. There will still be lots of poverty. He tells me that the low-caste people are worthless and that all the *chamars*, or sweepers, should be castrated according to the German theory of eugenics. It is not the first time he has argued this to me.

I suspect that he is trying to pry some anti-semitism out of me or link me with this as he knows my ancestors were German. I think he doesn't realise what he is saying or how dead set in the old system he is. That's why only a revolution could change and break down the system.

This man takes in from 75,000 to 100 thousand rupees per year. Most of the work is done by hand labour. At least, all of the harvesting is done this way. This doesn't cost him more than 10,000 rupees in a year, not more than five rupees per day per man.

Today when I come back from Banga the low caste people who live down on the west side of the village are out in the road sweeping up grains of wheat which has spilled from carts and trolleys taking wheat to market. These poor people have laboured for one month in the hot sun, the merciless sun, for days, for a pittance. Now they are out picking up grains of wheat from the road. They have cut thousands of rupees worth of wheat, yet they are so poor that they have to go out and sweep up the grains of wheat which spill from the carts just to get enough to eat. This is a terrible situation, yet here it is seen as normal. But the situation has changed somewhat. There is now more of a gap between these people and the big farmers since the Green Revolution has come and the landowners are making more money. But a low caste person who lives down on that side of the village cannot come up into the centre of the village.

Today I show some of my pictures to some kids in the village. One was a picture of a little girl who is a *chamar*. One boy thought it was really strange that I had taken a picture of a *chamar*. He said: "Oh, Sahib just takes pictures of anyone," that is, regardless of their caste. That attitude is so deeply ingrained in the society that only a great revolution could ever change and break it down. But I am not sure that could either.

After leaving Khatkar Kalan I ride to Banga. I'm sure it was 110 degrees and the hot wind was like out of an oven. I meet

Sudarshan in Banga. Also see Swaran Singh and his cronies in the Kartar Singh sweet shop and have some tea and sweets with them. Stopping for some mangoes, I head out for the village in the blistering heat.

The next day is Friday, the 15th, the beginning of the end and a very special programme for me.

36

Chakwal

"How can I describe the vastness of the tavern of insane love."

–Mirza Ghalib

There were only two weeks left before I was to leave India. The wheat harvest had been completed in the searing heat of April. I dreamed of getting together with Lakshmi before leaving for Delhi. But how does one do this in rural Punjab? That was the question. We were able to arrange it with the help of her friend Lakhbir.

The most appropriate place was Lakhbir's village of Chakwal near Hoshiarpur. I thought that not much was likely to happen of a serious nature at this late stage of my stay. If I was to be kicked out at this stage, there would not really be much to lose. I was on the way out anyway.

This arrangement was only possible because Lakhbir's family was not typical. It was not that they were socially liberal, I think. They could not be, as rural villagers. But for other reasons they did not seriously object to our meeting. I really do not know what Lakhbir's mother thought about our relationship. I really have no way of knowing. But the only man in the family was her older brother. This was because her father had been killed some years before in an encounter with some thieves near the village. Her brother was not married and possibly had a relationship with a woman in the village. Lakhbir would have a traditional arranged wedding and move with her husband to London in future. So her flirtation with the doctor at the health clinic was of the nature of many young loves which go on for some time, but never lead to marriage, simply because they are not in the cards, given the social constraints of the society.

We stayed in the house in Chakwal for eight days, May 15 to the 23rd. It was a strange and lovely existence. Most members of the family slept out in the open courtyard of the house. It was an old traditional house of mud walls, the kind that had mud floors and walls fortified with manure. They were always comfortable and I loved staying in them.

It was the peak of the heat before the monsoon. In the daytime, one could rest out near the fields under the large shade trees near the burning hot fields and enjoy some cool breezes. There was a village crazy, a *pagal,* named Cushy Ram, Happy Ram. Every village had at least one crazy. He roamed around the fields. It was a more natural situation, as these people were cared for in the villages and did not get institutionalised as they do in America.

A little past eleven in the evening, Lakshmi would leave the other women in the courtyard and come to where I was sleeping. It was only a few days until I would be leaving India and we were now lovers. It was not so far from tradition in north India. It is not uncommon that men sleep alone and visit their wives for a time in the late evening for sex. I was very anxiously waiting for her to appear in the evenings, but she wanted to wait until the other women in the courtyard, her friend and her mother, were asleep. Then she would come and we would embrace. I loved her Indian scent. It was sweet heaven in a small remote and poor Indian village. I couldn't wait to get her clothes off, gently. It was lovely having her in my arms and feeling her soft velvet skin. All her sweet, brown delicious chocolate flesh, good enough to eat. So nice to taste the soft tips of her lovely young soft breasts and fill my mouth with them. To kiss her body down to where she had trimmed her bush short, her Delta of Venus above her enticing cleavage. She had brought me cardamom. I was stiff, stiff as a young man can be as I tasted her young lips and urged her to caress my tool in her hand. Oh God, I wanted her. I wanted her so. The moonlight was bright enough to see into her large beautiful eyes as I held her. The window adjacent to the cot was open enough for air and, of course, mosquitoes. Now she had begun to love me. She took me, letting me come inside her, inside her warm tenderness. We flirted with the danger. I knew I had to be alert and not make a false move, which could be very serious indeed. Still there was danger of spilling a small amount of one's seed for her young womb to suck up. I pleasured her, slipping in half way, fearing the consequences of giving her all. My thick member throbbed, bucking to break free and gallop, gallop to the hilt and finish it in ecstasy. A natural inclination in a young lusty man who was sex starved in the male chastity belt which was rural Punjab. In the village, it was more often married women who had love affairs with other men or the younger brothers of their husbands. That was not a matter of great concern. It was not full, not flat out, but it was enough. It was love. I don't know. This was so heavenly. It was so sweet, in this incredible back water of the world. It was a back water of a back water. Perfect for a secret liaison with a young delicious fecund Punjabi girl. Yes, I was now her lover and wanted her to be mine. I would bring her to the US and the hell with anything else. It was what I wanted. I was not under any racial restrictions from my mother, but would not have cared if I was. Unlike my friend, Bob.

I thought it strange, how young Punjabi girls left the hair on their legs. The young peasant farmers in the villages, who wore traditional tumbas, on the other hand, had their legs shaven smoothly, sporting them in the buses of Punjab Roadways. Quite strange, I thought. Why do these rough peasants bother to shave their legs? Are they showing off their style, their legs in the dusty roadway buses?

We kissed and petted and half way made love till she went back to the courtyard. I slept. In the hot afternoons, one could find an empty *mungie* out under the cool shade of a large mango or peeple tree near the fields. The local peasants thought I was a strange creature from Mars or some such place.

In many ways, it was a backward village and the house had no modern facilities. The water supply was an open well where the water was drawn up in buckets with a rope. Partly because of this, I was going back to Delhi and America with several bugs in my system, but I didn't worry about it as I knew that I would get the needed treatment. That week was to be our last get together in India while I was in the Peace Corps. One year later, she would arrive in America.

I had kept it a private matter between us and did not want to mix up the Peace Corps in it. Once I was out of the country and out of the Peace Corps, then we could make our own arrangements and it would not involve any official bureaucracy. In my heart and mind, I had already made a commitment not to just walk away, or in this case, fly away, and so I would wait until I had left the Peace Corps. Once on my own, what happened would have nothing to do with involving the Peace Corps or the US Government.

I had already been working on how to get a passport for Lakshmi and bring her to America. But at the time, I was not sure how to proceed. By this time, India, and particularly, Punjab, had started to get into my blood. Perhaps I needed a break back home, but at the same time, was deeply implicated now and Indian culture had planted itself deeply into my mind. I didn't know how the reverse culture shock of being back in America was going to affect me.

I don't think there was any real shock. It was quite exhilarating and I had greatly broadened my experience in the world. I had busted out of the Midwest parochial Bible Belt, never to return.

Life in India, even in rural Punjab, had been more interesting in ways that my life in America had never been. When I landed back in America, I would not find young women that I could like as much as Lakshmi. That was the thread that ran through my Peace Corps years. This was the way it happened and life can take many strange twists and turns. I was always a sort of a rebel, so I guess that I was a rebel in love too.

It was an affair under wraps. I would be free to pursue it in my own way once I had cut my ties with the Peace Corps.

37

Farewell Punjab

"I have got my leave. Bid me farewell, my brothers."

—Rabindranath Tagore

Back in my village from Chakwal, I do my final packing, give away the rest of my things and get ready to take my leave.

At some point we could not avoid rubbing elbows with the Jalandhar Police. Before leaving India at the end of two years, we were required to go to the local police station and get a document called "No Objection to Leave India." I went with Bob, my fellow volunteer, one day before we were to go to Delhi, to get the document. We stayed in a hotel in Jalandhar for a night. Some new hotels were being built and they were quite nice places to stay and not very expensive. In the evening, we went to the hotel restaurant to eat. While we were there, two big Jalandhar police with great protruding bellies came in and greeted us and invited themselves to sit down with us. They knew we were there, of course, because one has to register with the hotel and the police get the reports. Then they ordered up meals and ate with us. They knew that we would not refuse to pay their bill because we needed their cooperation to get the documents needed to leave India. So we got stuck with the bill. It seemed to be a way of getting a free meal out of us.

I was in a rather strange mood in those days, as I was really torn between staying some time longer and just pulling everything up and leaving. In some ways Punjab had become a sort of home to me. And it would be in my mind more when I left India because I started missing it so much. I don't know how much of that was missing Lakshmi and how much was missing the country. I don't think that it was possible to separate them in my mind India had taken over such a huge part of my brain, of my mentality, of my life, in my young formative years that it was to dominate me in a way for many years to come. In some ways it took over my whole life.

And it would be sweet, I knew, when I would bring Lakshmi to the US and I was working on doing that. I didn't know if it was a good thing to do, but I wanted to do it. It would not turn out exactly as I expected, but that is true of almost every event in life. My life and mentality continued to revolve around India even after I returned to the US. I can remember that some people in the US tended to resent it that I related so many things to India and seemed to not think so much about the US. This was true of the Principal of the High School where I got a job teaching the following year. A straight Missouri small-town conservative, he simply couldn't tolerate my liking for India. I should wave the American flag and rally my young students to love America. But, then, India had never put me in any danger like America. They had never tried to get me killed. So I guess there was a reason for my feeling that way.

I must say that at the time, I preferred Indian youth to American.

Some other volunteers may have had similar feelings and some did extend to stay in India for an extra month or two to do some travelling before heading out to other places. Two years seems to be a short time in one's life, but for a young person of twenty three it is a very impressionable age and it was not really clear at the time how much it had really gotten under my skin and changed me.

Perhaps Bob just wanted to leave India and get back to the farm in Ohio. For me it was different. I thought that I was in love and didn't really know what I was going to do. But I was going to be leaving a big chunk of my heart and soul in India. One way or the other, I would work it out.

The Peace Corps office sent a truck to Punjab to pick up our trunks and take them to Delhi. We painted our address in the US on the top of them. Mine would arrived by rail at the small Princeton, Missouri railway station before I arrived, after being air freighted back to the US.

After leaving the village, I spend the night in the house of Gulzar Singh in Jalandhar. I take the train the next morning for Delhi on the 24th of May. It is a Sunday. Gulzar Singh comes with me to the station to see me off.

On the train, I meet Staff Clarry, Pete Backry, Ed Norkus, and Bob Baker. In Delhi, we check into the Lodhi Hotel. We have a hamburger, for the first time in a long time, at the nearby Oberoi Hotel and I buy some pastry which seems inordinately expensive after Punjab.

It is Monday, 25 May. The Peace Corps termination process starts with medical checks. Our old group is now back together once again. We are taken to the "Holy Family Hospital" to give stool and urine samples, and get our blood tested. Then it's to the Peace Corps Northern Regional Office for a tine test. The rest of the day is free.

The next day we are off to dentist. Bob and I shop at the Government Cottage Industries Emporium where I buy a carpet. In the evening, there is a party for India 53 and 54 volunteers at Warren Sawyers place, one of the Peace Corps staff.

At Holy Family Hospital, they tell me that I have Guardia. Holy shit. I am not surprised after Chakwal. They give me some pills. Back to the Regional Office for shots and a certificate that we have been medically cleared to leave India. Unfortunately, we are now too healthy to stay.

On Thursday, there are many forms to sign. I get a cheque for 570 dollars and an airline ticket back to the US.

I buy more things to pack in my trunk.

In the evening we see "*Planet of the Apes*" at the American Embassy. Here is culture shock, not the film, but the theater. So different from an Indian Cinema. It is clean. No one comes around selling nuts and all kinds of things to eat. How boring. I go with Bob to a Chinese Restaurant for prawn chow main.

Finally, there is a farewell party at Ernie Peterson's place for India 53 in the evening. The food is great and there is plenty to drink.

On Saturday, the India 53 and 54 groups are invited over to Ed Barnett's house for a farewell ceremony sponsored by the Government of India. We were given a small gift and certificate saying that we had been working in India for two years in Punjab in Agriculture.

Bob and I go to Agra on the Taj Express for the following day. I had been to Agra once already but Bob had not. It was a comfortable old train where one had a guaranteed seat. After rural Punjab, one takes small things as luxuries. The train left at seven in the morning. Arriving in Agra, we take government bus tour to Fatihpur Sikri, Agra Fort and the Taj Mahal. We get almost to the old ghost city of Fatihpur Sikri when Bob starts feeling like he is going to faint in the severe heat. We get him a glass of *lussie* or buttermilk from a small shop. He feels better, but after lunch, he starts getting worse. His headache was building up into a migraine. So we get a rickshaw and find a local doctor and get him some pills. However, it knocks him out of making the trip out to the Taj Mahal.

We take the Taj Express back to Delhi in the evening. By this time, Bob had reached somewhat of a crises stage and when we got to Delhi, we rushed him to the hospital. His headache was about kill him by that time. A doctor treated him and in a little bit, he was feeling better.

At five in the morning on June 5, 1970, we are on the Pan Am plane.

The two young American hostesses looked like something completely artificial to me. They were almost completely white, as if their flesh was artificial. I began to understand why the Indians looked at us the way they did when they first saw us and wanted to feel of us. Our white flesh looked completely unreal, as if we had been out of a wax museum.

Finally, the big plane lifted off the runway. We are finally out of India.

38

Across the Kali Pani

"If a man went round the world,
Would he find a city to equal Istanbul?"

—Nazim Hikmet

The big Pan American bird hoisted itself aloft in the early morning heat, soared across the mountains and deserts and glided down in Tehran. Here we had to switch planes for Ankara and Istanbul. We fly on, arriving at eleven in the morning. After coming from India the countryside looks lush and green and the temperature quite cool. My first time in Europe and looks just like the pictures I have seen in the modern sections near the airport. We take a taxi to the Dilson Hotel in Taksim and sleep until evening.

The next day is Saturday and we walk around Taksim Square. It is a very much a mixture between the East and West. Small shops sell a variety of things, flowers sellers, simit sellers, bufes packed with almost anything. Food everywhere for snacks, hot dog type sandwiches, meat and cheeses, yogurt, milk and fruit drinks, fruits and so on.

We eat at a small restaurant. Beer is good and cheap. Also wine is fairly cheap. They serve bottled water in restaurants. We buy beautiful bread and cheese and beer and have dinner in the hotel room.

On Sunday, we buy milk, bread, meat, and pizza and eat lunch in the park. It is pleasant, almost too cool after India. Turks love to eat and there is food everywhere, and not a trace of India. If one needs an extra bladder in India, one needs an extra stomach in Turkey.

We walk down Istiklal Street to Cicek Pasaj. You could buy about anything in there, beer on tap out of wooden barrels, light and dark, and all kinds of fish and fried muscles and boiled shrimp. A cornucopia of *kuruyemis*, dry snacks, nuts, dried fruits, and sweets. Amazing Turkey, amazing Istanbul. A city where people come for a short visit and never leave.

There are vegetable and fruit markets, fish markets. Beautiful Strawberries.

We make reservations on Pan Am for Frankfurt. We tour the city. The Bosphorus, which connects the Black Sea with the Marmara Sea, is twenty-one miles long and four hundred meters wide at the narrowest point. It divides the continents of Europe and Asia. In 1970, some two hundred thousand people were crossing from the Asian side to the European side each day for work.

We cross Golden Horn, an inlet from the Marmara Sea. From here, one can see the seven mosques on the seven hills of the city which was once Constantinople, the capital of the Roman Empire.

Crossing the Golden Horn southward, one comes to the old part of the city, Eminonu. *Yeni Cami*, new mosque, is some four hundred years old. There are many mosques with tall slender spires, the largest being Sultan Ahmet or the Blue Mosque across from Santa Sofia. They are an impressive sight.

In the old part of the city, we visit an underground reservoir, which served as a water supply for the city in the Fifteenth Century. Topkapi Palace, residence of the Sultans is next. There were ten thousand people living inside with six hundred cooks. The place is complete with harems, kitchens, living quarters. Now it is a museum where one sees a collection of precious stones, dresses of the Sultan and family. In one room is an Emerald weighing seven and one-half pounds, said to be the largest in the world. There is a large gold urn weighing 48 kilograms.

We go to *Kapali Carsisi*, the Covered Bazaar. There are hundreds of shops and a mosque inside. It is still a thriving market for Turks as well as tourists. On the way back to the hotel, we buy things to eat in the hotel.

On Tuesday, we fly to Frankfurt. It is very different coming into Frankfort Airport after passing through airports of developing countries at the end of the sixties. We find a room in the Vera Hotel and head out for a restaurant. We find a lovely German place with a bar and small tables. A refreshing western atmosphere. Couples are sitting around drinking beer. Some having dinner. There are colourful stained glass windows. The waitress was beautiful, friendly, and very efficient. She was running the whole place single handed while at the same time managing to socialise at every table.

We ordered some steak and delicious beer. This was the first good steak since I left the US over two years ago. We were amazed at the efficiency of the waitress after spending time in India. We figured it would take at least five or six bearers to handle such a place in India. The atmosphere was great, casual, everyone talking and shooting the bull, enjoying themselves. This was clearly reverse culture shock. But very welcome. On Wednesday, we get used to a continental breakfast at the hotel, rolls, butter, jam and coffee. We find a laundry to get our clothes done. We find that few people speak English. Most people take us for Germans when we first walk into a store and the start speaking German. The consumer products, fine technical equipment, such as radios, cameras, and other electronic equipment amazed us after India.

These goods did not exist in the market in India at the time. We repair to a bar and indulge in beer and hamburgers, a heavenly delight. A tour takes us to the house of Goethe.

I meet a cute American girl from Virginia who has come to visit her brother who is stationed here in the Army. She is a sweet dream and gives me her address and phone number and puts a blister on my heart. Later when I called her up she says she is off for a tour and on her way to Paris. Out of luck again.

We go to one of the *Apfelwein* pubs by tram in the evening. We are looking for a place to go when we met a couple of American girls. One of them, who was thin and not very good looking, almost gasped: "Oh, are you Americans?" The other one was Jewish and from Boston. She was as fat as the other was thin. We went with them down to one of the *apfelwein* places.

This was rather embarrassing because here we were with these two hopeless cases when there were really beautiful German girls around. It seemed we were stuck with them for the evening.

They said they had been studying in Spain for a year and were now bumming around Europe. They said they had been picked up by the police for hitch-hiking on the Auto Bahn the day before and brought into Frankfurt to the American Consulate.

The food here was good. We drank *apfelwein* or fermented apple cider. I had wieners and sour kraut in a great atmosphere at a table outside in the square. An old man played an accordion, laughing and trying to get everybody to open up. He played a piano and then took up a collection.

We talked to the girls about India. A German guy sat down near us who knew a lot of Americans in the military. He said I was the first American he had ever seen with a beard.

He was born in Czechoslovakia. His father was in the *Schutzstaffel*, Hitler's Nazi paramilitary organisation, and killed at Leningrad. We were soon stuck with the two girls again. I enjoyed the music, the old familiar tunes such as "*Roll out the Barrel*." People sang along and we enjoyed a different atmosphere.

We took a tram back to the station with the girls, which was near our hotel. They were staying at a Pension near the station. We said goodbye and went to a tavern to have a few beers before returning to the hotel.

The next day we take a tour of the Rhine Valley. We left early. We see Wiesbaden, then a small village with a winery on the Rhine River. This was in the Rudesheim Valley. We climbed to the top of the hill on the Bank of the river. These are called the Rhine Valley Mountains. Overlooking the Rhine is the Niederwald Monument with the 32 oot high statue of Germania.

We take a cable car ride up the hill over the vineyards and down to the valley of Rudesheim. We have lunch as a band plays German songs. Unfortunately, the beautiful spot is starting to get spoiled by tourists, like us. At a wine cellar, we taste some wines from the region. The Rhine steamer takes us down the River. The scenery is pleasant with some old castles still standing along the banks. At a village, we get the bus back to Frankfurt. Back to the pub for food and beer. We are getting into the European life style.

On Friday, we buy cheese, salami, bread and wine to eat at the hotel.

We make our plans for Zurich and Vienna.

On Monday, June 15, we arrive in Zurich. The Leonhard Hotel

is in the centre of town. There is a small clean restaurant for lunch.

Bahn Hoffstrasse, is the main shopping district. I buy an Omega watch. We buy food and wine and eat in the room.

Below our window is a tavern with a piano and an old lady who seems to be about 75 years old. At least, she looks that way to us. She plays it or rather plunks it. We go down. It is just a local bar but a fun place. People are a little boisterous, shouting and singing with the real old time religion.

On Tuesday, we take a tour of the city and surrounding area. We see a Protestant church that was built in the fifteen and sixteen Centuries and was one of the first. We take a tram car ride up the side of a hill 2800 feet to the top of a bluff overlooking the city. It is a nice view with a forest at the top of the hill and meadows where people were out cutting hay.

We see a film, "*Easy Rider*," in the afternoon. It is exciting what is happening in the world at the end of the sixties. A rare window of sanity, soon to again be crushed under too much business rationality.

The back street of our hotel seems to be a "red light district." We see several drunks around and one fight in the street below our window. It is noisy until the bars close around midnight.

On Wednesday, while eating breakfast, Pete Backry comes walking past the hotel. We catch him. Small world. He had been to Istanbul, Athens and Rome. We do more shopping. We have lunch in a restaurant near our hotel. There is a band and a girl who sings and yodels. Music is harmonica and accordion. We drink beer for part of the afternoon, and then go to the old piano bar again. It is called Grandma's Place. I can still hear the strumming now.

It is Thursday, and I take some pictures and sit along the banks of the river. Then we tour the countryside. The road goes through dark, deep, green forests and green meadows. The country is quite beautiful. All the farmsteads are neat and tidy with small tidy vegetable gardens. We stop at the Stein am Rhine. A lot of the houses are frescoed. These paintings date back to the sixteenth century.

At Schaffhausen we see Munot Castle, a Sixteenth Century fortress. Then the Rhine Falls, a drop of some 70 feet, where the water roars down with tremendous spray. The foam and mist almost engulfs one at this close distance. The bus entertained us with Swiss music making for a gentle and relaxed ride. I meet a beautiful American girl on the tour. I am in love. Blisters on my sorry heart again. But alas. No possibility.

We arrive in Vienna around noon on Friday and check into a hotel. We have reservations for London on Sunday.

Our tour of Vienna the next day includes the Shoenbraun Palace. The beer is good here too in the land of milk and honey. On Monday, we leave Vienna for London, change planes in Frankfurt and arrive in the afternoon. We eat at a small restaurant near our hotel.

After an "English Breakfast" of ham and eggs we go to the Wax Museum, called Madam Tussaud. There are wax statues of many famous people and some are over one hundred years old. The statues, not the people. There is also a French Guillotine, and the original key to the Bastille. There is a portrayal of the Battle of Trafalgar where Lord Nelson was killed.

We go to the British Museum, the next day. But by the time we arrive, we are too tired from walking to enjoy it. We see some original manuscripts from some of the great English writers and poets, the Magna Charta, and also the original Guru Granth Sahib of the 10th Sikh Guru, Guru Gobind Singh. What is it doing in London? The British are obviously unashamed of having plundered the world.

There are Egyptian tombs dating back to 2000 BC. At Piccadilly Circus I buy some pants and a tweed jacket.

Thursday is a tour of London to the Parliament Building and Big Ben on the Thames River. Also Westminster Abbey. At Buckingham Palace we see the changing of the guard.

Westminster Abbey is an impressive church and the graves of many great men of England are there. Some that I recall seeing were Sir Henry Newton, Charles Darwin, Thomas Hardy, Thomas Elliot, Lord Alfred Tennyson, Byron, Alexander Pope and many others. Also the Brontes. The crowning chair is also here, which is several hundred years old and the place in Westminster Abbey where the kings and queens are crowned.

We will be heading back to the US. The truth is that I couldn't really go back home and realised that very quickly once I was back in America. I started looking for a way to leave the US fairly quickly again. I did not find it soon, but ironically, the military was one way, and even with the brutal values there, this was far better than staying around a small town in America to teach high school, as far as I was concerned. Small town America was very boring to me after seeing a swath of the wider world.

It would not be long before I would be leaving America again. The Peace Corps had changed me forever. I could never again live without travelling and seeing more of the world. Just how much one has changed is not realised until one is back home.

It was a lot of water under the bridge in that short two years and one month. I would never be the same again. I would be seeing America with a new set of eyes.

39

Afterward: Grass Roots Leader

> "Kariha being a grass roots leader was fully seized of the problems of disadvantaged sections of the society and his outstanding services for the welfare of lower strata would be ever remembered by one and all."
>
> **—Parkash Singh Badal,**
> **Chief Minister of Punjab**

(The following article appeared in The Indian Express on September 15, 2011.)

"Sitting Shiromani Akali Dal MLA from Nawanshahar, Jatinder Singh Kariha, died on Wednesday after suffering a heart attack. He was Sixty-three.

He is survived by his wife, four daughters, a daughter-in-law and two grandchildren. His only son, Major Hira Singh Sandhu, had died in January. "He was all right. He returned from Chandigarh last night and after having his meal and watching TV, went to sleep," said a family member. In the morning, his wife found him dead.

Kariha had inherited his political legacy from his father Hardev Singh Kariha. He won his first elections in 1977 by defeating Congress stalwart Dilbagh Singh. He also won in the 2000 and 2007 elections. Kariha will be cremated around 11 am on Friday at Kariha village. Chief Minister Parkash Singh Badal will attend his funeral."

It was from this notice that I learned that my old friend Jatinder Singh, from my Peace Corps days, had died. Hardev Singh, his father, had earlier died in an auto accident in the 1970s, which I learned from correspondence with Jatinder in the 1980s.

As noted above, Jatinder was a member of the Punjab *Vidhan Sabha* or State Legislative Assembly in Chandigarh as a member of the *Shiromani Akali Dal Party*. Politically, he followed in his father's footsteps in becoming an MLA of the Akali Party. Upon learning of his death, several Akali Party leaders visited his residence in Kariha.

His body was taken to the cremation site in his village, Kariha, in a decorated van in a cavalcade with hundreds of people in the cavalcade with garlands and flowers.

That is not the end of the story as elections for the *Vidhan Sabha* were to be held on January 30, 2012, in just over four months. As it turns out, the Akali Dal gave the election ticket to his widow, Satinder Kaur Kariha. This caused some dissent in the party as Satinder Kaur, who is Sixty-four, has had no experience in politics. The constituency consists of Nawanshahr and Rahon towns and 122 villages.

Satinder Kaur ran against another woman, another widow. Gur Iqbal Kaur Babli is the widow of a former Congress Party MLA, Parkash Singh Saini (not the Chief Minister, who is an Akali), who died in 2010.

MLA Jatinder Singh defeated Parkash Singh Saini in 2007.

The campaign, beginning in November 2011, mainly consisted of the two women candidates reminding voters of the work done by their husbands. Satinder said that her husband, Jatinder, had set up hospitals, laid the sewer system in Newanshahr and Rahon, and secured the construction of the Machhiwara Bridge across the Sutlej River connecting the Malwa Region with the Doaba. The Doaba is the land between the Sutlej and Beas Rivers.

Satinder Kaur was quoted as saying: "I request you to give every vote to help me in completing the unfinished work of my husband."

Gur Iqbal Kaur Babli, the Congress Party candidate, was reported to be seeking blessings from elders, touching their feet, eating with homeless children, and listening to the woes of women.

In some ways it was a battle of sympathies, with Satinder seen to have the most sympathy having lost her son and husband in the same year.

Gur Iqbal Kaur of the Indian National Congress Party, won with 30.6 per cent of the vote. Satinder Kaur took 29.1 per cent. There were other considerations, of course, besides the sympathy factor for the widows. Some were surely thinking of what would serve their interests better.

The other major party in the constituency is the Bahujan Samaj Party, a low-caste or Dalit party. This party took 25 per cent of the vote. The population of the region is around 30 per cent Dalit.

The state government is a coalition between the Akali Dal, a Sikh-based political party more in the rural areas, and the Bharatiya Janata Party (BJP) a Hindu-based political party which is more prominent in urban areas such as Jalandhar. The two parties divide the territory between the urban Hindus and rural based Jat Sikhs in their election strategies.

There was another interesting twist to the election. The People's Party of Punjab (PPP) fielded a candidate, Abhay Singh Sandhu, who is the nephew of Bhagat Singh. This leftist party is aligned with the two communist parties in the state, the Communist Party of India (CPI) and Communist Party of India-Marxist (CPM). This is a new party in the state that was launched from Katkar Kalan in 2011 by the party leader Manpreet Singh Badal.

Abhay Singh's father is Bhagat Singh's youngest brother. Although, the Newanshahr constituency no longer includes his ancestral village, Katkar Kalan.

Bhagat Singh is known as "*Shaheed-e-Azam* Bhagat Singh", Martyr Bhagat Singh, a legendary freedom fighter. He is the Sanjha Morcha candidate.

Sandhu was reported to be a "political greenhorn and reluctant electoral warrior." The party says it wants to "help realise the dreams of Bhagat Singh and bring a corruption free system."

Sandhu was reported to believe that he could "trounce the two women candidates," as people were fed up with corruption. The party might appeal to the Dalits, but they mostly vote for the Bahujan Samaj Party.

The party, however, could come up with only 7.6 per cent of the votes.

September 2012, the Chief Minister, Parkash Singh Badal, announced that taxes would have to be raised for development and progress. Health, education and infrastructure and ensuring the welfare of the people.

The political situation, typical of much of India, shows the salience of religious communalist voting, with the BJP and Akali Dal parties and caste solidarity within the Bahajan Samaj Party. The old nationalist Congress Party often has less appeal and a more ideological party such as the PPP does not cut much ice with the voters in Punjab.

The name of the Jalandhar District has been changed to Shahid Bhagat Singh Nagar District and the town of Banga has doubled in size to roughly twenty thousand in 2013.

Post Script
Once a Renegade, Always a Renegade

In this book, I have recorded my memories of life in Punjab in the 1960s. I am not under the illusion that I rendered any great service to the people of India. If I did anything worthwhile, I am grateful for the opportunity. The people of India and Punjab were kind and hospitable and did for me far more than I could ever do for them. They generously gave me a place to live in their community and helped me when I was in need. They put up with my youth, ignorance and foreign ways. They saved me from the terrible fate of being sent to Vietnam to fight in a war that I did not believe in. They saved me from being forced to destroy life unwillingly in the cause of American imperialism.

I regard my years in Punjab as simply another phase of my life. On the other hand, they are the most crucial years in shaping my life and views of society and the world. This leads me to believe that the United States of America would be a far different country if every youth could spend a year or two in a developing country like India and come to love another country, culture, and people.

I am grateful to my young friends in the village, Sant Ram, Prem Kumar, Shokene Singh and to the Sarpanch, Swaran Singh and many others. I am thankful to Jatinder Singh Kariha and his family for providing me a place to live when I first arrived in Banga Block in 1968.

The American Peace Corps was an integral part of the US imperialist structure, a branch of the US State Department. For me this was the unfortunate side of the Peace Corps. But this had nothing to do with my mission. I had only good will towards all for peace in the world. If that makes me a renegade, then so be it. I was glad to be part of our Peace Corps group of colleagues in India 53 and love all of the guys that went to India with me in our group. We all had the best intentions at heart for both India and our country. We thought that the war in Vietnam was a colossal mistake and wanted no part of killing Vietnamese in the name of stopping communism.

I am glad that my sojourn in Punjab came about and would do it again without hesitation. I consider myself very fortunate to have been sent to India, a very great and fascinating country. I have since returned to India some ten times. It simply strengthens my soul in ways that I cannot adequately describe, and brings back memories.

I am happy that I have been able to experience the "functioning anarchy" that is India. And I hope that I have retained not a small part of that anarchy in my soul. Once a renegade, always a renegade. Sat Shree Akal.

August 19, 2013 Seferihisar, Turkey.

eddiegirdner@gmail.com

1. Driving a tractor in Mahil Gaila.

2. My cook Feroze Mussie and his wife and two children

3. Trying my hand at cutting wheat

Index

C

D

E